# THE TRAVEL INDUSTRY

## An Industry Accounting and Auditing Guide

# THE TRAVEL INDUSTRY

# An Industry Accounting and Auditing Guide

BDO Stoy Hayward Travel Group

**Editor**
**David Templeman**

*BDO Stoy Hayward*

Accountancy Books
40 Bernard Street
London
WC1N 1LD
Tel: +44(0)171 920 8991
Fax: +44(0)171 920 8992
E-mail: abgbooks@icaew.co.uk
Web site: www.icaew.co.uk/books.htm

© 1998 The Institute of Chartered Accountants in England and Wales.

ISBN 1 85355 939 3

**British Library Cataloguing-in-Publication Data.**

A catalogue record for this book is available from the British Library.

*Throughout this book the male pronoun has been used to cover references to both the male and female.*

Typeset by Phoenix Photosetting, Chatham, Kent
Printed in Great Britain by Bell & Bain Ltd, Glasgow

# Contents

|                                        | page  |
|----------------------------------------|-------|
| *Foreword by Helen Simpson, CAA*       | *xiii* |
| *Foreword by Mike Monk, ABTA*          | *xv*  |
| *Foreword by Tony Brown, IATA*         | *xvii* |
| *Preface*                              | *xix* |
| *Acknowledgements*                     | *xxi* |
| *Introduction*                         | *xxiii* |

**1    Industry overview**                                                    **1**
  1.1    International/Global travel and tourism    1
      1.1.1    Economic impact    1
      1.1.2    Trends    2
      1.1.3    Regional trends    2
      1.1.4    Forecasts    4
  1.2    The UK travel and tourism market    5
      1.2.1    Market size    5
      1.2.2    Market sectors    6
  1.3    Industry background    10
      1.3.1    Regulations    11
  1.4    Tour operators and the package holiday industry    12
      1.4.1    All-inclusive tours    12
      1.4.2    Consumer demand and expenditure    13
      1.4.3    The supply structure and key players    13
      1.4.4    The big four    15
  1.5    Travel agents    21
      1.5.1    Supply structure and key players    21
      1.5.2    Consumer profile    22
      1.5.3    The key players    22
      1.5.4    The future    24
  1.6    Scheduled and non-scheduled passengers airlines    25
      1.6.1    Supply structure    26
      1.6.2    Scheduled airlines    26
      1.6.3    Charter airlines    26
      1.6.4    Leading charter airlines    27
      1.6.5    The future    28

**2    Civil Aviation Authority (CAA)**                                        **29**
  2.1    Government ad EU regulation – the role of the Civil    29
      Aviation Authority

|       |       |                                                      |    |
|-------|-------|------------------------------------------------------|----|
|       | 2.1.1 | Policy implementation                                | 29 |
|       | 2.1.2 | Structure and scope of the CAA regulation            | 30 |
| 2.2   | Air Tour Organisers' Licensing (ATOL) system         |    | 30 |
|       | 2.2.1 | Who needs an ATOL?                                   | 30 |
|       | 2.2.2 | Different forms of ATOL                              | 31 |
|       | 2.2.3 | The application process                             | 32 |
|       | 2.2.4 | Financial monitoring and review                     | 34 |
|       | 2.2.5 | Seat-only sales on scheduled flights                | 37 |
|       | 2.2.6 | ATOL to ATOL sales                                  | 37 |
|       | 2.2.7 | CAA returns                                         | 38 |

**3    The Association of British Travel Agents (ABTA)                     39**

| 3.1  | Introduction                                             | 39 |
|------|----------------------------------------------------------|----|
| 3.2  | The growth of ABTA                                       | 39 |
|      | 3.2.1 The Package Travel, Package Holidays and Package Tours Regulations 1992 | 39 |
|      | 3.2.2 The benefits for ABTA members and the distinction with the CAA | 40 |
| 3.3  | The internal structure of ABTA                          | 41 |
|      | 3.3.1 Current membership                                | 42 |
| 3.4  | Membership rules and criteria                           | 42 |
| 3.5  | Membership rules – general                              | 42 |
| 3.6  | Membership rules – tour operators                       | 44 |
| 3.7  | Membership rules – travel agents                        | 44 |
| 3.8  | Financial criteria and regulations                      | 44 |
| 3.9  | Financial criteria and regulations – general            | 45 |
|      | 3.9.1 Reporting requirements – audited accounts         | 45 |
|      | 3.9.2 Reporting requirements – audited turnover certification | 46 |
|      | 3.9.3 Reporting requirements – other                    | 46 |
| 3.10 | Financial regulations – tour operator                   | 47 |
|      | 3.10.1 Capital requirement                              | 47 |
|      | 3.10.2 Net recoverable currect assets                   | 47 |
|      | 3.10.3 Net asset deficits                               | 48 |
|      | 3.10.4 Bonding – tour operators                         | 48 |
|      | 3.10.5 Peak period bonding                              | 49 |
|      | 3.10.6 Third-party bonding                              | 50 |
| 3.11 | New members – tour operators                            | 50 |
|      | 3.11.1 New members' capital requirements                | 50 |
|      | 3.11.2 Reporting requirements of new members            | 50 |
| 3.12 | Financial regulations – travel agent                    | 51 |
|      | 3.12.1 Capital requirements                             | 51 |
|      | 3.12.2 Bonding                                          | 51 |
|      | 3.12.3 Applicable risk turnover                         | 51 |
|      | 3.12.4 Bonding requirements                             | 52 |

         3.12.5    TABRS – detailed calculations                  52
  3.13  New members – travel agents                               53

4   **Trade associations: International Air Transport Association
    (IATA)**                                                      **54**
  4.1   Introduction                                              54
  4.2   Structure of IATA                                         54
  4.3   Agency Accreditation Programme                            55
         4.3.1    The application process for travel agents       55
  4.4   Bonding requirement                                       57
  4.5   The approval process                                      58
  4.6   Annual financial review                                   58
  4.7   The Billing and Settlement Plan                           59
  4.8   Ticketing procedures and training                        59
  4.9   IATA agency fees                                          59
  4.10  The passenger sales agency agreement                      60
  4.11  Notification of changes                                   60
  4.12  Quality reviews                                           60

5   **Other industry bodies**                                     **61**
  5.1   Introduction                                              61
  5.2   The British Incoming Tour Operators' Association          61
  5.3   The Multiple Travel Agents Association                    62
  5.4   ARTAC World Choice                                        62
  5.5   The National Association of Independent Travel
        Agents – Advantage Travel Centres                         62
  5.6   The Association of Independent Tour Operators             63
  5.7   The Travel Trust Association                              63
         5.7.1    Operation of a TTA member's trust account       64
         5.7.2    The TTA travel protection plan                  64

6   **Commercial operation within the UK travel industry**        **65**
  6.1   Introduction                                              65
  6.2   The MMC report into the foreign package holiday
        industry                                                  65
  6.3   Defining the market, and defining monopoly                66
  6.4   Evidence of complex monopoly and restrictive practices    67
  6.5   The anti-competitive practices identified                 68
  6.6   Insolvency implications and responsibilities of directors 70
  6.7   Definition of insolvency                                  71
  6.8   Shadow director                                           71
  6.9   Offences under the Insolvency Act 1986                     72
         6.9.1    Misfeasance/Breach of duty                      73
         6.9.2    Fraudulent trading                              73
         6.9.3    Wrongful trading                                73

|        | 6.10   | Restriction on reuse of company names | 74 |
|        | 6.10.1 | Rule 4.228 | 74 |
|        | 6.10.2 | Rule 4.229 | 75 |
|        | 6.10.3 | Rule 4.230 | 75 |
|        | 6.11   | Preferences | 76 |
|        | 6.12   | Director's disqualification | 77 |
|        | 6.13   | Procedure for disqualification | 78 |
|        | 6.14   | Insolvency implications: what should directors do? | 79 |

**7**  **Commercial considerations for tour operators**  **80**

|        | 7.1    | Introduction | 80 |
|        | 7.2    | Sources of income | 80 |
|        | 7.2.1  | Selling holidays | 80 |
|        | 7.2.2  | Forfeit of deposits/Cancellation charges | 81 |
|        | 7.2.3  | Bank interest | 81 |
|        | 7.2.4  | Insurance | 82 |
|        | 7.2.5  | Holiday extras | 82 |
|        | 7.2.6  | Profit on foreign currency movements | 83 |
|        | 7.2.7  | Airport charge rebates | 83 |
|        | 7.3    | Costs associated with generating income | 83 |
|        | 7.3.1  | Accommodation | 83 |
|        | 7.3.2  | Transport | 84 |
|        | 7.3.3  | Brochures | 84 |
|        | 7.3.4  | Advertising and promotion | 85 |
|        | 7.3.5  | *Ex gratias* and compensation | 86 |
|        | 7.3.6  | Bonding | 86 |
|        | 7.3.7  | Holiday representatives | 87 |
|        | 7.3.8  | Sales team | 87 |
|        | 7.3.9  | Information technology | 87 |
|        | 7.4    | Identifying and managing the risks related to the income source | 88 |
|        | 7.4.1  | Nature of the market | 88 |
|        | 7.4.2  | Structure | 88 |
|        | 7.4.3  | Matching costs and revenues | 91 |
|        | 7.4.4  | Selling | 92 |
|        | 7.4.5  | Direct costs | 94 |

**8**  **Commercial considerations for travel agents**  **98**

|        | 8.1    | Background | 98 |
|        | 8.1.1  | Thomas Cook Group Limited | 99 |
|        | 8.1.2  | Going Places (part of the Airtours group) | 99 |
|        | 8.1.3  | Lunn Poly (part of the Thomson Travel Group) | 99 |
|        | 8.2    | Operation | 100 |

**9    Airline operation**                                              **104**
  9.1    Methods of acquiring aircraft                        104
      9.1.1    Outright purchase                           104
      9.1.2    Loan, hire purchase or finance lease        105
      9.1.3    Operating lease arrangements                106
  9.2    Audit considerations                                 107
  9.3    Capacity management                                  107
      9.3.1    Charter operations                          107
      9.3.2    Scheduled operations                        109
      9.3.3    Other capacity management issues            110
  9.4    Maintenance                                          110
      9.4.1    Available capital                           110
      9.4.2    Fleet size                                  111
      9.4.3    Nature of operation                         111
      9.4.4    Capacity of maintenance facility            112
      9.4.5    Relative costs                              112
      9.4.6    Audit considerations                        112
  9.5    Vertical integration                                 112
      9.5.1    Audit considerations                        113
  9.6    Alliances                                            113
      9.6.1    Equity ownership                            113
      9.6.2    Joint buying and maintenance                114
      9.6.3    Reservation systems                         114
      9.6.4    Franchising                                 114
      9.6.5    Audit considerations                        115

**10    Reservation and ticketing systems**                            **116**
  10.1    Introduction                                        116
  10.2    The traditional customer, agent, operator arrangement    116
  10.3    Galileo                                             118
  10.4    Sabre                                               119
  10.5    Amadeus                                             119
  10.6    Worldspan                                           119
  10.7    Current developments                                119

**11    The euro and its impact on the travel industry**               **121**
  11.1    Introduction                                        121
  11.2    1 January 1999                                      121
  11.3    1 January 2002                                      122
  11.4    1 July 2002                                         122
  11.5    The implications for UK firms                       122
      11.5.1    Euro accounting under compunction         122
      11.5.2    Euro accounting to maintain competitive edge    123
  11.6    Immediate issues for the financial director and
      auditor                                         123

**12    Accounting policies**                                                    **126**
   12.1   Introduction                                                126
   12.2   Tour operators                                              126
         12.2.1   Income and cost recognition                      126
   12.3   Travel agents                                               129
         12.3.1   Income and cost recognition                      129
         12.3.2   Stocks                                           131
   12.4   Airline operators                                           132
         12.4.1   Definition of turnover: point of income and
                   costs recognition                                132
         12.4.2   Segmental reporting of turnover                  133
         12.4.3   Tangible fixed assets                            134
         12.4.4   Aircraft maintenance costs                       140
         12.4.5   Deferred expenditure                             140
         12.4.6   Frequent flyer programme                         141
         12.4.7   Stocks                                           142
   12.5   Foreign exchange contracts                                  142
         12.5.1   Translation of assets and liabilities in foreign
                   currencies                                       142
         12.5.2   Profits and losses from overseas subsidiaries    143
         12.5.3   Forward currency contracts                       144
   12.6   Travel industry bonds and guarantees                        144

**13    Statutory audit considerations**
   13.1   Introduction                                                146
   13.2   Understanding the client business and its reporting
         requirements                                                146
   13.3   Supporting the statutory audit report to members            149
   13.4   Risk-based auditing                                         150
   13.5   Travel agency                                               152
         13.5.1   Commission income                                152
   13.6   The Billing and Settlement Plan (BSP)                       153
   13.7   Tour operating                                              154
         13.7.1   Income and cost recognition                      154
   13.8   Resort expenditure                                          157
   13.9   Accounting for foreign currency transactions                159
   13.10 Airlines                                                     159
   13.11 Audit programmes                                             159
         13.11.1 Travel agents                                     159
         13.11.2 Tour operators                                    160
         13.11.3 Airlines                                          160

**14    Auditing client returns to the regulatory bodies**              **162**
   14.1   Introduction                                                162
   14.2   Reporting to the regulators                                 163

14.3    Turnover certification    163
14.4    Net asset position    164
14.5    New businesses    165
14.6    Other returns    166
14.7    Duty of care    166
14.8    Summary    166

**15    UK tax implications    167**
15.1    Introduction    167
15.2    Tax implication of accounting policies    167
15.3    Trading status    168
15.4    Groups of companies    169
15.5    Choice of year end    170
15.6    Areas specific to the travel industry    170
    15.6.1    Bonding    170
    15.6.2    Foreign exchange gains and losses    171
    15.6.3    Capital allowances    173
    15.6.4    Operating leases, finance leases and hire
           agreements    174
    15.6.5    Deposits    175
    15.6.6    Brochures and advertising    176
    15.6.7    Subscriptions    176
    15.6.8    Sponsorship, conferences and entertaining    176
15.7    The overseas dimension    177
15.8    PAYE and P11D issues    179
15.9    Other sundry matters    179
15.10 Summary    180

**16    VAT    181**
16.1    Introduction    181
16.2    Scope    181
16.3    Application    184
    16.3.1    Registration    184
    16.3.2    Time of supply    184
    16.3.3    Place of supply    185
    16.3.4    Accounting    185
16.4    Exceptions and concessions    185
16.5    Calculations    185
16.6    Non-TOMS issues    189
16.7    Summary    190

**Appendices**

Appendix 1  CAA forms    192
Appendix 2  ABTA travel agent forms    197

*Contents*

Appendix 3  ABTA tour operator forms                                    207
Appendix 4  Accounting policies                                         209
Appendix 5  EC Directive 77/388, Article 26A                            227
Appendix 6  VAT Act 1994, section 53                                    228
Appendix 7  The Value Added Tax (Tour Operators) Order 1987
            (as amended)                                                229
Appendix 8  TOMS: end of year calculation                               233
Appendix 9  Provisional margins and output tax for the next year        237
Appendix 10  The Package Travel, Package Holidays and Package
             Tours Regulations 1992                                     239

Glossary                                                                262

Index                                                                   265

# Foreword by Helen Simpson, CAA

The UK travel industry is one of the great growth stories of the last 30 years, and it is a dynamic and exciting business. In the public perception, it perhaps retains some of the entrepreneurial flavour that was its hallmark in the late 1960s and early 1970s: during that time, foreign travel began to change from being the preserve of the rich or adventurous few to being within the grasp of many ordinary people. The change has been helped along by increased leisure, higher disposable incomes and real terms cost reductions achieved by advances in aviation and other technologies, and the UK-originating market for foreign holidays has increased more than tenfold in the last 25 years. Despite the industry's size today, however, its image still keeps from its early days a touch of the street market.

In fact, this perception is now largely a myth. Demand for foreign travel continues to grow at a rate faster than the economy generally, and the industry is still dynamic and inventive; but, at least for the larger companies, it is also a highly sophisticated business in which survival depends on competitiveness, and competitiveness depends on the availability of detailed and systematic management information. The ability to set prices with precision, and to maximise marginal revenue by adjusting prices with equal precision as circumstances dictate, is vital in protecting profit margins. So too is the ability to manage foreign currency exposure and to limit other risks: the extent to which the large firms have become part of integrated organisations containing charter airlines and travel agents as well as tour operators has resulted in different risks and different capital structures.

Industry accounting practitioners and auditors both need to understand the industry's dynamics if they are to present the information that businesses need, and to present statutory accounts and returns that show a true picture. There are many aspects of accounting policies that are specific to the travel industry, and an incorrectly applied policy may produce considerable variances in the key indicators presented in the accounts. The relationship between accounting policies and the tax regime, which equally has a number of travel-specific aspects, is complex.

Travel is also a highly regulated industry, in which the customer enjoys a level of protection that is difficult for other sectors to equal. Since the early 1970s people have been able to book holidays without worrying about losing their money or being stranded abroad because of tour operator failure. For air holidays this protection is achieved by the Air Travel Organisers'

*Foreword*

Licensing system, managed by the Civil Aviation Authority, which leads to the need for most firms selling air travel to hold a licence. The Package Travel Regulations of 1992 provide parallel protection for non-air packages, as well as setting a range of customer benefits that apply to all packages, and the various industry bodies have a role in providing customer protection to meet the requirements of those Regulations. These bodies also impose their own standards as membership requirements, and some of them monitor trading by means of regular returns, as do the CAA.

For the industry, this imposes a framework of regulations and compliance demands that can sometimes be rather daunting, particularly for the smaller firm. One company may hold an ATOL and may also be a member of two or even three trade bodies, each with different and overlapping requirements for compliance and monitoring. All of these will place demands both on the industry accounting practitioners and on the auditors, who need to validate returns and to provide various essential certifications direct to the CAA and the trade bodies.

This book will fill an important gap in the guidance currently available for travel industry accountants and auditors, and provide them with a work of reference that has both comprehensive coverage and depth of detail. It recognises that an auditor must start by understanding the commercial realities of the underlying business – but he must also know the technical detail attached to a wide range of accounting policy, tax and compliance aspects. It also recognises the extent to which regulators depend on the work of auditors in order to ensure that consumer protection works smoothly. I believe it will become an indispensable handbook for all those involved in the financial management and auditing of travel firms.

Helen Simpson
Head of Licensing and Finance
Civil Aviation Authority
October 1998

# Foreword by Mike Monk, ABTA

Although primarily a trade association, much of the ABTA's work is as a regulator of the industry, the Association being a body approved under Regulation 18 of the Package Travel, Package Holidays and Package Tours Regulations 1992. A considerable amount of the regulatory work of the Association is carried out in close cooperation with our members' professional advisers and their auditors. Indeed, we often rely heavily on confirmations and opinions expressed by members of the accountancy profession when carrying out own risk assessment procedures. In providing these to us, members' auditors in particular are often providing the Association with data that is expressly stated to be the basis upon which decisions are based. This would often apply, for example, when the early release of a bond or other form of security has been requested by a former member. It is vital therefore, that auditors and accountants have a thorough knowledge of EU and UK legislation and of the requirements of the Association, the CAA and other regulatory bodies.

Given the complexity and importance of what is, after all, a very significant industry, it is surprising to note, therefore, that until the publication of this book, no single reference work existed which provided comprehensive help, information and guidance to both those working within the industry and their professional advisers. This is especially so when one considers that responsibilities and potential liabilities that auditors and accountants take on when dealing with the bodies responsible for regulating the industry.

The authors have obviously gone to great lengths to produce, in a single volume, material which will prove to be an invaluable reference book for accountants who work in or have clients in the travel industry. Indeed the book will make for interesting reading for anyone involved in travel whether on the accounting side or not.

This work provides all of the necessary information for accountants to advise their clients on industry best practice as well as compliance issues, some of which will not be familiar to those outside of the travel trade. The Tour Operators' Margin Scheme, for example, has always caused difficulties for all but the most dedicated readers of VAT legislation. Chapter 16 makes for considerably easier reading!

For those involved in the audit of those in the travel trade this work will assist in the planning of audit or work programmes and hopefully help auditors to identify matters of importance in addition to managing areas of potential risk to themselves and their clients.

The travel industry is an ever-changing one and it is particularly interesting to see the authors' views on future trends. The growth of electronic means of distribution, the single European currency and the likely impact of the recent Monopolies and Mergers Commission report are all addressed in the book all of which will be important matters to consider when advising clients.

Mike Monk FCA
ABTA
October 1998

# Foreword by Tony Brown, IATA

The travel industry, with its business and leisure sectors, makes a significant contribution to the UK economy. Travel agents are intermediaries who are the link between the supplier and the customer. They have accumulated a wealth of knowledge and expertise, enabling them to represent a variety of suppliers and offer a diversity of destinations, activities and programmes.

For many people, the purchase of a holiday is a substantial part of their annual budget. They are disappointed and dissatisfied if their experience does not match their expectations. The protection of customers' money and the promotion of high standards are objectives which are clearly in the interests of the travelling public. However, the regulatory bodies involved in the distribution system are responsible for securing and safeguarding different areas of liability.

Each organisation has its own rules and financial criteria which apply to all new applicants and existing agents. Confronted with added demands and new pressures, the owners of travel companies and firms find it increasingly difficult to keep up with the separate requirements. Their professional advisers must understand these regulations and give suitable and reliable advice to ensure compliance.

Unless the criteria is clearly formulated, and readily available and accessible, the exercise becomes more complicated. This book provides a comprehensive guide for agents, accountants and auditors which will prove invaluable in the conduct and management of a travel business. It will not only assist agents in meeting the respective criteria but will increase their awareness of the general regulatory framework. When questions and issues arise, particularly in annual financial reviews, it will provide clarification and guidance which will enable agents to maintain their accreditation.

I strongly recommend this book, which fills an obvious gap, and fulfils a real need, in this changing and volatile industry.

Tony Brown ACIB
Financial Assessor
Agency Services Office
IATA, UK
October 1998

# Preface

This work is a result of the development of BDO Stoy Hayward's travel expertise over the course of a number of years since I, and a number of like-minded individuals, decided to focus our attention on advising clients in this very exciting area of business.

In editing this work it has given me considerable pleasure to see just how much our partners, managers and staff understand and appreciate the special requirements of servicing travel industry clients. Our travel group comprises over a dozen people across our south east practice and I'm indebted to each of the contributors for their hard work, careful research and timely presentation of material.

Having advised clients in each of the three sectors considered within this book for many years we became increasingly aware of the need to set out for our fellow professionals a clear and concise guide to this very regulated sector. When dealing with client issues and assisting client teams throughout our practice we found that no appropriate work was available. I hope that this volume will go some way in rectifying this unwelcome situation.

Apart from those members of our travel group who have contributed to this book thanks are also due to our friends and contacts at the various industries bodies, to our clients, and to those other members of the firm who have encouraged the development of our travel expertise. In particular, thanks are due to Richard Emanuel for his invaluable assistance in directing our energies, and all those other people who have at various times been bored by my enthusing over this project at lunch or dinner parties.

David Templeman
London
October 1998

# Acknowledgements

The BDO Stoy Hayward Travel Group comprises partners, managers and staff across various disciplines of our firm. Each of the following members of our Travel Group have contributed chapters to this work.

Specific thanks are due to Stephen Kavanagh, Simon Watson, Martin Israel and Helen Bottomley who are enthusiastic members of our group and have contributed much to the present volume. They are founder members of our group and have a wealth of first-hand experience in advising growing businesses within this sector.

Keith Jones, Clive Clark and Ray Adams together with Brian Pope have all been instrumental in the development of our travel group since they joined our firm in 1992. All are general business practitioners with special interest and great experience in the industry.

Clare Hartnell and Mike Payne represent the two strands of tax expertise in this work and between them have many years in advising on tax legislation as it impacts on travel businesses.

Anne Bourgeois and Steve Bynghall have provided invaluable contributions to this work. Anne and Steve are experienced business researchers and have assisted us in identifying and clarifying many of the issues surrounding the history, development, and future direction of the industry.

Michael Larkin works in our insolvency practice and has brought a different perspective to our advisory skills, focusing as he does on insolvency and corporate recovery aspects of industry operation, and where possible on saving companies which have failed or are in danger of failing to tackle the problems and challenges associated with growth.

# Introduction

This book has been written to assist the accountant in practice who advises travel businesses in each of the tour operating, travel agency or airline sectors. We hope it will also be of assistance to accountants working within the industry – especially those who are new to the discipline or who wish to broaden their knowledge of the sector.

In the knowledge that the adviser to any travel business should understand how his client sits within the industry, is regulated under both direct and indirect statute, and will face accounting and auditing issues unique to the travel industry we have adopted a structure which deals in turn with each of the following areas.

In Chapter 1 we have analysed the UK industry in terms of its development, its future direction and the competitive pressures facing UK businesses. While it will be clear from this chapter that a small number of very large companies have an important place within the industry, it should also be apparent that there are many independent businesses operating successfully and giving healthy returns to their shareholders and employees.

This chapter also highlights the significant importance of the travel industry to both the UK and global economies and the continued growth which can be expected into the next century.

In Chapters 2 to 5 we analyse in some detail the regulatory framework in which travel businesses operate and the various reporting requirements imposed on UK businesses and their auditors under both direct and indirect statute.

While every reader should have a basic appreciation of the operation of the Civil Aviation Authority (CAA), the Association of British Travel Agents (ABTA), and the International Air Transport Association (IATA) and may well have a passing knowledge of other industry associations such as the Association of Independent Tour Operators (AITO), it is unlikely that without detailed research into the rules and regulations of each of these self-regulators the accountant will easily understand the onerous responsibilities imposed on his clients, and indeed of the duties imposed on the adviser by virtue of acting for businesses which are either licensed, accredited, or members of the various industry bodies.

*Introduction*

These chapters set out from first principles the functions and the reporting requirements of the various bodies and should therefore enable the adviser to give good commercial advice to clients when considering such aspects as the need for licensing and assessing bonding requirements.

In Chapters 6 to 11 we look at the commercial considerations attaching to operation within the sector.

We begin in Chapter 6 by considering the Monopolies and Mergers Commission (MMC) report into the foreign package holiday industry and how this report may impact on the future of the UK industry; we also consider insolvency law and how this impacts on the actions of directors of UK travel businesses.

In each of Chapters 7 , 8 and 9 we consider various commercial considerations of operation in each of the tour operating, travel agency and airline sectors.

In Chapter 10 we look at reservation systems and how these impact on the auditor's work and consider how these will develop in the future. In Chapter 11 we look at European Monetary Union and how euro accounting will impact on UK businesses.

Chapters 12 to 14 analyse, in turn, common accounting policies adopted by UK businesses, audit considerations and techniques to satisfy both the statutory requirement to report to the members of the business and also audit work to support returns to the industry regulators. We stress the importance of adopting a streamline approach to testing to achieve cost-effective and efficient audit techniques.

In Chapters 15 and 16 we look at the taxation implications of operation in the industry – Chapter 15 with regard to corporate taxes and Chapter 16 with regard to the Tour Operators' Margin Scheme (TOMS).

Finally we have compiled a glossary of terms which are commonly found when dealing with travel businesses and in our appendices we reproduce (with kind permission) returns to the CAA, ABTA, our accounting policy review, together with abstracts from relevant VAT legislation and the Package Travel, Package Holidays and Package Tours Regulations 1992.

# Chapter 1 – Industry overview

## 1.1   International/Global travel and tourism

Tourism is one of the fastest growing industries in the world and it is predicted that it will be the largest by the year 2000. There are many reasons why the travel and tourism industry is growing. The underlying demand for both consumer and business travel is driven by long-term economic growth, the growing requirement for leisure, the commercialisation of national cultures by the mass media, the easing of border controls and the falling real cost of transport, aided by deregulation and competition.

The following facts give some indications of the economic impact of the travel and tourism industry on the global economy.

### 1.1.1   Economic impact

Travel and tourism, encompassing transport, accommodation, catering, recreation and services for travellers, is the world's largest industry and generator of jobs. The industry produced over US$448 billion in gross output and an estimated 255 million jobs in 1997.

Travel and tourism now contributes 10.7 per cent of gross domestic product (GDP) to the world economy.

Travel and tourism is human resource intensive, stimulating employment in upstream suppliers and downstream services providers of travellers and travel companies such as construction, telecommunications, retail and manufacturing. Globally, one in nine jobs is generated by the travel and tourism industry and many of them in small businesses and in urban or rural areas, where structural unemployment is usually severe.

In 1996, the private and public sectors spent an estimated US$766 billion in new travel and tourism capital investment worldwide.

Travel and tourism is both a generator and receiver of government funds. Globally in 1996, tourism generated approximately US$653 billion of taxes, while receiving US$304 billion of government operating expenditures. Taxes on tourism are proliferating as it is relatively easy to collect revenues on tourist expenditure and usually less controversial than other forms of taxation.

International tourism is the world's largest export earner. In 1996, foreign currency receipts from international tourism reached US$423 billion.

Tourism jobs and businesses are often created in the most underdeveloped regions of a country and help to equalise economic opportunities throughout a nation and provide incentives for residents to remain in rural areas rather than move to cities.

## 1.1.2   Trends

Tourism is the world's largest growth industry and shows no sign of slowing down. Over the last decade, receipts from international tourism have increased by an average of 9 per cent annually to reach US$448 billion in 1997. During the same period, international tourist arrivals grew by a yearly average of 4.6 per cent and reached 616.5 million in 1997.

However, this growing trend was dampened in the last quarter of 1997 by the Asian economic crisis and this continues throughout 1998. Notwithstanding such cyclical movements in activity, in the longer term there can only be further sustained growth in the sector.

## 1.1.3   Regional trends

### Africa
Arrivals rose by 7.4 per cent to more than 23 million in 1997, while receipts increased by 4.5 per cent to US$8.7 billion. The most popular regions were Southern Africa and Eastern Africa.

### Americas
Growth fell below the world average with arrivals increasing by 2 per cent to 119 million and receipts climbing over 6 per cent to US$120 billion in 1997.

The USA showed the strongest growth, with an increase of 5.7 per cent in terms of arrivals and 7.4 per cent in terms of receipts.

Arrivals in the Caribbean region grew by 6.8 per cent to 15.4 million and by 6.5 per cent to 15.4 million in South America in 1997.

### East Asia and the Pacific
1997 was not a good year for tourism in East Asia and the Pacific. Tourism arrivals rose by only 1.1 per cent in 1997 and the receipts grew by only 2 per cent, with the worst results in North-East Asia.

### Europe
European countries experienced a growth of 3.2 per cent to almost 363 million and receipts up slightly less than 1 per cent to US$223 billion. The

most popular destinations in 1997 were Northern Europe with France (+ 7 per cent), Switzerland (+ 4.5 per cent), Ireland (+ 4.9 per cent) and the United Kingdom (+ 3 per cent).

European and Mediterranean countries had another season of solid growth, especially Spain and Greece which experienced growth of 7 and 11 per cent respectively.

### Middle East

Tourist arrivals to the Middle East grew by 4.1 per cent to almost 15 million and receipts by 10.7 per cent to US$8.6 billion in 1997. Egypt, which accounts for half of the region's arrivals, reported an increase of 3.7 per cent in arrivals and 20 per cent in receipts despite numerous cancellations at the end of the year due to violence in Luxor.

The only exception in the region was Israel, which suffered a drop of nearly 2 per cent in tourist arrivals.

### South Asia

Tourist arrivals increased by 5.1 per cent, to 4.6 million and receipts by 6.6 per cent to US$4.1 billion.

India, which accounts for half of all arrivals, showed an increase of 3.9 per cent. Sri Lanka showed a spectacular turnaround with an increase of 23.5 per cent in arrivals and 35.7 per cent in earnings.

The Maldives and Nepal grew steadily in 1997, while Pakistan declined for the third consecutive year.

**Example 1.1**   *Top 20 tourism destinations 1990–1997*

| Rank | | | | | International tourism arrivals (million) | | | Market share % of world total | |
|------|------|------|------|---------|------|------|------|------|------|
| 1990 | 1995 | 1996 | 1997 | Country | 1990 | 1996 | 1997 | 1990 | 1997 |
| 1 | 1 | 1 | 1 | France | 52.497 | 62.406 | 66.800 | 11.52 | 10.83 |
| 2 | 2 | 2 | 2 | USA | 39.363 | 46.325 | 48.977 | 8.64 | 7.94 |
| 3 | 3 | 3 | 3 | Spain | 34.085 | 40.541 | 43.403 | 7.48 | 7.04 |
| 4 | 4 | 4 | 4 | Italy | 26.679 | 32.853 | 34.087 | 5.86 | 5.53 |
| 7 | 5 | 5 | 5 | UK | 18.013 | 25.293 | 26.052 | 3.95 | 4.22 |
| 12 | 8 | 6 | 6 | China | 10.484 | 22.765 | 23.770 | 2.30 | 3.85 |
| 8 | 7 | 7 | 7 | Mexico | 17.176 | 21.405 | 22.700 | 3.77 | 3.68 |
| 27 | 9 | 9 | 8 | Poland | 3.400 | 19.410 | 19.560 | 0.75 | 3.17 |
| 5 | 6 | 8 | 9 | Hungary | 20.510 | 20.674 | 19.478 | 4.50 | 3.16 |
| 10 | 11 | 10 | 10 | Canada | 15.209 | 17.285 | 17.556 | 3.34 | 2.85 |
| 16 | 12 | 12 | 11 | Czech Rep. | 7.278 | 17.000 | 17.400 | 1.60 | 2.82 |

| | | | | | | | | | |
|---|---|---|---|---|---|---|---|---|---|
| 6 | 10 | 11 | 12 | Austria | 19.011 | 17.090 | 16.575 | 4.17 | 2.69 |
| 9 | 13 | 13 | 13 | Germany | 17.045 | 15.205 | 15.828 | 3.74 | 2.57 |
| – | 18 | 14 | 14 | Russian Fed. | – | 14.587 | 15.000 | – | 2.43 |
| 11 | 14 | 16 | 15 | Switzerland | 13.200 | 10.600 | 11.077 | 2.90 | 1.80 |
| 19 | 15 | 15 | 16 | Hong Kong | 6.581 | 11.703 | 10.534 | 1.44 | 1.71 |
| 13 | 16 | 18 | 17 | Greece | 8.873 | 9.233 | 10.126 | 1.95 | 1.64 |
| 14 | 17 | 17 | 18 | Portugal | 8.020 | 9.730 | 10.100 | 1.76 | 1.64 |
| 24 | 20 | 19 | 19 | Turkey | 4.799 | 7.966 | 9.040 | 1.05 | 1.47 |
| 21 | 21 | 20 | 20 | Thailand | 5.299 | 7.192 | 7.263 | 1.16 | 1.18 |
| | | | | Total 1–20 | 327.52 | 429.263 | 445.326 | 71.90 | 72.22 |
| | | | | **World total** | **445.54** | **594.140** | **616.635** | **100.00** | **100.00** |

Source: World Tourism Organisation

**Example 1.2**    *Top 20 tourism earners 1990–1997*

| Rank | | | | Country | International tourism arrivals ($bn) | | | Market share % of world total | |
|---|---|---|---|---|---|---|---|---|---|
| 1990 | 1995 | 1996 | 1997 | | 1990 | 1996 | 1997 | 1990 | 1997 |
| 1 | 1 | 1 | 1 | USA | 43.007 | 69.908 | 75.056 | 15.99 | 16.74 |
| 3 | 2 | 2 | 2 | Italy | 20.016 | 30.018 | 30.000 | 7.44 | 6.69 |
| 4 | 4 | 4 | 3 | Spain | 18.593 | 27.414 | 28.147 | 6.91 | 6.28 |
| 2 | 3 | 3 | 4 | France | 20.184 | 28.357 | 27.947 | 7.50 | 6.23 |
| 5 | 5 | 5 | 5 | UK | 14.940 | 19.296 | 19.875 | 5.55 | 4.43 |
| 6 | 6 | 6 | 6 | Germany | 14.288 | 17.567 | 18.989 | 5.31 | 4.24 |
| 7 | 7 | 7 | 7 | Austria | 13.417 | 13.990 | 12.393 | 4.99 | 2.76 |
| 25 | 10 | 9 | 8 | China | 2.218 | 10.200 | 12.074 | 0.82 | 2.69 |
| 11 | 8 | 8 | 9 | Hong Kong | 5.032 | 10.836 | 9.635 | 1.87 | 2.15 |
| 8 | 9 | 10 | 10 | Switzerland | 7.411 | 8.891 | 9.015 | 2.75 | 2.01 |
| 65 | 15 | 14 | 11 | Poland | 0.358 | 8.400 | 9.000 | 0.13 | 2.01 |
| 14 | 14 | 12 | 12 | Australia | 4.088 | 8.703 | 8.900 | 1.52 | 1.99 |
| 9 | 12 | 11 | 13 | Canada | 6.339 | 8.868 | 8.825 | 2.36 | 1.97 |
| 13 | 13 | 13 | 14 | Thailand | 4.326 | 8.664 | 8.700 | 1.61 | 1.94 |
| 12 | 11 | 15 | 15 | Singapore | 4.596 | 7.916 | 7.950 | 1.71 | 1.77 |
| – | 23 | 17 | 16 | Russian Fed. | – | 6.875 | 7.318 | – | 1.63 |
| 10 | 16 | 16 | 17 | Mexico | 5.467 | 6.934 | 7.307 | 2.03 | 1.63 |
| 21 | 21 | 20 | 18 | Turkey | 3.225 | 5.962 | 7.000 | 1.20 | 1.56 |
| 16 | 17 | 18 | 19 | Netherlands | 3.636 | 6.256 | 6.597 | 1.35 | 1.47 |
| 15 | 18 | 21 | 20 | Belgium | 3.721 | 5.893 | 5.997 | 1.38 | 1.34 |
| | | | | Total 1–20 | 194.86 | 310.94 | 320.72 | 72.43 | 71.55 |
| | | | | **World total** | **269.03** | **435.07** | **448.26** | **100.00** | **100.00** |

Source: World Tourism Organisation

## 1.1.4   Forecasts

*Market forecasts*

Despite setbacks in 1998, the travel and tourism industry is on course as a key industry in the 21st century, along with telecommunications and information technology.

Tourism growth in the next decade is expected to be impressive. The World Tourism Organisation (WTO) predicts that international arrivals will top 700 million by year 2000 and one billion by 2010. Likewise earnings are predicted to grow to US$621 billion by year 2000 and US$1,550 billion by 2010.

While the number of people travelling will boom in the 21st century, the WTO also predicts that the amount of leisure time that people can spend travelling will decrease. As a result, travellers will look for products that offer maximum thrill in minimum time.

Short break and weekend trips will be enjoyed more frequently while the main vacation of the year is likely to get shorter.

### Sector forecasts
As the world becomes increasingly explored and there are fewer destinations left for tourists to discover, the future trend will be to travel to high places or to the ends of the earth. It is already possible to book organised treks to scale the world's highest peaks or to visit the wreckage of the Titanic from a submarine.

The cruise sector is growing at a phenomenal rate. Some seven million people took a cruise in 1997 and that number is expected to increase to nine million by the year 2000. To respond to this demand, 42 cruise vessels are currently under construction worldwide.

Ecotourism is another growing sector. Ecotourism ranges from small, highly focused study tours to the large volume of resort tourists who make a day trip to a nature reserve during their holidays.

The other sector of growth is cultural tourism, especially to Europe, the Middle East and Asia from virtually all regions of the world. This type of tourism includes a wide range of travellers, from small educational groups to day trips to cultural sites by mass market holidaymakers.

Finally, theme parks will be an increasingly popular vacation destination and several new ones are currently in the planning stages around the world.

## 1.2   The UK travel and tourism market

### 1.2.1   Market size

As for the rest of the world, the travel and tourism industry is one of UK's key industries.

**Example 1.3**  *Value of tourism and the gross domestic product 1991–1997*

| Year | International tourism | | | Domestic tourism | All tourism | GDP | Share of tourism |
|------|-----------------------|---|---|---------|---------|---------|----------|
| | Overseas earnings | Fares | Total | | | | |
| | £m | £m | £m | £m | £m | £m | % |
| **1991** | 7,386 | 1,800 | 9,186 | 10,470 | 19,656 | 575,700 | 3.4 |
| **1992** | 7,891 | 2,100 | 9,991 | 10,665 | 20,656 | 598,900 | 3.4 |
| **1993** | 9,487 | 2,375 | 11,862 | 12,430 | 24,292 | 631,000 | 3.8 |
| **1994** | 9,786 | 2,550 | 12,336 | 13,220 | 25,556 | 669,100 | 3.8 |
| **1995** | 11,763 | 2,825 | 14,588 | 12,775 | 27,363 | 704,200 | 3.9 |
| **1996** | 12,369 | 3,090 | 15,459 | 13,895 | 29,354 | 742,300 | 4.0 |
| **1997e** | 12,785 | 3,210 | 15,840 | 14,180 | 30,020 | 786,308 | 3.9 |

*Source: Office for National Statistics*
*e - estimates*

Over the review period, the value of tourism has increased by 53 per cent to reach the value of just over £30 billion in 1997. Tourism as a proportion of GDP has increased gradually from 3.4 per cent in 1991 to 4 per cent in 1997.

In the first three months of 1998 the number of visitors arriving in the UK fell by 7 per cent compared with the same period of 1997. Industry sources suggest that there were 10 per cent fewer Europeans and arrivals from the Middle East, Africa and Asia dropped by 12 per cent.

The strength of sterling and the economic crisis in Asia are thought to be the main reasons for this fall in tourism. However, the British Tourist Authority still predicts that the number of tourists visiting the UK will increase by 3 per cent in 1998 from the 1997 total of 26.2 million overseas arrivals.

The British Incoming Tour Operators' Association (BITOA), the 310 members of which handle around 40 per cent of all arrivals from abroad, is, however, less optimistic. It forecasts a 6 per cent fall overall, with Western Europe showing the biggest drop.

The good news for the rest of the world is that British tourists have been travelling abroad in record numbers during 1997. Taking advantage of good exchange rates, 80 per cent of them chose European destinations.

## 1.2.2  Market sectors

The tourism industry consists of three main sectors: domestic, outbound and inbound. In 1997 these markets represented a total of 199 million tourist trips, over 1.1 billion bed nights and a total expenditure estimated at £50bn.

**Example 1.4**  *Growth in expenditure since 1993*

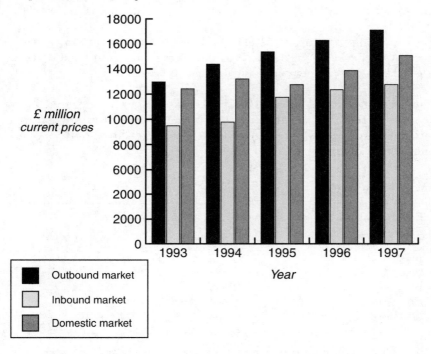

## Definitions

- **Domestic market** – includes all tourist trips and day visits of UK residents within the UK.
- **Outbound market** – includes all tourist trips and day visits of UK residents overseas.
- **Inbound market** – includes all tourist trips and day visits of overseas residents to the UK.

**Example 1.5**  *Sector shares of the UK tourism industry (%) 1997*

|  | Trips | Expenditure |
|---|---|---|
| Sector |  |  |
| **Domestic market** | 43.8 | 35 |
| **Outbound market** | 36.0 | 35 |
| **Inbound market** | 20.2 | 25 |

### The domestic market

The domestic market accounts for 47 per cent of expenditure of the total travel and tourism industry. In 1997 British residents took 56.7 million trips for holiday purposes, an increase of 9 per cent on the previous year, and the spending at £14,170 million was also up by 2 per cent compared to 1996.

The duration of a domestic travel trip follows a similar pattern to outbound travel trips. Between 1992 and 1997, the average duration for a domestic trip fell by almost 17 per cent from 4.2 days to 3.5 days.

The development of short domestic breaks has been triggered by an increase in the level of car ownership, an improvement in the transport infrastructure and a wider range of short break offers from both large and smaller tour operators.

### The outbound market

| **Example 1.6** *UK residents' visits abroad and spending 1993–1997* | | |
|---|---|---|
| | *Visits (000s)* | *Spending (£m)* |
| **1993** | 36,720 | 12,972 |
| **1994** | 39,630 | 14,365 |
| **1995** | 41,345 | 15,386 |
| **1996** | 42,569 | 16,310 |
| **1997** | 46,803 | 17,136 |

The UK market for overseas travel has increased by 10 per cent since 1996 to reach a volume of 46.8 million visits in 1997 and by 5 per cent in value to reach a value of £17.2 billion. Over the review period it represents a growth of 27 per cent in volume and almost 33 per cent in value.

*Where did they go?*
European Union countries remain the most popular overseas destination, followed by North America and non-European Union countries.

Overall, the number of visits by UK residents to the European Union remained almost unchanged between 1995 and 1996 with France and Spain remaining the two main destinations.

The largest increases in the number of visits were to Belgium, Sweden, Finland and the Irish Republic. The largest falls were in Austria and Greece.

The number of visits to non-European Union countries and North America increased by 12 per cent between 1995 and 1996.

The largest increases were to Turkey, Central and Eastern Europe and the USA.

As regards the rest of the world, the Caribbean, Central and South America and New Zealand registered the largest increases.

In terms of spending, the greatest rise was in the USA and the largest falls were in Greece and Spain.

*Average length of stay*
The longest stays by UK residents abroad were for visits to Australia, followed by New Zealand and India. Australia and New Zealand also accounted for the highest average spending per visit.

The shortest stays and lowest level of spending were for visits to Belgium and France, the most popular destinations for UK residents' visits of nil to three nights in 1996.

*Transport*
Air transport is the most popular means of transport when travelling overseas. In 1997, almost two-thirds of all visits abroad were made by air. Just over a quarter of the other visits were made by sea and about one-twelfth through the Channel Tunnel.

The Channel Tunnel, since it opened in 1994, has welcomed aboard an increasing number of travellers despite the fire in November 1996. The number of trips through the tunnel reached 3.5 million in 1996, up 79 per cent compared with 1995.

**The inbound market**

*Example 1.7  Overseas residents' visits to the UK and spending, 1993–1997*

|      | Visits (000s) | Spending (£m) |
|------|-----|-----|
| 1993 | 19,863 | 9,487 |
| 1994 | 20,764 | 9,786 |
| 1995 | 23,537 | 11,763 |
| 1996 | 25,293 | 12,369 |
| 1997 | 26,189 | 12,785 |

The number of overseas residents' visits to the UK has increased by 3 per cent since 1996 to reach a volume of 26 million visits in 1997 and by 3 per cent in value to reach a value of £12.8 billion. Over the review period it represents a growth a 31 per cent in volume and almost 35 per cent in value.

*Where do they come from and go to?*
Residents of the European Union accounted for over 65 per cent of all visits to the UK in 1997. The highest number of visits were made by residents of France, who accounted for 15 per cent of all visits made to the UK, closely followed by the USA and Germany which both made up 12 per cent of all visits.

Overall, the number of visits by North American residents to the UK remained almost unchanged between 1995 and 1996, whereas there was an increase of 12 per cent in the number of visits to the UK from the rest of the European Union in 1996.

The largest increases in the number of overseas residents' visits to the UK were from Iceland (104 per cent), Central and Eastern Europe and Denmark.

Visits from other countries fell by 2 per cent overall with the largest falls from South-East Asian countries following the financial crisis which hit the region.

In terms of spending, the USA accounted for 16 per cent of all spending, while residents of France accounted for 6 per cent only.

Over half of the overseas residents staying in the UK spent at least one night in London. England was the most visited region with 46 per cent of visitors spending one night or more. The second most popular region was Scotland with 9 per cent and finally Wales with 4 per cent.

*Average length of stay*
The longest average stays in the UK were by residents of distant countries, in particular New Zealand and the Caribbean for which the average stay was about 25 nights. Residents of Belgium had the shortest stays; an average of three nights.

*Transport*
In 1996, around 65 per cent of all visitors to the UK came by air, 24 per cent by sea and 11 per cent used the Channel Tunnel. As for the outbound market, the Channel Tunnel has taken an increasingly share of the overseas market. There was a 51 per cent increase in the number of visits by overseas residents using the Channel Tunnel between 1995 and 1996.

## 1.3   Industry background

Accurate statements of total numbers of tour operators and travel agents are difficult to make. A large number are members of ABTA; more than

90 per cent by turnover according to ABTA. Today there are over 2,000 ABTA travel agents and 644 and 321 travel agents/tour operators. However, there is a multitude of other travel trade associations and many of those are not members of ABTA. Those associations are principally:

(a)  The Association of European Travel Agents (AETA). It has approximately 45 members, none of which are members of ABTA.

(b)  ARTAC. Membership of approximately 660, mainly travel agents which are all members of ABTA.

(c)  The Association of Independent Tour Operators (AITO). Membership of 155 and about half are members of ABTA.

(d)  The Association of British Tour Operators to France (ABTOF). Membership of 150 about half of which are members of ABTA.

(e)  Federation of Tour Operators (FTO). FTO has a membership of 18 tour operators, all of which are members of ABTA.

(f)  The Global Travel Group (GTG). Membership of 200 travel agents which are not members of ABTA.

(g)  The National Association of Independent Travel Agents (NAITA). NAITA has a membership of 720 travel agents of which 90 per cent are members of ABTA too.

(h)  The Travel Trust Association (TTA) has 300 travel agent members which are all members of ABTA.

Finally there are a number of tour operators and agents which are not members of any trade associations.

## 1.3.1  Regulations

The travel trade is subject to both statutory regulation and self-regulation. As regards statutory provisions, the Civil Aviation (Air Travel Organisers' Licensing) Regulations 1995, known as the ATOL Regulations, require businesses selling or advertising package holidays taken by air to hold an Air Travel Organisers' Licence (ATOL). As at June 1997 there were 1,719 ATOL holders. The Civil Aviation Authority (CAA) is the licensing authority under the ATOL Regulations. To acquire an ATOL, the business must satisfy financial criteria and provide a bond to the CAA, the amount depending on projected turnover. We deal with the CAA regulations in depth within Chapter 2.

The other main statutory provisions are the Package Travel, Package Holidays and Package Tours Regulations 1992 (the 'Package Travel Regulations'). These were introduced following an EC Council Directive in 1992.

On the self-regulation side, the main regulatory body for the travel trade is ABTA. ABTA imposes financial requirements upon its members and it operates a code of conduct. ABTA is an approved body for the purposes of

11

the Package Travel Regulations and so are AITO and FTO. ABTA's rules are analysed in Chapter 3; we look at the International Air Transport Association (IATA) in Chapter 4, and other industry bodies in Chapter 5.

# 1.4 Tour operators and the package holiday industry

The number of holidays taken abroad by UK residents has increased steadily since the early 1980s. Between 1986 and 1997, the number of UK residents' visits abroad rose from 25 million to over 46 million visits in 1996. During the same period, the number of holidays abroad of four or more nights increased by 51 per cent from almost 18 million in 1986 to 27 million holidays in 1996.

Europe has remained the most popular holiday destination: three-quarters of overseas visits were made to the European Union in 1997. However, the longest average stays abroad in 1997 were for visits to non-European countries. European countries benefit particularly from short business trips, weekend breaks and short stays. France and Spain have remained the two most popular destinations, accounting for 42 per cent of all visits abroad by UK residents in 1996.

## 1.4.1 All-inclusive tours

The all-inclusive sector has shown a dynamic growth over the last few years. Exotic long-haul destinations are contributing to the strong growth of the all-inclusive sector as holidaymakers are now prepared to take a long-haul flight for a summer holiday. Figures over the last past years show that long-haul holidays have increased on average by 12.5 per cent since 1993.

As holidaymakers become more experienced and adventurous, newer destinations like Mexico and India are becoming more attractive. Inexpensive charter flights, price wars and discounting among the major tour operators have also boosted the market. However, the demand for all-inclusive tours in Europe has increased and leading tour operators have recently introduced the concept to European resorts.

**Example 1.8**  *Number of visits abroad on all-inclusive holidays by UK residents 1995–1997*

|  | *Visits (000s)* | *% change from previous year* | *£m* | *% change from previous year* | *Average price/holiday* |
|---|---|---|---|---|---|
| **1995** | 170 | – | 163 | – | 959 |
| **1996** | 350 | 105% | 315 | 93% | 900 |
| **1997** | 700 | 100% | 578 | 83% | 826 |

## 1.4.2 Consumer demand and expenditure

In 1980, just 9 per cent of UK residents took an annual holiday abroad. By 1996, this figure had risen to 23 per cent.

According to the 1995/1996 Family Expenditure Survey (FES), the average household spent just under £500 a year buying holidays, of which £374 was on hotels and holidays abroad. Expenditure on holidays abroad is the third largest of individual household expenditure items; housing and motoring being the two highest. However, in times of economic hardship consumer expenditure on holidays is one of the first things to be cut.

## 1.4.3 The supply structure and key players

The recent deals that have recently taken place have put a large part of the UK package travel industry in the hands of just four operators. Thomson, Airtours, First Choice and Thomas Cook control almost 70 per cent of the market.

The consolidation of Britain's travel industry was intensified as three major deals were concluded in June 1998. First Choice Holidays took the lead with two deals worth a combined total of £134 million, buying two long-haul operators, Unijet and Hayes & Jarvis. It paid £110 million for Unijet, the tour operator which specialises in package holidays and also controls an airline and car rental business. First Choice also paid a further £24 million for Hayes & Jarvis, the upmarket travel company which offers more expensive long-haul trips to exotic islands.

Thomas Cook completed the third deal by acquiring Flying Colours, the tour operator and charter airline. The sum paid for Flying Colours remained undisclosed; however, analysts estimate the cost of the acquisition between £50 and £65 million. The deal also included the Flying Colours airline.

Two main factors are behind this rush for acquisitions. The first is the result of the year-long MMC investigation released in December 1997 and which gave the green light for further acquisitions in the industry.

The MMC investigation followed the protests of smaller agents and tour operators which had complained that the intensified vertical integration of the larger groups was leading to uncompetitive practices. The UK's largest holiday companies, principally Thomson Travel and Airtours, were referred to the MMC on competition grounds in November 1996. However, in its final report, the MMC ruled this integrated structure was 'broadly competitive'. The MMC report findings and implications for the future of the industry are analysed in Chapter 6.

13

The second factor is the growing trend toward long-haul holidays, at the expense of the more traditional package holidays. Over the last four years long-haul holidays have shown a growth of 12.3 per cent whereas the short-haul market has decreased by 1.4 per cent. The problem for the larger tour operators is that so far they have been under-represented in long-haul holidays. For example, while Thomson has 25 per cent of the UK holiday market, its share of long haul is only 14 per cent.

In market share terms, Thomson is still the largest player with 25 per cent of the UK all-inclusive air holiday market. Following its recent acquisitions, First Choice is now within touching distance with Airtours, which remains in second place with 18.2 per cent. First Choice now has 15.4 per cent, and finally Sunworld, Thomas Cook's tour operator, has 8 per cent.

Following the acquisitions, analysts reckon that First Choice's market share of the UK holiday industry could rise to 18 per cent and Thomas Cook's to 16 per cent.

Despite this quasi-monopoly situation, competition between the four largest players should remain fierce in their rush for market share. Further consolidation and alliances are possible within the industry but there are now relatively few other medium-sized companies to buy.

In an industry now dominated by four major players, many smaller companies are questioning their future and are wondering how they can grow. However, if the big four control almost 70 per cent of the package holiday market, nearly 55 per cent of the long-haul market is still dominated by a multitude of medium- to small-sized companies. With holidaymakers developing a taste for more remote destinations, and taking the chance of getting away from more commercial tourist areas and exploring foreign cultures, smaller companies should take this opportunity to develop niche markets and thereby protect themselves (if that is their intention) from being eaten up by the big ones.

## 1.4.4  The big four

**Example 1.9**  *Vertical integration of the largest companies in the UK travel trade*

| *UK parent* | *Main tour operator and trade names* | *Main travel agent and trade names* | *Airlines* |
|---|---|---|---|
| **Thomson Travel Group** | Thomson Tour Operations Ltd *Trade names:* Thomson Skytours Portland Direct Ausbound Austravel Budget Travel | Lunn Poly Ltd *Trade name:* Lunn Poly Holiday Shops | Britannia Airways Ltd *Trade name:* Britannia |
| **Airtours plc** | Airtours plc *Trade names:* Airtours Aspro Eurosites Tradewinds | Going Places Leisure Travel Ltd *Trade names:* Going Places Going Places Direct Go Direct Late Escapes | Airtours International Airways Ltd *Trade name:* Airtours International |
| **First Choice Holidays Plc** | First Choice Holidays & Flights Ltd *Trade names:* First Choice Eclipse Sovereign Hayes & Jarvis Unijet | | Airtours 2000 Ltd *Trade name:* Air 2000 |
| **Thomas Cook Group Ltd** | Thomas Cook Group Ltd Sunworld Ltd Time Off Ltd *Trade names:* Thomas Cook Holidays Sunworld Time Off Flying Colours | Thomas Cook Group Ltd *Trade names:* Thomas Cook Thomas Cook Direct | Airworld Ltd *Trade name:* Airworld |

*Example 1.10*   *Changing share of holiday market*

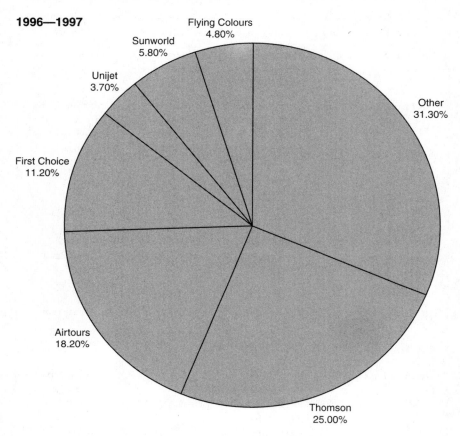

**1996—1997**

Flying Colours
4.80%

Sunworld
5.80%

Unijet
3.70%

Other
31.30%

First Choice
11.20%

Airtours
18.20%

Thomson
25.00%

### Thomson Travel Group Limited ('Thomson' or TTG)

Thomson is Britain's largest travel operator with 25 per cent of the market. Its airline, Britannia Airways, is the UK's second biggest airline after British Airways. It owns the Lunn Poly tour agency chain as well as Holiday Cottages, the biggest renter of holiday cottages in Britain. Last year, it sold 3.7 million holidays and flew 18 million passengers and reached a profit of £112.24 million on turnover of £1.7 billion.

TTG is organised as a holding company and subsidiary companies control-ling its four main holiday business activities: tour operations (Thomson), charter airline (Britannia), retail travel (Lunn Poly) and holiday cottage letting (Holiday Cottages Group Limited). The four operating subsidiaries are managed as self-contained entities.

TTG has generally grown organically. However, in 1988 it acquired Horizon Travel Ltd and in the last five years to 1996 total acquisitions cost

16

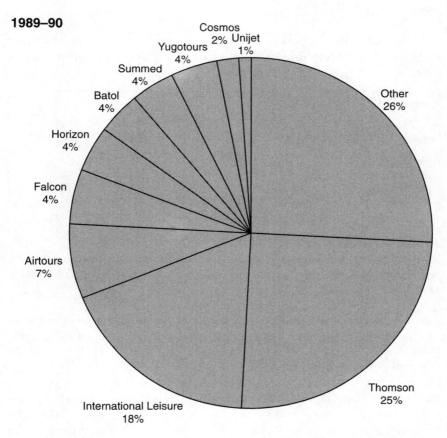

**1989–90**

Cosmos 2%
Unijet 1%
Yugotours 4%
Summed 4%
Batol 4%
Horizon 4%
Falcon 4%
Airtours 7%
International Leisure 18%
Thomson 25%
Other 26%

TTG £58 million. Among those acquisitions were English Country Cottages Limited, Blakes Cottages Group Limited and Country Holidays Limited (which became the Holiday Cottages Group Limited) and Budget Travel Limited.

TTG's main brands are:

- Thomson, which has been used since 1972 to replace the Thomson Skytours name;
- Britannia, Thomson's charter airline acquired in 1964. In 1997 Britannia operated a fleet of 29 aircraft;
- Lunn Poly, Thomson's travel agency acquired in 1972;
- Skytours, which was rebranded in 1986 to offer budget-type holidays; and
- Portland Direct, formed in 1979 to compete with direct sales operators in the UK market.

From 1992 to 1997, turnover increased by 36 per cent from 1.25 billion in 1992 to 1.7 billion in 1997.

TTG defended its position as the UK's largest package holiday company by buying Crystal, the seventh largest group, for £66.2 million in August 1998.

| ***Example 1.11*** *Financial results* | | | | |
|---|---|---|---|---|
| | *1997*<br>*(£m)* | *1996*<br>*(£m)* | *1995*<br>*(£m)* | *1994*<br>*(£m)* |
| **Sales** | 1,780.2 | 1,584 | 1,504 | 1,456 |
| **Profit** | 83.5 | 67.0 | 58.0 | 90.0 |
| **Profit margin** (%) | 4.6 | 4.2 | 4.0 | 6.1 |

### First Choice Holidays plc

With its recent acquisition of Unijet Group, number five in the industry, and Hayes & Jarvis, the upmarket package holiday group, First Choice Holidays now claims 15.4 per cent market share.

First Choice Holidays' profit last year was £15.4 million on turnover of £1 billion while Unijet made £10.2 million profit on turnover of £308.6 millions. Hayes & Jarvis had a turnover of £51.7 million in 1997 and an adjusted profit before taxation of £2.7 million.

First Choice Holidays was known as Owners Abroad until 1994 when it was rebranded to its present name and its product range rationalised. The rebranding and rationalisation were in response to poor performances in 1993.

First Choice Holidays is a vertically integrated tour operator, First Choice, and airline, Air 2000, but it does not have a travel agency. Between 1993 and 1995, it tried a strategic alliance with Thomas Cook Group but the link has gradually weakened over the years.

Air 2000 was founded in 1986. Initially, First Choice Holidays invested 76 per cent in the airline and acquired the remaining 24 per cent in 1990. The airline leases 13 Boeing 757s and four Airbus A320s.

In the five years to 1996 the cost of First Choice Holidays' acquisitions totalled £43 million for travel-related businesses, £29 million was spent on new acquisitions and the balance represented acquisitions for the remaining shareholding in companies in which First Choice Holidays owned 25 or 50 per cent of the share capital.

Turnover increased by 31 per cent over the last five years, from £772 million in 1992 to over £1 billion in 1997.

| **Example 1.12**   *Financial results* | | | | |
|---|---|---|---|---|
| | **1997** **(£m)** | **1996** **(£m)** | **1995** **(£m)** | **1994** **(£m)** |
| **Sales** | 1,021.0 | 1,031.1 | 933.6 | 821.8 |
| **Profit** | 15.4 | 10.0 | 1.3 | 16.3 |
| **Profit margin** (%) | 1.5 | 1.0 | 0.1 | 2.0 |

*Airtours plc*
Having failed to purchase Unijet, Airtours plc is no longer the largest player in the industry.

Airtours plc owns Airtours International Airways and the Going Places travel chain. Its brands include Aspro Holidays, Eurosites and Tradewinds. Last year it carried five million passengers and sold 2.9 million holidays. It made a profit of £120 million on turnover of £2.1 billion.

Airtours plc is organised in six divisions, each as a separate entity:

- UK tour operations – this comprises Airtours UK all-inclusive tour operations (Airtours, Aspro Travel Ltd and Tradewinds) and the Eurosites business (self-drive camping holidays for UK and continental customers);
- UK retail – this includes the Going Places travel agent network and Late Escapes, a telephone sales operation;
- Scandinavian Leisure Group – this has tour operations and a retail network in Denmark, Finland, Norway and Sweden;
- North American Leisure Group – this comprises tour operations in Canada and in the USA;
- Aviation division – this comprises Airtours International and Premiair which supplies the Scandinavian Leisure Group;
- Cruise and hotel division – this consists of three cruise ships and around 40 hotels serving the group's tour operating activities.

Between 1992 and 1996, Airtours spent over £200 million on acquisitions. The main acquisitions include:

- Pickford for £16 million in 1992;
- Aspro for £20 million and Hogg Robinson for £25 million in 1993;
- SLG for £80 million in 1994; and
- Sunquest Vacation Limited in 1995 for £38 million.

The Pickford and Hogg Robinson acquisitions enabled Airtours plc to establish its travel agency network, which was rebranded as Going Places in December 1993.

Airtours plc established its airline, Airtours International, in 1990.

Over the last five years, Airtours plc has increased its turnover by more than three times, from £406 million in 1992 to £2.1 billion in 1997.

| *Example 1.13* *Financial results* | | | | |
|---|---|---|---|---|
| | 1997 (£m) | 1996 (£m) | 1995 (£m) | 1994 (£m) |
| **Sales** | 2,174 | 1,717 | 1,317 | 971 |
| **Profit** | 120.3 | 86.8 | 59.4 | 71.3 |
| **Profit margin** (%) | 5.5 | 5.0 | 4.5 | 7.3 |

### Thomas Cook Group

In terms of holidays sold Thomas Cook remains fourth in its market, although it is said that the purchase of Flying Colours could give Sunworld, its tour operating business, 16 per cent market share. Thomas Cook expects to carry more than 1.5 million passengers in summer 1998 on its combined fleet of 14 aircraft.

Thomas Cook as a travel company has a long history, going back to 1841 when it was owned by the British Government. It was then owned by Midland Bank until 1993 when it was acquired by Westdeutsche Landesbank Girozentrale.

Thomas Cook Group's management is organised in two major businesses:

- Financial services, including foreign exchange and traveller's cheques businesses and retail, wholesale and commercial activities; and
- Travel-related businesses which consists of a travel agency operation, Thomas Cook Retail, and a tour operator, under the name of Thomas Cook Holidays.

In June 1996 Thomas Cook acquired Sunworld for £38 million. Sunworld offers short- and long-haul holidays and its charter airline operates under the name of Airworld. During summer 1996 Airworld operated three Airbus A320 aircraft.

Over the last five years, Thomas Cook Group's turnover increased by 80 per cent from £486 million in 1992 to £873 million in 1996.

In September 1997 Thomas Cook was set to buy Carlson Leisure, the travel group that owns the AT Mays travel group.

| **Example 1.14** *Financial results* | | | | |
|---|---|---|---|---|
| | *1997* (*£m*) | *1996* (*£m*) | *1995* (*£m*) | *1994* (*£m*) |
| **Sales** | 970,910 | 873,285 | 750,042 | 656,562 |
| **Profit** | 41,751 | 44,978 | 32,127 | 60,700 |
| **Profit margin** (%) | 4.3 | 5.15 | 4.28 | 9.25 |

## 1.5  Travel agents

Overall, 1997 was a good year for travel agents. Both retail and business travel agents reported that trading was on the increase in 1997, resulting from a higher consumer confidence in the economic climate, a stronger pound, and the so-called 'feel good' factor boosted by the general election and windfall payouts.

Margins also improved in 1997 as fewer holidays were sold at last minute discounted prices, following the capacity reductions made by the leading tour operators.

### 1.5.1  Supply structure and key players

Many travel agents are members of ABTA. According to ABTA, its members accounted for around 90 per cent of the total turnover of travel agents, including the largest vertically integrated groups of tour operators and travel agents. In 1996, there were some 2,152 ABTA travel agencies with 6,935 retail branch offices. This figure is lower than the high point of 2,971 in 1990, but there are now an increasing number of non-ABTA travel agents.

In terms of outlet numbers the sector is still dominated by the independent agents, although not in market share. Approximately 71 per cent of travel agents had only one retail outlet and 19 per cent had either two or three retail outlets in 1997. Only about 10 per cent had more than three retail outlets in their travel agency chain.

Meanwhile multiple chains are continuing to increase their hold on the sector, with four leading travel agents – Lunn Poly, Going Places, Thomas Cook and AT Mays. Collectively their retail outlets rose from 1,461 in 1991 to 2,310 in 1997. This increase was offset by a broadly matching reduction among smaller travel agents. Their ever growing market share is triggered by intensified vertical integration in the travel industry and heavy price discounting.

***Example 1.15***   *All-inclusive airtours: market shares of UK travel agents by volume, 1992–1997*

|  | *1992* | *1993* | *1994* | *1995* | *1996* | *1997* |
|---|---|---|---|---|---|---|
| **Lunn Poly** | 21.0 | 23.0 | 24.0 | 23.0 | 22.0 | 23.0 |
| **Going Places** | 9.5 | 10.0 | 11.0 | 14.0 | 14.0 | 14.5 |
| **Thomas Cook** | 10.0 | 10.0 | 11.0 | 12.0 | 10.0 | 10.0 |
| **AT Mays/Worldchoice** | 4.5 | 4.0 | 5.0 | 5.5 | 5.0 | 5.5 |
| **Co-op Travelcare** | 3.0 | 3.5 | 3.5 | 4.5 | 4.0 | 4.0 |
| **Top five** | 48.0 | 50.5 | 54.5 | 59.0 | 55.5 | 57.0 |
| **Other travel agents** | 52.0 | 49.5 | 45.5 | 41.0 | 44.5 | 43.1 |

The four largest travel agents together accounted for 57 per cent of sales made to customers visiting travel agents in 1997. This is an increase of 8 per cent compared with 1992. If telesales and direct sales are included, the market shares of the four largest travel agents is reduced but only to a small extent. In part this is because these companies are also active in the direct sales sector through their linked tour operator.

Over the last three years the number of different foreign package holiday destinations offered by travel agents has increased. On average, travel agents offer 770 destinations for foreign package holidays, compared to 564 destinations three years ago.

## 1.5.2   Consumer profile

Overall, most UK residents take a foreign package holiday once a year or every other year and also a holiday in the UK once a year, with a large majority flying to their holiday destination.

Most package holidays are booked through a travel agent, Lunn Poly and Going Places being the most commonly used. However, holidaymakers do not feel tied to any particular travel agent. The choice of travel agent is generally a matter of convenience and there appears to be limited shopping around between travel agents.

## 1.5.3   The key players

### Lunn Poly

Lunn Poly is TTG's integrated travel agent and the largest retailer of UK air-inclusive holidays with a 21 per cent market share in 1997. Up until 1995, the company had a policy of store expansion to keep ahead of its main competitor Going Places. Since then, store openings by Lunn Poly have slowed down as they try to consolidate their market position.

In 1996, Lunn Poly received Investors In People (IIP) accreditation for its efforts in training and skills development, which is part of an overall programme to improve its customer satisfaction ratings.

In 1997, Lunn Poly successfully implemented 'Vision', a tailor-made automated booking and administration system, giving accurate holiday and travel information and reducing shop staff administration effort.

| **Example 1.16** *Financial results* | | | | |
|---|---|---|---|---|
| | *1997* *(£m)* | *1996* *(£m)* | *1995* *(£m)* | *1994* *(£m)* |
| **Sales** | 137,288 | 127,212 | 118,446 | 119,257 |
| **Profit** | 18,711 | 13,822 | 11,610 | 13,408 |
| **Profit margin** (%) | 13.6 | 10.9 | 9.8 | 11.2 |

### Going Places Leisure Travel Ltd

Going Places is Airtours' retail travel agency and was formed after Airtours acquired 333 Pickfords travel agent outlets in 1992, and another 210 of Hogg Robinson Leisure the following year.

Over the last few years Going Places has extended the range of air-inclusive products with an increased choice of cruise, ski, short breaks and long-haul holidays. At the same time it has also widened its choice of non air-inclusive products, which now account for 30 per cent of their business.

In the second half of 1997, Going Places sold 11 Going Places branches to Travelworld, the sixth largest travel agency in the UK. At the same time, Going Places set up a telesales network, called Go Direct, which is expected to sell 75,000 holidays direct to the public in its first year of operation.

The development of the 'matchmaker' concept has improved the level of service provided to clients, ensuring that they receive the best product to match their requirements.

Another area of significant growth has been the introduction of foreign exchange facilities.

**Example 1.17**   *Financial results*

|  | 1997 (£m) | 1996 (£m) | 1995 (£m) | 1994 (£m) |
|---|---|---|---|---|
| **Sales** | 175,817 | 157,088 | 141,465 | 118,840 |
| **Profit** | 14,056 | 8,741 | 7,032 | 6,001 |
| **Profit margin** (%) | 7.9 | 5.5 | 4.9 | 5.0 |

### Thomas Cook

One of Thomas Cook's main strengths over its competitors is in the foreign exchange and currency market where it has 20 per cent of the market.

In order to consolidate its market position, Thomas Cook has developed several new services. In 1997, it launched Money Direct, a next-day home delivery service for foreign exchange. Later in the year, it began to sell foreign exchange over the Internet.

An Internet booking service for holidays and flights was developed in the second half of 1997, the first of its kind in the UK.

Thomas Cook has also capitalised on direct booking. Today, around 10 per cent of Thomas Cook's booking are made by phone.

## 1.5.4   The future

The future is bright for the travel industry. Market research surveys suggest that there will be a rise of almost 30 per cent in the volume and about 23 per cent in real terms of charter transactions by the year 2002.

However, the holiday market is highly suceptible to unforseen events such as regional conflicts, adverse publicity about particular destinations and exchange rate fluctuations.

Although profitability has improved throughout the sector, travel agents are still facing increased pressure on margins, especially as suppliers tighten their pricing structures and airlines cut their commission rates. There is also the growing threat of direct bookings over the Internet and digital TV bookings.

To remain in the marketplace, travel agents must add value to their products, offer specialist knowledge of destination, as well as visa requirements, currencies, climate, etc.

Travel agents using the latest technologies will have a decisive advantage in the market. However, the pace of change in travel technology and channels for promoting travel is so swift that many small travel agents may not be prepared for this technological revolution.

Viewdata, the main booking format used by travel agents, is becoming outmoded with limited and slow search parameters.

Teletext has become a very successful response medium for holidays advertising and sales. It is estimated that 10 per cent of all package holidays bookings are a direct result of teletext advertising.

The launch of digital television should also create new opportunities in the travel industry.

## 1.6 Scheduled and non-scheduled passenger airlines

Over 530 airports worldwide reported passenger traffic rising 2 per cent in January 1998 compared with the same month last year, according to the Airports Council International. Although these figures continue to show movement increases, they clearly reflect a slowdown from the fast pace maintained at the start of 1996.

The highest passenger traffic growth were recorded in Latin America and the Caribbean with an increase of 12 per cent, followed by Europe (+ 6 per cent), the Middle East (+ 2 per cent), and North America (+ 1 per cent) in January 1998. The highest falls were recorded in Africa where passenger traffic fell by 8 per cent and in Asia/Pacific (− 3 per cent).

Both UK airports and UK airlines have benefited from the continued expansion in international and domestic air travel. The UK airline industry is among the world leaders in the market with British Airways (BA) being one of the global key players in the international passengers market.

---

**Example 1.18**   *UK airports 1997*

| | Terminal passengers (000s) | % change |
|---|---|---|
| **London (Gatwick)** | 26,795.5 | 11.1 |
| **London (Heathrow)** | 57,808.0 | 3.7 |
| **London (Stansted)** | 5,366.6 | 11.5 |
| **Edinburgh** | 4,157.8 | 9.1 |
| **Glasgow** | 6,011.7 | 9.8 |
| **Manchester** | 15,741.4 | 8.7 |

---

### 1.6.1 Supply structure

Airlines are classified into two main types: scheduled airlines and non-scheduled or charter airlines.

Although international scheduled services constitute the largest sector of the market, charter operators have considerably increased their share of the market over the last five years. This increased level of penetration of the market by non-scheduled services is a reflection of strong growth in the package tour industry.

### 1.6.2 Scheduled airlines

Since its privatisation in the 1980s, BA has remained the UK's number one airline despite the liberalisation and deregulation of the industry which has increased competition. In 1996, BA accounted for approximately 60 per cent of revenues generated by UK airlines.

BA's globalisation strategy includes a 25 per cent shareholding in Qantas, held since 1993, and also included a share in USAir which it sold in 1997 because of commercial negotiations with American Airlines.

Its position in Europe was consolidated through a 49 per cent stake in Deutsche BA and a 49.7 per cent stake in the French regional airline, TAT, in 1992.

However, BA is under continuing constant pressure from other UK carriers on European routes. British Midland and Air UK, which used to be mainly domestic airlines, are now flying to all the major European cities. Virgin Atlantic, which was once strictly an intercontinental airline, has also introduced European flights. Air UK's success in Europe led to its takeover by KLM, the Dutch national carrier, in 1997.

Strong competition is also coming from the low-cost carriers such as Easyjet and Debonair. Their success pushed BA to launch its own low-cost carrier, GO, in 1998.

### 1.6.3 Charter airlines

Most of the charter airlines are part of larger travel groups; the top four tour operators all own charter airlines. Owning a charter airline has become a characteristic of large tour operators' vertical integration strategy.

Even newer and smaller tour operators have their own charter airline. Inspirations, only started up in 1993 but soon after acquired its own airline when it bought Caledonian Airways from BA in 1994.

Those tour operators which own an airline generally view it as an extension of their tour operating business. The larger tour operators usually allocate the majority of their airline seats to the in-house tour operator. In the case of TTG, nearly all Britannia's capacity is taken up by Thomson. Since 1992, Airtours International has sold only between 4 and 11 per cent of its seats to third parties and about two-thirds of Air 2000's seat capacity has been allocated to its in-house tour operator.

Thomas Cook and Inspirations plc are the only two large tour operators offering a larger proportion of their airlines' capacity to third parties.

## 1.6.4 Leading charter airlines

### Britannia Airways Ltd
Britannia Airways is the charter airline division of TTG and the largest charter airline in Europe.

It started operations in May 1962 as Euravia Ltd, based in Luton.

Most of the airline capacity is used for TTG's holiday packages, but it is also contracted with other tour operators such as Kuoni, Unijet, Ausbound and P&O cruises.

**Example 1.19**  *Financial results*

|                     | 1997 (£m) | 1996 (£m) | 1995 (£m) | 1994 (£m) |
|---------------------|-----------|-----------|-----------|-----------|
| Sales               | 674,051   | 630,350   | 605,473   | 557,689   |
| Profit              | 30,231    | 19,000    | 24,186    | 18,313    |
| Profit margin (%)   | 4.5       | 3.0       | 4.0       | 3.3       |

### Airtours International Airways Ltd
The Airtours International Airways was established by Airtours in 1990 and became operational in March 1991.

Airtours International in the UK and Premiair in Scandinavia make up Airtours' aviation division.

**Example 1.20**  *Financial results*

|                     | 1997 (£m) | 1996 (£m) | 1995 (£m) | 1994 (£m) |
|---------------------|-----------|-----------|-----------|-----------|
| Sales               | 388,525   | 347,229   | 175,479   | 72,091    |
| Profit              | 38,266    | 37,865    | 21,493    | 5,038     |
| Profit margin (%)   | 9.8       | 10.9      | 12.2      | 7.0       |

### Air 2000 Ltd

Air 2000 is the charter airline division of First Choice but also provides services for many third-party tour operators.

| *Example 1.21* *Financial results* | | | | |
|---|---|---|---|---|
| | *1997 (£m)* | *1996 (£m)* | *1995 (£m)* | *1994 (£m)* |
| **Sales** | 275,341 | 277,781 | 281,005 | 283,934 |
| **Profit** | 28,879 | 35,815 | 46,817 | 43,562 |
| **Profit margin (%)** | 10.4 | 12.9 | 16.7 | 15.3 |

### Monarch Airlines

Founded in 1968, Monarch has been in the top rank of UK charter operators for many years.

Although it is part of the travel group Cosmos, it provides charter services for a range of other tour operators.

| *Example 1.22* *Financial results* | | | | |
|---|---|---|---|---|
| | *1997 (£m)* | *1996 (£m)* | *1995 (£m)* | *1994 (£m)* |
| **Sales** | 309,345 | 306,332 | 304,847 | 283,268 |
| **Profit** | 10,169 | 11,103 | 11,028 | 12,108 |
| **Profit margin (%)** | 3.3 | 3.6 | 3.6 | 4.3 |

## 1.6.5 The future

In 1997, the demand for air traffic at UK airports and airlines continued to increase in line with international forecasts and future growth seems guaranteed. The UK airport and airline industry is expected to grow over 4 per cent annually to the year 2000.

However, the ever growing demand for international air travel puts increasing pressure on airport terminals, runway capacity and air traffic control. With the number of people flying worldwide to double in the next 15 years, UK airports are expected to reach their capacity limits by 2013.

# Chapter 2 – The Civil Aviation Authority (CAA)

## 2.1 Government and European Union regulation – the role of the Civil Aviation Authority

As noted in Chapter 1, the Civil Aviation Authority (CAA) is empowered by statute to regulate the UK air travel industry. It plays a leading role in the development of the aviation industry through safety and economic regulation.

Its specific responsibilities include:

- Air safety – airworthiness of aircraft and operational aspects including licensing flight crew, aircraft engineers, air traffic controllers and aerodromes; certificating UK airlines and aircraft and maintaining air traffic services standards.
- Air traffic services – providing air traffic control services and radio and navigational aids through its subsidiary the National Air Traffic Services (NATS), jointly with the Ministry of Defence.
- Economic regulation – through licensing of routes, approval of air fares for journeys outside the European Union, regulating certain airport charges, and licensing air travel organisers.

In addition, the CAA advises the Government on aviation issues, carries out economic and scientific research, produces statistical data and provides specialist services including fire-fighting and consultancy and training to clients worldwide.

In this chapter, we will look at the CAA's role in economic regulation and in particular the licensing of air travel organisers.

### 2.1.1 Policy implementation

The Civil Aviation (Air Travel Organisers' Licensing) Regulations 1995 stipulate that anyone who advertises or sells air travel in the UK, with the exceptions noted in **2.2.1** below, must hold an Air Travel Organisers' Licence (ATOL).

In addition, the Package Travel, Package Holidays and Package Tours Regulations 1992 require that the package tour organiser must provide

29

financial security for customers' money. This requirement is met if the organiser holds an ATOL.

Failure to comply with these Regulations is a criminal offence and may lead to prosecution.

### 2.1.2 Structure and scope of the CAA regulations

In simple terms, an ATOL (and more directly the supporting bond) protects the public from losing money or being stranded abroad because of the financial failure of a firm selling flights or package holidays by air.

The scope of the regulations is broad, and they are intended to cover all eventualities. As such ATOL licences are required by all parties advertising or selling air travel which include:

- individuals and companies;
- flights sold on their own or as part of an inclusive package;
- sales made through agents; and
- flights that start inside or outside the UK.

In all cases, the protection works by each ATOL holder providing financial guarantees in the form of a bond before a licence is granted. If the business then experiences financial difficulties and cannot provide the flights and holidays that it has sold, the CAA uses the bond to repatriate those customers who are on holiday and repay those customers who have not yet taken their holiday. If the bond is insufficient, there is a back-up fund managed by the CAA (the Air Travel Trust Fund) to make up the shortfall.

## 2.2 Air Travel Organisers' Licensing (ATOL) system

### 2.2.1 Who needs an ATOL?

Anyone who advertises or sells air travel in the UK needs an ATOL, except as detailed below, regardless of whether:

- they are an individual or a company;
- the flights are sold on their own or as part of a package;
- the sale is through an agent either inside or outside the UK;
- the flight begins inside or outside the UK.

An ATOL is *not* required where:

- An airline sells tickets for its own flights either directly or through an agent. However, airlines are required not to sell to any agents which require a licence but do not hold one.

- A 'ticket provider' does not need an ATOL as long as a valid ticket is issued as soon as payment is received from the customer. These are generally sales by International Air Transport Association (IATA) appointed agents which sell scheduled air flights on a commission basis. Business house and credit sales, where the customer does not pay for the flight until it has been taken, are also covered by the ticket provider exception in the regulations.
- An agent acting on behalf of an ATOL holder does not need its own ATOL provided that when it accepts money from its customers it issues an ATOL receipt confirming that it has accepted the money as an agent for the ATOL holder and the ATOL holder issues an ATOL confirmation invoice to the customer within seven days.
- The CAA may grant exemptions from the need to hold an ATOL but these are only in very rare and specific circumstances

## 2.2.2 Different forms of ATOL

Travel entities often undertake more than one type of business. For example, they may sell full fare scheduled air flights as an IATA appointed agent, holiday packages or discounted tickets as the agent of another ATOL holder and inclusive packages created in-house or purchased from other operators.

It is therefore essential that the management of the business understands the full scope of the businesses undertaken to ensure that they hold the appropriate ATOL.

The CAA recognises that there are many different types of businesses undertaken by travel businesses with different risks inherent in each and as such there are three principal ATOL business categories (in addition to 'subsidiary' arrangements introduced in 1996).

The three business categories are:

- *Fully bonded*

  This is the most common category of licence and covers the broadest level of operations. It includes scheduled and charter packages and charter flight seat only sales.

  Fully bonded businesses have a four-digit ATOL number.

- *Scheduled bonded*

  This category is for consolidators and other businesses who sell scheduled flights on a seat only basis but do not issue the tickets straightaway (i.e., non-IATA accredited agents).

Scheduled bonded businesses have a five-digit ATOL number which is prefixed with a seven. Scheduled bonded business is also sometimes referred to as lower bonded.

- *Other, including agency bonded*

  This category is for consolidators and other businesses which sell discounted flights as the agents of scheduled airlines. An agency licence is granted where the airline provides a deed of undertaking, which means that it guarantees the business of the consolidator and, in some cases, any sub-agents to which the consolidator distributes tickets.

  Agency licences have a five-digit ATOL number which is prefixed with an eight.

As detailed above, many travel entities undertake more than one type of business. When this is the case they must ensure that they are registered to cover the highest level of business carried out. In the example above the business would need to register as a fully bonded ATOL holder. Note, however, that the CAA would take all operations into account when calculating the financial requirements of the business for the licence.

### 2.2.3 The application process

The application process begins with the application form, which must be submitted to the CAA along with the additional information requested in the application form (see below) and a cheque for the initial non-refundable application charge.

The application form consists of two parts. The first requests information about the applicant, whether it is a limited company, a partnership or a sole trade, the names of the directors or principals, how long the business has traded, the registered number and office, and other business details as set out in the CAA's guide for new applicants.

The second part is about the form of licence that is being applied for and the type and volume of business carried out. In this part the applicant must disclose details of the number of passengers it expects to carry on a quarterly basis and the turnover generated from those passengers split into each category, i.e., fully bonded, scheduled bonded or agency. Note that the turnover must include all associated costs, i.e., hotel, villa, car hire, insurance, etc., the exception being in respect of ATOL to ATOL sales where turnover is only the price paid by the buying ATOL holder.

The following additional information will be requested within the application form and must be submitted with the application form to ensure a timely decision by the CAA. The CAA will not consider any application until all additional information requested is submitted.

The following information generally is required:

- Full CVs of the directors or principals of the business.
- The latest set of accounts of the applicant.
- The past three years' audited accounts including detailed profit and loss account, if the entity is already trading (if the accounts do not need an audit they must be 'certified' by a chartered or certified accountant).
- If the entity has just started to trade, an opening balance sheet, 'certified' by a chartered or certified accountant.
- If the applicant is a sole trader or a partnership, a certified statement of personal assets and liabilities to the same day as the last set of accounts and signed by the same accountant.
- The latest audited accounts for a parent, ultimate holding or associated company.
- Completed financial projections from the date of the latest accounts to the end of the next financial period.

Not all of the items listed above will be required for agency licences.

As can be seen from the list above, the applicant entities are assessed for financial rigour at an early stage, and this is discussed in more detail below.

Once the application has been received by the CAA it will analyse the information received and set up a meeting with the applicant. This meeting is simply to understand the entity and its requirements and to explain how the ATOL system works.

After the meeting the CAA will issue a decision letter, stating (where appropriate) that a licence will be granted once certain conditions are met.

These conditions will always include the payment of grant charges, directors' guarantees, and the provision of a bond; they may also include a Deed of Undertaking from at least one airline, the introduction of new capital to strengthen the entity's financial position and a formal requirement such as auditors' confirmation of any required changes to the entity.

The applicant must then obtain the necessary bond and comply with any other requirements detailed in the decision letter. This will normally need to be done within two months of the decision letter being issued.

Once all conditions have been met within the required timeframe the licence will be granted, an ATOL number will be issued and the business can legally sell and advertise licensable business.

The total time from applying for a licence to obtaining a decision is approximately three months, but this is of course dependent on the applicant submitting all the necessary information to the CAA when required.

## 2.2.4   Financial monitoring and review

As detailed above as part of the application process, it is a legal requirement that the CAA is satisfied as to the fitness of the applicant, the fitness of the individuals controlling the entity and the financial stability of the entity before a licence can be granted.

The financial stability of the entity is assessed on application and is reviewed each year on renewal of the ATOL.

As a minimum paid up capital and free assets must be at least £30,000. Above that the entity must demonstrate that it has a sufficient ratio of 'net free assets' to projected 'turnover' (both as defined), thus ensuring that it has sufficient financial backing to support the level of business which it intends to undertake.

The ratio depends on the risks inherent in the business undertaken, the trading record and the management of the business. For new applicants the ratio would typically be at least 5 per cent, reducing to a normal level of around 4 per cent in stages for established licence holders with at least a two-year profitable trading record, and a minimum level of 3 per cent.

### Turnover

Turnover is calculated as the higher of total projected turnover for the next financial year or next licence year from:

- all fully bonded turnover, i.e., all packages and charter flights;
- all non-air packages, including non-travel business, where the licence holder acts as a principal;
- charter flight sales sold on to other ATOL holders; and
- 10 per cent of gross turnover relating to scheduled flight sales or retail sales for other ATOL holders and non-air principals.

### Free asset calculation

Free assets are calculated as the readily recoverable net current assets plus the written down value of any assets capable of supporting borrowings, net of any loans secured on those assets.

Assets capable of supporting borrowings include freehold properties, long-leasehold properties and assets like aircraft. Independent valuations of such assets may be sought, particularly in cases where the balance sheet worth depends on the value of properties or other assets.

The following assets are specifically excluded from the free assets calculation:

- Brochure expenditure and prepaid advertising costs.
- Amounts due from related undertakings which are clearly not capable of repayment in the short term.
- Amounts advanced to directors or employees.
- Investments, except when the investment is in a publicly quoted company and can be realised at any time.
- Properties outside the UK.
- Short leasehold properties, i.e., those with less than 10 years to run on the lease.
- Minor fixed assets such as cars, computers and fixtures and fittings.
- Intangible assets such as goodwill.
- Any assets used as security for bonds. Where the bond is secured by a floating charge or debenture the full value of the bond is subtracted from the assets.
- Any current or long-term liabilities, including loans from a parent or related company, unless they are covered by a formal subordination deed to which the CAA is a party.
- Deferred tax, except where it can be demonstrated that a liability would not crystallise in the event of financial failure.

### Bonding arrangements

As detailed above in the application process, once the decision letter has been issued the applicant must obtain a bond.

A bond is an irrecoverable guarantee provided by a third party which enables the CAA to draw down a specified sum in the event of financial failure of the business, which it then uses to repatriate any passengers that would otherwise be stranded abroad and to reimburse any passengers where holidays have not yet commenced.

The third party which provides the bond is ordinarily a bank or an insurance company. The CAA will only accept bonds from bank and insurance companies which have an office in the UK.

The minimum bond level for any kind of licence is £10,000. Further to that, bond levels are determined by taking into consideration:

- the scope of the applicant/licence holder's operations, i.e., the licence category;
- the projected level of operations; and
- the risk inherent in the specific operations of the applicant/licence holder.

The bond level is set as a percentage of licensable turnover authorised by the ATOL for the year.

Typically fully bonded licences will have a bond level of 15 per cent of turnover initially, reducing to a minimum level of 10 per cent in time for existing licence holders with sufficient profit levels and a record of maintaining their licences at sufficient levels.

Scheduled bonded licences will have a bond level of 10 per cent of licensable turnover and agency bonds, where the Deed of Undertaking stands mainly in place of the bond, are the higher of £10,000 and 0.50 per cent of licensable turnover.

### Bonding variations
As detailed above, in part two of the application form the applicant must disclose details of the number of passengers it expects to carry on a quarterly basis and the turnover generated from those passengers split into each category, i.e., fully bonded, scheduled bonded agency or ATOL to ATOL.

If, as the year progresses, it becomes apparent that the initial projections were incorrect and the licensable turnover is going to exceed that authorised by the licence then the licence holder must apply to vary the licence to increase the authorisation and an additional bond will be required before the variation can be granted.

It is important that the licence holder identifies the fact that sales will be in excess of authorised sales as quickly as possible and applies to vary the licence before the licensable turnover is undertaken because the principals' personal guarantees may be called if the licence holder exceeds its authorisation and then fails.

Where an applicant fails to make a reasonable estimate of licensable turnover or applies to vary the licence at a very late stage the CAA will usually increase the bonding level in subsequent years until the entity proves that its estimates are reasonable and/or applies for a variation on a timely basis.

### Directors' guarantee obligations
Standard term 13 of Air Travel Organisers' Licences requires that the principals in an ATOL application provide personal guarantees, unless the firm

is authorised by the CAA not to do so. These provisions were introduced in 1997 in the face of a number of high profile collapses involving overtrading leading to bonds being insufficient.

Typically guarantees will be required from two key executive directors of an established ATOL holder and more may be required from a new applicant initially.

The main aim of the guarantees is to ensure that licence holders do not overtrade. The guarantees can only be called if:

- the ATOL holder fails; and
- the ATOL holder was trading in excess of its licence at the time of failure; and
- the Air Travel Trust Fund has to compensate customers as the bond is insufficient.

Established ATOL holders with good records have the option of either providing guarantees or providing a higher bond. This is at the CAA's discretion; if it has a particular reason to be concerned about possible overtrading it can deny the right to provide a higher bond. In such cases the CAA will make it clear why it has insisted on a guarantee; the licence holder does have the right of appeal to a CAA Board Member.

The higher bond is normally an additional 20 per cent above the standard bond level (with lower premiums for larger businesses) which gives a basic bond of 30 per cent. Where no guarantees are given the minimum bond is £50,000.

## 2.2.5 Seat-only sales on scheduled flights

If tickets are issued immediately no ATOL is required. If tickets are not issued immediately then an ATOL (scheduled bonded or agency bonded) is required.

## 2.2.6 ATOL to ATOL sales

In addition to public sales, licences may also be granted which authorise the sale of bonded seats and packages from one ATOL holder to another.

This is where an ATOL holder is licensed to sell seats to another ATOL holder for resale on the latter's licence. In this case the selling ATOL holder must:

- ensure that the buying ATOL holder has sufficient capacity in its authorised passenger and turnover levels to sell the seat on;

- note that the sale is ATOL to ATOL on the customer confirmation invoice;
- inform the CAA that it is dealing with a buyer on an ATOL to ATOL basis; and

Where an ATOL holder deals with another on an ATOL to ATOL basis, it is normally prohibited from dealing with that firm as an agent. However, where it sells fewer than 400 seats per year in total on an ATOL to ATOL basis, it may notify sales individually to the CAA and deal with the buyers of those seats also as agents.

## 2.2.7 CAA returns

Licences are normally valid for a year and run to either March or September depending on the ATOL holder's year end, i.e., if the year end falls between 1 June and 30 November the licence runs to March and if the year end falls between 1 December and 31 May the licence runs to September.

As part of the application and renewal processes applicants are required to disclose details of the number of passengers it expects to carry on a quarterly basis and the turnover generated from those passengers split into each category, i.e., fully bonded, scheduled bonded agency or ATOL to ATOL.

Throughout the period of the licence the ATOL holder must submit quarterly returns to the CAA detailing the number of passengers actually carried and the turnover generated from those passengers in that quarter on a date of departure basis.

At the end of the period the licence holder must submit an annual statement which discloses the number of passengers actually carried and the turnover actually generated from them in the year. The annual return should equal the sum of the quarterly returns.

The annual return is audited by the entities' auditors and submitted to the CAA with a copy of the audited financial statements. The auditor's role is discussed in more detail in Chapters 12 and 13 – the former in respect of the statutory audit; the latter in respect of additional responsibilities.

# Chapter 3 – The Association of British Travel Agents (ABTA)

## 3.1  Introduction

This chapter will consider the Association of British Travel Agents (ABTA), its bonding requirements and other financial criteria, and ABTA's role in the regulatory framework of the travel industry.

## 3.2  The growth of ABTA

ABTA was founded in 1950 and after five years was formed into a company limited by guarantee. Its stated intention was the provision of a representative organisation for travel agents and tour operators in the United Kingdom, the Channel Islands and the Isle of Man.

The explosion of the travel industry in the last 40 years has led to this being one of the most significant industry growth sectors. Such growth led to substantial problems including the financial failure and poor performance of operators and agents.

Because of the industry's unusual position in the country's social fabric these problems became unacceptable and over time caused significant damage to the travel industry as a whole. ABTA recognised this and, since its formation, has developed into an independent self-regulating body providing support and confidence not only for the public, but also its members. As such the association now forms an important part of the regulatory framework of the travel industry.

The position obtained by ABTA originally came from a self-introduced rule called the 'stabiliser' whereby ABTA members selling or buying foreign 'inclusive' holidays could only do so through other members. This expanded the network of members and provided security to the public through self-regulation.

### 3.2.1  The Package Travel, Package Holidays and Package Tours Regulations 1992

The growth of the European Community in the 1980s, and the resultant Directives and regulations issued from Brussels led to the publishing of an

EC Directive aimed at harmonising consumer protection in the travel industry.

In the UK this EC Directive was enacted in the form of the Package Travel, Package Holidays and Package Tours Regulations 1992 (Package Travel Regulations), these ultimately being the responsibility of the Department of Trade and Industry (DTI) and Trading Standards Authorities. As a result, ABTA's stabiliser was abolished in October 1993.

A key measure embodied in the Regulations is that an organiser, retailer, or both, must ensure that a bond or other form of financial protection is in place. This must be with an authorised institution which binds itself to pay, when called, a body approved by the Secretary of State. It should be noted that strictly speaking the DTI's interpretation of the Package Travel Regulations does not require retailers to provide protection, although ABTA does.

The Regulations include several key definitions as follows:

- 'An organiser' – the person who, otherwise than occasionally, organises packages and sells, or offers them for sale, whether directly or through a retailer.
- 'A package' – the pre-arranged combination of at least two of the following components when sold at an inclusive price and when the service covers a period of more than 24 hours, or includes overnight accommodation:
  - transport;
  - accommodation;
  - other tourist services not ancillary to transport or accommodation and accounting for a significant part of the package.

It should be noted that the Package Travel Regulations provide a number of other legal measures aimed at consumer protection though these are not covered in this section.

## 3.2.2   The benefits for ABTA members and the distinction with the CAA

ABTA clearly has an important role in the development and regulation of the travel industry. However, the CAA as a government body, and through the operation of the ATOL system, has the direct backing of statute. The CAA's ATOL is a legal requirement if a business wishes to sell air travel.

As a result of the Package Travel Regulations, ABTA, being a body approved by the Secretary of State, has indirect statutory backing. This should carry sufficient weight for ABTA to continue expansion of its membership and, more importantly, the regulation of the industry.

Under the Package Travel Regulations tour operators carrying out both licensable and non-licensable activity must have a bond or other form of financial protection in place. The ATOL system meets the criteria for licensable activities and full membership to ABTA meets this statutory requirement for non-licensable activities.

ABTA is, however, a self-regulating body although it is not the only body approved by the Secretary of State to provide financial protection as required by the Regulations. However, the Association currently has a pre-eminent position in the industry and in the eyes of the general public.

Membership of ABTA not only meets the legal requirements but has a number of other benefits. In the public's eyes the legal position is, to a degree, irrelevant. Their concern is that financial protection is in place; not necessarily how it is achieved. The ABTA symbol is widely recognised as providing this protection and providing the confidence the public requires, thus giving members a strong trading position in the marketplace.

## 3.3 The internal structure of ABTA

The internal structure of ABTA is reasonably straightforward and is best shown in the following diagram:

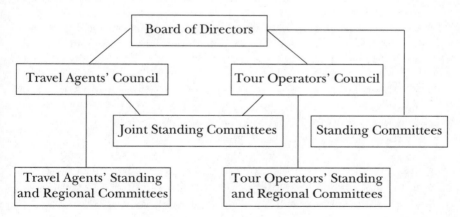

Members on application are officially categorised as either tour operators' or travel agents' class, although dual membership is possible. This class system is reasonably transparent as far as the general public is concerned.

As a member of their specific class they elect representatives to sit on the relevant council – 18 tour operators and 20 travel agents. The councils then nominate representatives to the board of directors, and appoint committees and working parties as necessary.

### 3.3.1 Current membership

According to ABTA's membership handbook current membership is about 3,400 members. The chart below illustrates the number of members in the last five years:

|  | *Tour operators' class* | *Travel agents' class* | *Joint class members* | *Total members* |
|---|---|---|---|---|
| 31 December 1992 | 647 | 2,712 | 288 | 3,071 |
| 31 December 1993 | 623 | 2,572 | 270 | 2,925 |
| 31 December 1994 | 609 | 2,430 | 268 | 2,771 |
| 31 December 1995 | 616 | 2,219 | 276 | 2,559 |
| 31 December 1996 | 616 | 2,090 | 308 | 2,398 |

## 3.4 Membership rules and criteria

The membership requirements of ABTA are conceptually very similar to those operated by the CAA. Indeed both bodies are currently exploring ways in which they can interact with each other for the benefit of members and the general public. This is a natural step given that both aim to afford protection to the general public when transacting with the travel industry.

ABTA's rules relating to membership are broadly applicable to all members, although some rules are specific dependent on the membership class, i.e., travel agent or tour operator.

ABTA's constitution is set out in its Memorandum and Articles of Association. The Articles are extremely detailed and provide the internal rules and regulations for ABTA members for all issues ranging from membership and financial criteria to disciplinary.

As a supplement to these and as an aid to interpreting the rules, the codes of conduct and members' handbook are produced. These are distributed to all members on application and are also available on request.

## 3.5 Membership rules – general

As stated in the Articles all members must be able to demonstrate that they are fit and proper individuals. In particular, a member must not:

- be an undischarged bankrupt;
- have made an arrangement with creditors;
- have been an owner, a controlling director (definition as per Income and Corporation Taxes Act 1988) or partner of a business that has failed to meet its liabilities; or
- have been guilty of any other conduct making the individual unfit to be a member.

Clearly the relevant council (that's the tour operators' or travel agents' as appropriate) has discretion over the interpretation and implementation of the rules.

A business cannot attempt to circumvent these requirements by acquiring an ABTA membership simply through the acquisition of an existing ABTA member. An important requirement of Article 13(5) is that any changes in the financial control of the members' business, i.e., a change in the beneficial owners of the majority shareholding, or change of partner with a majority share of the profits, must be notified to the secretariat of the membership department. This notification must be performed within seven days of the change of ownership.

Clearly it is an important restraint on unscrupulous businesses trying to avoid the regulations. During a merger or acquisition of a business the suspension or even loss of membership could prove an unnecessary challenge.

The following represents a summary of other membership rules which apply to all members in order to provide protection to the general public and members:

- Trading and business names are restricted. The business must not trade under, or pass itself off as, a member that has previously failed to meet liabilities (Articles 4(1)(e) and 8(g)).
- The employment of outside sales representatives is prohibited unless they have successfully completed a training course approved by the relevant council. They must also be an employee of the member (Articles 11(2) and 12).
- Where premises are shared with a non-ABTA member the member must ensure that sufficient prominence is given to the ABTA symbol, such that the general public cannot be misled as to the membership status of the non-ABTA member.
- New offices and/or changes in office address must be notified to the secretariat (Articles 11(1) and 12).
- Members must permit the inspection of their business premises by an authorised ABTA inspector (Article 13(4)).

- Members must submit three copies of published brochures to the secretariat of the legal department within seven days (Article 13(6)).
- Members must make unsold seats available, free of charge, for the repatriation of customers of failed members (Article 13(7)).
- Members must demonstrate that they are financially sound.

The above list is not comprehensive and reference should be made to the Articles where necessary.

## 3.6   Membership rules – tour operators

Potential members must demonstrate to ABTA on application that *inter alia*:

- they are the engaged in the business of a tour operator as *principals* and not as agents. The principals must show that they *organise,* and offer for sale to the public, tours, holidays or other travel arrangements. ABTA regards organising as including entering into contractual arrangements with other principals for the purchase of blocks of tours, holidays and other travel arrangements. If an operator is also engaged as an agent then it must become a member of both classes;
- they are able to provide a bond or guarantee acceptable to the Tour Operators' Council;
- adequate liability insurance has been obtained.

## 3.7   Membership rules – travel agents

Members must demonstrate on application that:

- they are engaged in the business of travel agency, as opposed to that of a tour operator. The distinction is not always clear: a travel agent is normally engaged in retail activities acting as the agent on behalf of the principal and does not normally enter into a contract with the customer;
- they have at least one qualified person at any premises. 'Qualified' is defined by ABTA as having gained two years' practical experience in the five years prior to any point of employment, or at least 18 months' practical experience plus an appropriate qualification. Periods of temporary absence, short-term emergencies and in abnormal circumstances a contactable absence are permitted.

## 3.8   Financial criteria and regulations

The following sections deal with the financial rules and requirements of each membership class. As with the general rules these can be broken down into those applying to all members and those specific to tour operators and travel agents.

The travel industry can be considered unusual in the event of the financial failure of a company, and not only on liquidation. In addition to the usual trade and other creditors of the business there is often a body of customers who form a section of creditors.

ABTA's financial rules and regulations exist to afford protection to these customers and ensure that ABTA has sufficient funds to:

- arrange for customers whose holidays or travel arrangements are in progress to complete the holidays and ensure the customers stranded abroad are repatriated; and
- reimburse customers where holidays/arrangements have not started, or arrange for an alternative.

One of the most significant measures is the requirement for a bond or other acceptable form of protection to be in place. There are, though, limitations to the protection afforded by the bonds. The bond is in place for a specific purpose, however, and normal trade creditors of the business are not covered by the bond, even if this happens to be a member of the public. For example, in the event of a liquidation if customers are owed money for compensation they would be considered an unsecured creditors and treated with the other creditors of the business under normal insolvency rules. The bond is effectively a form of insurance/protection for the traveller and provides protection on the financial failure of a business.

It should be noted that where the customers' arrangements fall under licensable activities, the first bond called is that of the CAA (see Chapter 2).

## 3.9 Financial criteria and regulations – general

### 3.9.1 Reporting requirements – audited accounts

The operator and agent must prepare audited accounts, the audit being performed by a registered auditor, and submit the accounts within six months of the year end, or within 18 months of the last previously submitted audited balance sheet, whichever is earlier. Failure to comply results in, following a seven-day notice period, termination of membership. Accounts received in the seven-day period are accepted but a maximum discretionary penalty of £1,000 may be applied.

Anybody wishing to extend a company's year end should be careful. No procedures exist for extending the filing deadline. Therefore any extension of the year end could result in either extreme pressure on completion of the audited accounts or, where the deadline is missed, the possible termination of membership.

### 3.9.2 Reporting requirements – audited turnover certification

This is separated into the following certificates:

- *Turnover certificate and analysis*
  Each year end the member must prepare a certificate detailing the member's turnover analysed between licensable, non-licensable and retail activities for the year. This contains a section that must be completed by the member's auditor. This form is required to be submitted at the same time as the audited accounts. (Appendix 2 Form Audit 003.)

- *Turnover certificate – annual monthly summary*
  The member's auditor must produce and sign a statement of non-licensable tour operating turnover analysed month by month. This is required to be submitted within six months of the member's bond year end. (Appendix 2 Form Audit 009.)

Form Audit 003 must be submitted with the financial statements. The same filing deadlines and penalties apply to both reports.

The auditor's responsibility in producing these reports is no different to his normal responsibilities; he must be aware that ABTA will rely on these figures in considering the relevant bonding levels required and also, in conjunction with the review of the audited financial statements, in considering the financial position of the business. This may lead to an increase in bonding required or calls for an increase in capital or change in the financial structure of the business.

Clearly this is central to the financial protection ABTA is implementing and the auditor needs to be aware of the duty of care that needs to be displayed in preparing all the audit certificates of the member.

### 3.9.3 Reporting requirements – other

In addition to the annual submission of the audited documents the member has several reporting requirements throughout the year:

- *Annual projected turnover*
  At the start of each year the member must submit projections stating anticipated non-licensable activity for the following year. This should be analysed on a quarterly basis.

- *Quarterly returns*
  Twenty-eight days after the end of each quarter the member must report the actual non-licensable turnover for the quarter along with a written declaration to the accuracy of the figures. This does not need to be audited on a quarterly basis. (Appendix 2 Form FM003.)

  Travel agents are also required to submit quarterly returns stating their retail activities. (Appendix 2 Form QUARCER 1.)

Any members who have reason to believe they are going to exceed the projected non-licensable turnover on which their bond is based must report this as soon as the possibility arises. They should not wait until it has become a matter of fact, since by this stage customers are now financially at risk. Should the business collapse in such circumstances, possibly through overtrading, an insufficient bond will exist to cover all customers.

## 3.10 Financial regulations – tour operator

### 3.10.1 Capital requirement

The minimum fully paid up share capital requirement for members is now not less than £50,000. This requirement was introduced on 1 April 1995, when an increase of £10,000 for each of the subsequent four years was applied. Therefore by 1 April 1998 all members should have a share capital of £50,000 or more. (Appendix 2 Form Audit 008.)

### 3.10.2 Net recoverable current assets

Each year the tour operator member is required to submit an audited statement of its net recoverable current assets (NRCA) along with the audited financial statements and other documents. (Appendix 2 Form Audit 008.)

Any tour operator member whose non-licensable turnover either represents 30 per cent or more of total turnover, or whose turnover is in excess of £500,000, must have a surplus of NRCA equivalent to 4 per cent of 'total applicable turnover'. Total applicable turnover is further defined as the greater of actual and projected tour operating turnover, including both licensable and non-licensable.

When members or applicants fail to meet this requirement they are required to rectify the position by using one of the following methods:

- introducing an injection of additional share capital or long-term funds;
- providing an additional bond of the shortfall;
- converting short-term debts; or
- carrying out whatever arrangement ABTA deems necessary.

### 3.10.3   Net asset deficits

When a member has accounts showing a net asset deficit membership is immediately terminated unless it can be shown that, by the due date for submission of the member's account, share capital has been issued for cash or fixed assets have been revalued by a qualified professional to the lower of market value or net realisable value. This increase in asset base must be sufficient to at least replace the deficit that has arisen.

### 3.10.4   Bonding – tour operators

All members of the tour operators' class are required to have either a bond, guarantee or other financial security of a level and form that is acceptable to the Tour Operators' Council to secure their operations as tour operators.

The calculation of the bond is based on a standard formula and the table below shows an example of a business and the type of bond percentage required. The table is broken down into three parts: firstly the terms of trade showing when cash flows are received; secondly the cash collection profile showing the factor percentage applied dependent on the terms of trade; and thirdly the actual calculation using the factor percentage from the collection profile and based on the terms of trade.

*Terms of trade*

|  | *Percentage of average fare* |
|---|---|
| Initial deposit | 20 |
| Additional deposit | – |
| Final balance | 80 |

*Cash collection profile*

| *Prior to departure* | *Factor % applied* | *Initial deposit* | *Additional deposit* | *Final balance* |
|---|---|---|---|---|
| Over 12 months | 100 | nil | nil | nil |
| 9–12 months | 75 | nil | nil | nil |
| 6–9 months | 50 | 30 | nil | nil |
| 3–6 months | 25 | 50 | nil | nil |
| less than 3 months | nil | 20 | nil | 100 |
|  |  | 100% | nil | 100% |

## The calculation

| | Initial deposit | Additional deposit | Final balance | Total % |
|---|---|---|---|---|
| Over 12 months | nil | nil | nil | nil |
| 9–12 months | nil | nil | nil | nil |
| 6–9 months | 3.00 | nil | nil | 3.00 |
| 3–6 months | 2.50 | nil | nil | 2.50 |
| less than 3 months – not required | | | | |
| Total | | | A | 5.50 |
| **Less base rate** | | | B | (5.50) |
| Shortfall (A – B) | | | C | nil |
| **Basic rate** | | | D | 10.00 |
| Bond rate required (C + D) | | | | 10.00 |

Interpreting this example it can be seen that because 30 per cent of the initial 20 per cent deposit is collected six to nine months prior to departure a factor of 50 per cent is applied. Thus a 3 per cent factor (30% × 20% × 50%) is applied to the final calculation for the period six to nine months and go on based on the cash collection profile.

The final balance is not collected until less than three months prior to departure. Because the risk involved in holding the money for this short period is obviously reduced, no bond percentage is applied. The use of a base rate and basic rate in the final calculation (rates determined by the Tour Operators' Council) ensure that a bond is required for all operators. The application of a factor based on when cash is paid and how long it is held for mean that the bond is variable. As can be seen from the above table the minimum bond rate is 10 per cent.

It is clear that considerations should be given to the cash flows of the operator, by adopting different payment terms; this has the effect of altering the bonding levels of the business in practice.

In addition to the security provided by the bond the operator is required to contribute to a policy to insure all business, other than that covered by an ATOL, for the purpose of providing further cover in the event of any bond or security proving inadequate. Also, the tour operator must, if required to do so, make contributions to the ABTA Tour Operators' Fund.

## 3.10.5  Peak period bonding

For some operators the situation will arise where their turnover is more concentrated at certain peak periods of the year. For example, ski operators will have a very high first quarter of the year, if no significant summer tours are undertaken. ABTA recognises that operational risk increases in these situations and, therefore, where 70 per cent of a member's non-licensable turnover falls into one quarter, on a rolling basis of the year, it is required to provide an additional bond to cover this specific period of time.

### 3.10.6 Third-party bonding

It is possible for operators to obtain bonds from a party other than ABTA. The most obvious example of this is licensable activities, where the operator is required to have the relevant bond with the CAA. ABTA states that it is keen not to have members overbonding but needs to ensure that it is not at risk. Therefore operators must provide copies of ATOL applications and licences where granted.

The third-party bonding of non-licensable operations is also permitted, and in these circumstances a copy of the current bond documentation must be provided. Unless it is apparent from the documents, confirmation of the amount of turnover bonded and the tenure of the bond must be provided. The Association may also require a number of other documents to satisfy itself that the bond is sufficient to meet ABTA's requirements.

## 3.11 New members – tour operators

New members are defined as those who have not been a member of the tour operators' class for three full years and those applying for continued membership following a change of ownership. The following section highlights the key additional requirements in these circumstances.

### 3.11.1 New members' capital requirements

As of 1 April 1998 the capital requirements are the same as existing members, i.e., £50,000. They must also show a positive net asset position after disallowing intangible assets.

### 3.11.2 Reporting requirements of new members

New members have a number of documents that need to be submitted in addition to those required by existing members.

*Accounts projections*
The tour operator must submit a projected profit and loss account and balance sheet for the coming year. These must be accompanied by a standard format statement from the member's auditor confirming that the projections have been prepared on a 'reasonable' basis.

### Quarterly turnover certificates
As is practice for existing members, quarterly turnover certificates are required. However, for the first two complete bonding years of membership these will need to be accompanied by an auditor's certification. (Appendix 2 Form FM002(S).)

### Management accounts
Management accounts for the six months from admission, including a profit and loss account and balance sheet, must be submitted within 60 days. There is also a requirement to submit a standard format report from the member's auditor considering the accounting policies, especially that of turnover, whether proper books and records have been maintained, and that the accounts have been prepared in accordance with those books, and whether the accounts show a true and fair view.

## 3.12   Financial regulations – travel agents
### 3.12.1   Capital requirements
New members, and those who have undergone change of financial control, are required to have £50,000 of paid up share capital or capital account balance. Working capital should be maintained at a level of not less than £15,000.

### 3.12.2   Bonding
Travel agent members of ABTA are required to provide a bond or other acceptable form of protection. Agents must ensure that consumers are aware of the principals with whom they are contracting. The agent must be careful not to inadvertently become an operator by preparing personally designed packages made up from a number of sources.

In 1994 ABTA introduced a number of changes to the rules and specifically looked at replacing bonding in the travel agent class. The system introduced was the Travel Agents' Bond Replacement Scheme (TABRS). The current position is that members can apply for full or partial entry into the system; however, new members and members with applicable risk turnover in excess of £50m are specifically excluded from full entry into the scheme.

### 3.12.3   Applicable risk turnover
Whether it be for the purposes of bonding or TABRS, turnover is defined under the applicable risk turnover (ART) definition.

ART is defined as gross income including commissions and VAT as a retail travel agent less:

- income from currency transactions, traveller's cheques, seat sales to other ATOL holders and inbound tours;
- 90 per cent of Billing and Settlement Plan (BSP; formerly Bank Settlement Plan) income; tickets must be issued at point of sale;
- 95 per cent of turnover derived from the sale of rail tickets and/or scheduled bus tickets; tickets must be issued at point of sale;
- 50 per cent of certified credit turnover with an ABTA principal;
- 30 per cent of income arising under certified credit arrangements with a specialised car hire provider.

### 3.12.4   Bonding requirements

The following table applies for members who have elected to continue to bonding arrangements:

| Applicable risk turnover | Bond required |
|---|---|
| Under £1,000,000 | £25,000 |
| £1,000,001 to £2,000,000 | £25,000  plus 2% of ART over £1,000,000 |
| £2,000,002 to £5,000,000 | £45,000  plus 3% of ART over £2,000,000 |
| Over £5,000,001 | £135,000 plus 1.5% of ART over £5,000,000 |

If members have elected to provide a bond rather than fully enter TABRS and has a working capital deficit it is required to provide an additional bond being:

$$\frac{\text{ART} \times \text{working capital deficit}}{\text{Total turnover per accounts}}$$

New members are required to provide a primary bond of £50,000.

### 3.12.5   TABRS – detailed calculations

Contributions to TABRS are made in contribution bands as follows:

- *Band 1 – flat rate contribution*
  A flat rate contribution payable by all members at the rate of £250 for each member and £25 per branch.

- *Band 2 – turnover charge*
  In assessing the level of contribution a degree of risk assessment is required. The charge is therefore based on ART with a maximum charge of £20,000 and a minimum charge of £250. It is possible for members to apply for partial exemption from TABRS in respect of this band, but only where a bond has been provided. It should also be noted though that from 1 May 1998 no maximum charge applies.

- *Band 2b – turnover charge, working capital deficit*
  Where a working capital deficit exists an additional surcharge factor is introduced based on the deficit as a factor of total turnover.

- *Band 2c – turnover charge, net asset deficit*
  A similar calculation is applied when this position is more extreme and a net asset deficit exists.

## 3.13 New members – travel agents

The definition of new members is the same as that for tour operators. As previously stated they require £50,000 of share capital and working capital of at least £15,000. New members are also not permitted entrance into band 2a of TABRS and must have a primary bond of £50,000.

On application, as with tour operators, new members are required to submit projections along with a standard form audit report. They must submit management accounts six months after admission within 60 days. They are also required to provide a standard form auditors' report on the state of the books and records and stating whether the management accounts show a true and fair view.

The auditor will also be asked to confirm net assets are not less than £50,000 and working capital is at least £15,000 on two dates other than the accounting reference date.

# Chapter 4 – Trade associations: International Air Transport Association

## 4.1 Introduction

The International Air Transport Association (IATA) is an international association which was set up by an Act of the Canadian Parliament in 1946. Its membership comprises most of the world's major airlines on a voluntary basis. IATA helps to coordinate the working methods and practices of different IATA airlines operating throughout the vast global route network.

IATA operates for the benefit of its member airlines, principally by regulating the sale of air tickets through accredited agents. The system recognises that in practice airlines will sell air tickets through agents, and the development of the Agency Accreditation Programme allows the member airlines to regulate air ticket sales to the public.

It is important to recognise the different stance taken by IATA when compared with the Civil Aviation Authority (CAA) and Association of British Travel Agents (ABTA). While the CAA and ABTA are acting to promote the industry by providing protection for the customer, IATA acts to promote the industry by enabling accredited agents to sell tickets on credit. IATA does not, *per se*, therefore provide public protection. There are of course indirect benefits in dealing with IATA accredited agents.

## 4.2 Structure of IATA

IATA provides a link between member airlines, accredited travel agents and national travel agents' associations.

IATA splits its activities into three principal regions:

- Area 1 – North, Central and South America and environs.
- Area 2 – Europe, Middle East and Africa.
- Area 3 – Far East, Australia, New Zealand and the Pacific Islands.

The regulation and control of IATA activities takes place within each of these regions.

# 4.3    Agency Accreditation Programme

The majority of ticket sales for airlines are generated through independent travel agents. IATA has developed the Agency Accreditation Programme on behalf of its member airlines to register approved travel agents. The Programme is administered in the UK by the Agency Service Office, which has the following functions:

- The accreditation and financial assessment of agents.
- The coordination of IATA agent training programmes.
- The proposal of accreditation criteria for endorsement by the airline delegates at their annual conference by a body known as the Agency Programme Joint Council – UK APJC.
- To process applications for accreditation and recommend approval or disapproval in accordance with the laid down rules.

The Billing and Settlement Plan (BSP) system provides accredited agents with procedures for issuing ticket sales on a credit basis. Payment for tickets in any month by the agent does not generally take place until the 17th day of the month following ticket sale, at which time the amount outstanding on ticket sales is collected by direct debit, and the agent commission accounted for. The operation of the BSP can be seen as a major benefit of IATA to growth in the agency sector.

Agents can therefore benefit by obtaining up to six weeks' credit on ticket sales. The accreditation process is intended to ensure that only financially sound applicants are approved as the system operates for the benefit of airlines which seek protection from accredited agents.

## 4.3.1    The application process for travel agents

A travel agency which seeks IATA accreditation must complete an application form providing IATA with information on the company, its location and its owners. The application form, once signed, becomes part of the Passenger Sales Agency Agreement which is the contract that binds travel agents to their IATA airline principals.

The application form is sent to the local IATA office together with the following items:

- Photographs of the premises – one interior and one exterior.
- A copy of the latest company accounts for assessment by IATA's financial assessors.
- A crime prevention survey report.
- Specifications of the safe installed to store tickets, and traffic documentation.

- A sample of the travel agency letterhead.
- A BSP training seminar certificate.
- Fees.

### Accreditation criteria

IATA maintains its professional standards by ensuring the attainment by applicants of certain criteria broadly falling under the following categories:

- Premises status (the regulations, for example, prohibit accredited IATA agents from sharing premises with another travel agency).
- Security of premises.
- Safe storage procedures.
- Staff qualifications.
- Finances.

The financial criteria are considered in further detail below.

Newly formed companies and firms must submit a copy of their opening balance sheet for assessment certified by an independent registered accountant.

The financial criteria fall into three areas:

- share capital/capital account;
- profitability; and
- liquidity.

(a) **Share capital (for limited companies) or capital account (for partnerships/sole traders)**

Minimum levels for fully issued and fully paid up share capital in limited companies have been set by IATA. For partnership and sole traders these levels must be reflected in the firm's capital account.

The minimum levels are calculated by reference to projected annual turnover (including turnover derived from non-IATA BSP airlines) less credit card sales. The minimum capital requirements are halved for companies which are able to demonstrate a trading history in retail travel by submitting three consecutive years' satisfactory financial statements.

The present minimum capital levels taken from IATA's June 1997 Accreditation Guide are set out in the table opposite:

56

***Example 4.1***   *Minimum capital levels*

| Turnover up to £ | Normal minimum (for businesses with less than three years' retail travel trade) £ | Traded minimum (for companies with three years or more of retail travel trade) £ |
|---|---|---|
| 2,000,000 | 40,000 | 20,000 |
| 3,000,000 | 60,000 | 30,000 |
| 4,000,000 | 80,000 | 40,000 |
| 5,000,000 | 100,000 | 50,000 |
| 6,000,000 | 120,000 | 60,000 |
| 7,000,000 | 140,000 | 70,000 |
| 8,000,000 | 160,000 | 80,000 |
| 9,000,000 | 180,000 | 90,000 |
| 10,000,000 and over | 200,000 | 100,000 |

### (b)   Profitability

IATA requires that all accredited agents must be profitable. IATA does not define profitability beyond stating that the submitted financial statements must show a trading profit before tax.

### (c)   Liquidity

IATA applies a simple liquidity test to ensure that current assets exceed current liabilities. IATA additionally requires accredited agents to meet a solvency criterion defined as an excess of total tangible assets over total tangible liabilities excluding intangible assets (which are excluded from the assessment.) Agents which submit accounts reflecting an insolvent position will be required to rectify the deficiency, usually by way of a capital injection.

## 4.4   Bonding requirement

To offer protection for the IATA airlines, an applicant that has traded for less than three years or fails to meet either of the profitability or liquidity criteria will be required to enter into a bond for the benefit of IATA. The bond may be arranged through a bank or insurance company or through the National Association of Independent Travel Agents Ltd (NAITA) insurance company.

The level of the bond is based upon the projected annual turnover of airline sales (including non-IATA BSP airlines) less credit card sales.

Current bonding levels are as follows:

● New agents and those without a three-year trading history: 16 per cent of turnover.

- Agents with a three-year trading history: 12 per cent of turnover.
- Agents which elect to pay twice monthly: 8 per cent of turnover.

Bonding levels are calculated to the nearest multiple of £5,000 subject to a minimum of £15,000. There is no upper limit. The amount of the bond is set at a level which is intended to roughly equate to the average credit provided to the agent by IATA members.

## 4.5   The approval process

As soon as IATA accreditation staff have reviewed the agency's application, details are published to all IATA's member airlines. During a period of 45 days following publication any member airline may file evidence with the Agency Services Office identifying areas where the applicant fails to meet the criteria.

In addition, the travel agent's offices will be visited by one of IATA's assessors to inspect matters such as the security of the premises, the safe, and how the location is identified. The assessor will also review the applicant's training experience.

On the expiry of the 45-day period and subsequent to the IATA assessor's visit to the business location and the financial assessor's review of the accounts, financial information submitted and bonding levels, the Agency Services Office will take a decision with regard to the application.

On approval of the application a Passenger Sales Agency Agreement will be sent to the agent for signature and return together with a direct debit mandate and an estimate of ticket stock requirements. On approval, an IATA numeric code is issued to each agent together with a ticket imprinter and ticket staff and accounting documentation. All IATA member airlines and all non-IATA BSP airlines are informed of the approval decision and they then may provide their carrier identification plate and/or automated ticketing authority.

There are arbitration procedures in place in case of situations where an applicant is not approved.

## 4.6   Annual financial review

Accredited agents must submit certified accounts to IATA every year for review by its financial assessors. IATA requires accounts to be delivered within six months of the agent's year end. Where the accredited agent is a subsidiary company the financial statements of the parent company must also be submitted.

If accredited agents fail to submit accounts within the deadline IATA has the ability to impose monetary fines and to cancel accreditation.

Bonding levels are assessed on an annual basis. However, as sales levels are monitored by IATA from information available through the BSP system throughout the year, a review of the bonding level may be prompted at any time.

## 4.7　The Billing and Settlement Plan

The BSP is a system through which the majority of travel agencies' ticket sales are reported and paid for. At least one person from each agency must attend a BSP training seminar and a certificate is issued at the conclusion of the course. This course enables a member of each agency to organise billing and settlement within the IATA rules.

All BSP air ticket sales are made on a credit basis. The agency does not need to pay for sales until the 17th day of the following month when payment will be made by direct debit. Each agency will therefore have up to six weeks' credit (which is reduced to four weeks if twice monthly settlement is adopted). This is obviously the prinicipal reason why the financial criteria are drawn up with the objective of ensuring that only financially sound applications are accredited.

## 4.8　Ticketing procedures and training

IATA sets out strict requirements for the storage of ticket stocks, validator plates, and training courses for agency staff on the BSP rules and standards. Staff qualifications are evaluated by a points system and IATA maintains a list of approved training providers.

## 4.9　IATA agency fees

The following fees, taken from the June 1997 *Accreditation Guide,* are payable at the time of application:

| | |
|---|---|
| Non-refundable application fee | £235 plus VAT |
| Entry fee – head office | £1,000 plus VAT |
| – branch | £500 plus VAT |
| Entry fee for AUKDA domestic agents – head office | £500 plus VAT |
| – branch office | £250 plus VAT |

In addition, an annual agency fee will be payable of 200 Swiss francs.

## 4.10   The passenger sales agency agreement

An approved agent is required to enter into a Passenger Sales Agency Agreement with IATA. This agreement is a contract that binds the agency to IATA member airlines and is an important agreement that all financial staff and third-party auditors should be aware of.

## 4.11   Notification of changes

IATA requires changes to be notified to it in respect of any of the following:

- shareholding;
- ownership;
- name; and
- location.

## 4.12   Quality reviews

IATA maintains standards by undertaking reviews from time to time to ensure that agents continue to meet their quality criteria. In addition, the BSP has an audit programme designed by IATA to monitor agents' compliance with BSP procedures.

# Chapter 5 – Other industry bodies

## 5.1 Introduction

There are a number of other industry bodies and associations which the accountant should be aware of. These bodies are mainly formed for marketing purposes or to act as influencing groups to the public and government on behalf of their members. However, the Travel Trust Association offers alternative consumer protection to that provided by Association of British Travel Agents (ABTA) bonding and the Association of Independent Tour Operators operates a bonding programme.

While there are other valuable trade associations in existence, this chapter seeks only to inform the reader of the activities of the following bodies:

- The British Incoming Tour Operators' Association (BITOA).
- The Multiple Travel Agents Association (MTAA).
- ARTAC World Choice.
- The National Association of Independent Travel Agents (NAITA) – Advantage Travel Centres.
- The Association of Independent Tour Operators (AITO).
- The Travel Trust Association (TTA).

## 5.2 The British Incoming Tour Operators' Association

BITOA was established in 1977 to represent the commercial and political interests of incoming tour operators and suppliers to the British inbound tourism industry. The Association is a non-profit making body which is funded entirely by members' subscriptions and revenue-generating commercial services. There are about 300 corporate members of the organisation.

The objectives of the Association are to promote tourism in Britain, to ensure that members adopt best practice procedures, eco-friendly practice, and improve their educational and training programmes. In addition, BITOA represents the political interests of its members, both in the UK and within the European Union.

There are a number of commercial opportunities for BITOA members, including free use of a legal hotline, preferential credit card processing rates and discounts from suppliers.

## 5.3  The Multiple Travel Agents Association

MTAA was formed in July 1990 to consider the development of the leisure travel market, resolve problems common to members, foster, articulate and maintain professional trading standards, and to act as a members' representative to the Government. The current members of the Association are:

- American Express (Europe).
- Carlson World Choice.
- Thomas Cook Group.
- Going Places Leisure Travel.
- Lunn Poly.
- Co-op Travel Care.

## 5.4  ARTAC World Choice

ARTAC World Choice is a non-profit making organisation which aims to convey and communicate an image of professionalism, experience and a high standard of customer care and service to the public and other influencers within the industry. Its members obtain a number of benefits resulting from the ability for the organisation to negotiate preferential rates and service from suppliers, and to assist in packaged branded marketing and promotional items.

## 5.5  The National Association of Independent Travel Agents – Advantage Travel Centres

NAITA, which has rebranded under the name of Advantage Travel Centres, was formed in 1978 as an association to promote and develop the trade, commercial and general interests of UK independent travel agents. NAITA has a membership of over 600.

NAITA is made up of smaller independent businesses which have come together to provide greater marketing and buying power in the marketplace. It is therefore in effect a central buying and marketing group that relies upon its members to actively support, wherever possible, contracted operators. NAITA provides marketing support for its members by assisting with product and tactical promotions which are designed to communicate the competitiveness of members to the public.

All members must have either ABTA or IATA bonding, or both. There is a turnover requirement based on the latest audited accounts as follows:

|                              | £         |
|------------------------------|-----------|
| ABTA and IATA bonding held   | 500,000   |
| ABTA only                    | 750,000   |
| IATA only                    | 1,000,000 |

NAITA has recently formed the Independent Advantage Insurance Company Limited (IAICL) to provide the travel industry with financial bonds as an alternative to those provided by banks or the general insurance market.

## 5.6   The Association of Independent Tour Operators

AITO was established in 1976 to serve as a forum for the specialist tour operator and as an organisation providing information to the public and marketing services to its members. The majority of AITO members are owner-managed tour operators.

In 1990 AITO set up its own bonding scheme administered by AITO Trust Limited. AITO Trust is responsible for monitoring the financial performance of member companies within the scheme, setting bond levels and collecting premiums. The Trust has approved body status under Regulation 18 of the Package Travel, Package Holidays and Package Tours Regulations 1992 and is designed to bond non-licensable turnover (i.e., holidays including service transport options such as self-drive, coach or train-based holidays).

## 5.7   The Travel Trust Association

The TTA has created an alternative method to bonding while providing consumer protection which complies with the Package Holiday, Package Travel and Package Tours Regulations 1992. The TTA is a trade association of travel agents, tour operators and travel organisers that operate trust accounts in order to provide financial protection of the consumer. The TTA lays down strict guidelines on how customer funds may be handled and each member must adhere to these guidelines.

It was formed in April 1993 and has in excess of 375 members. Members may be limited companies, sole traders, or partnerships that operate in the travel industry and agree to operate a trust account under the control of a TTA approved trustee. Each member is assessed by the TTA on its individual merits and must pass certain key background searches. Existing businesses should have a good trading history. Membership costs are a set up fee of £150 and an annual membership fee of £500.

### 5.7.1 Operation of a TTA member's trust account

All funds received from a consumer for a travel service (be that transport, accommodation or ancillary product including insurance) have to be deposited in the TTA member's trust account. Depending upon the type of transaction, funds may be treated in one of the following ways:

(a)   In transactions where the TTA member acts as the principal organiser funds are held until the contract between the TTA member and the consumer have been fully performed. They may then be released by the trustee. Each trustee must be either a solicitor, chartered accountant, registered auditor or banker. A trustee must be a member of a firm and not a sole practitioner and in respect to accountancy firms one partner within the firm may act as trustee, while another may act as auditor. In no case may one individual act as both trustee and auditor as this represents a conflict of interest that may void professional indemnity policies. Each trustee must agree to sign a trust deed with the TTA member outlining the conditions under which he may release funds.

(b)   In retail transactions where the TTA member sells to the public on behalf of an Air Travel Organisers' Licence (ATOL) holder then the commission element of the transaction will be released to the TTA member once that ATOL holder has received the consumer's payment. In this instance, that ATOL holder is responsible for the financial protection of the consumer's funds.

(c)   In all other transactions, the consumer's funds must remain in the trust account until such time as the service has been provided. The intention is that other than forwarding funds to an ATOL holder, at no time can a client's funds be used as a prepayment or be placed at risk.

### 5.7.2 The TTA travel protection plan

If a TTA member fails financially then the consumer's funds should still be in the trust account to either pay for the holiday as planned or to provide the consumer with a full refund. The TTA has, however, developed 'the travel protection plan' whereby if a member did not place money into the trust account, or money was improperly removed from the trust account, then the consumer may claim the value of his holiday from an insurance plan developed through AIG Europe Limited up to a value of £11,000 per passenger.

The TTA travel protection plan is financed through the commission obtained by the member selling travel insurance. If the consumer does not purchase travel insurance, it is a tenet of the Association and part of the Code of Conduct that every member provides to the consumer a travel protection plan (fidelity only) from the member's profit element of the transaction.

# Chapter 6 – Commercial operation within the UK travel industry

## 6.1  Introduction

We have given a detailed review of the structure of the UK travel industry within Chapter 1, and in the following three chapters we deal more specifically with the commercial operation of businesses in each of the three sectors which this book addresses: tour operators, travel agents and airlines.

In the first part of this chapter we address the question of industry concentration in more detail by examining the findings of the Monopolies and Mergers Commission (MMC) report, Foreign Package Holidays: A report on the supply in the UK of Tour Operators' services and Travel Agents' services in relation to foreign package holidays'. In the second part of the chapter we look at some of the commercial considerations of operation in the travel industry from the perspective of insolvency.

## 6.2  The MMC report into the foreign package holiday industry

Against the background of an industry which may appear particularly concentrated in the hands of a small number of vertically integrated groups (each having tour operations, travel agency and charter airline functions) in November 1996 the Director General of Fair Trading commissioned a report by the MMC into the competitiveness of the UK travel industry. In fact, a detailed review of vertical integration was first carried out by the Office of Fair Trading in 1993 at which time it was decided that a reference to the MMC was not warranted. However, the new Director General, John Bridgeman, later decided that there were indeed grounds for a reference to the MMC leading to the report issued in December 1997.

In a Press Release dated 7 November 1996 the Director General made the following statement to put the reference to the MMC into context:

> 'The vertically integrated groups now supply a large proportion of this £7bn market. I believe they have the market power to put competitors at a disadvantage for example by de-racking or threatening to de-rack their brochures in an attempt to negotiate larger commissions, by pressurising tour operators not to supply independent travel agents on better terms, or by pushing their own holidays through in-house incentive schemes.

The two leading travel companies with whom I have had discussions have argued that such practices are a reflection of the competition that prevails in the travel trade. My view is that they can distort the competition process.

I am also concerned about the widespread practice of linking travel insurance with holiday discounts because it may result in consumers being sold unsuitable or expensive insurance. Complaints have been made to my Office about holidays which are not available at the advertised price unless certain travel insurance is bought at the same time. I am pleased that the Advertising Standards Authority has recently issued guidelines on compulsory travel insurance. I believe, however, that the tying of specified insurance policies to discounts is an issue which justifies closer examination by the MMC.'

A reference to the MMC addresses the essential questions of whether:

(a)   a monopoly situation exists;
(b)   if so, in whose favour does the monopoly situation exist;
(c)   whether the monopoly situation is being exploited by way of uncompetitive practices or otherwise;
(d)   whether any act or omission on the part of the monopolists is attributable to the existence of the monopoly; and
(e)   whether the monopoly situation operates or may be expected to operate against the public interest.

The approach taken by the MMC in testing the possible monopolistic nature of the UK travel industry was, as is commonly adopted in such situations, to canvass opinion within the industry (by reference to the potential monopolists themselves, their competitors, and the various trade bodies such as ABTA and by commissioning research studies, and a 'mystery shopper' exercise carried out at a number of travel agents to test the proposition that certain agents sell, or try to sell, packages organised by linked tour operators in preference to others.

## 6.3   Defining the market, and defining monopoly

In assessing whether a monopoly situation existed the MMC faced the task of defining the market into which the context of monopoly could be placed. The larger groups of course sought to broaden the definition of the market, arguing that foreign package holidays did not in themselves constitute a separate market but rather that the market should include packages taken in the UK and also independent holidays.

The MMC did not accept this argument and indeed also took the view that the market should exclude direct sales and telesales when examining competition.

Having defined the market, the MMC then tested the two definitions of monopoly in respect of the tour operating sector and the travel agency sector respectively.

These definitions are:

A *'scale monopoly'* – when at least one-quarter of all of the services of a particular description which are supplied in the UK are supplied by or for the same person, or by members of the same group of interconnected bodies corporate.

A *'complex monopoly'* – when at least one-quarter of all of the services of a particular description which are supplied in the UK are supplied by or for members of the same group consisting of two or more persons (not being a group or interconnected bodies corporate) who, whether voluntarily or not and whether by agreement or not, so conduct their respective affairs as in a way to prevent, restrict or distort competition in connection with the supply of services of that description (etc.).

The report concludes that while there is no evidence of scale monopoly (citing Thomson as a fraction under 25 per cent in the tour operating sector; Thomson at 22 per cent as a tour operator for whom travel agents' reference services are supplied, and Lunn Poly at 23 per cent as a travel agent), the situation in respect of complex monopoly was different.

## 6.4 Evidence of complex monopoly and restrictive practices

The Commission found that there was evidence of complex monopoly operating by way of certain restrictive practices, and made a number of recommendations to eliminate these. These are examined in more detail below. It is though worth noting that in the report's summary, while the Commission identified a number of practices which distorted competition it did note that it had received a great deal of evidence to the effect that competition in the industry was strong, and that it broadly agreed with this view.

The Commission also noted that:

> 'While concentration has increased over the past five years, it is not at a particularly high level. Profits are not excessive taken year on year. Players come and go. There are no significant barriers to entering either the tour operator or travel agent market. Most of the large, vertically integrated groups contend that consumers are well served in this competitive environment. On the other

hand many independent participants in the travel trade, both tour operators and travel agents, argue that increasing vertical integration is bringing about various anti-competitive practices which will eventually squeeze them out of the market, leading to higher prices and less choice for consumers.'

What then are these anti-competitive practices, and how did the MMC recommend their removal or mitigation?

## 6.5  The anti-competitive practices identified

The report identified a number of practices as follows.

***Tour operation*** (citing Thomson, Airtours, First Choice, Thomas Cook and Inspirations):

(a)  Paying differential commission rates to different categories of travel agents, not justified by costs or quality of service.
(b)  Imposing restrictive terms on certain travel agents. The report identifies the practice that travel agents must promote the holidays of one or more members of the complex monopoly group on terms no less favourable than those on which they promote the holidays of competitors.
(c)  Imposing less favourable credit terms on certain categories of agents than others (the others being vertically linked agencies).
(d)  Withholding or delaying delivery of, or threatening to do so, brochures to certain agents.
(e)  Passing to vertically linked agents commercial information about other agents to provide a competitive advantage.
(f)  Pricing holidays such that the component parts of the package are not transparent (especially the travel insurance element).
(g)  Securing from linked airlines preferential seat allocations.
(h)  Tying the purchase of travel insurance to the purchase of holiday packages.
(i)  Offering incentives to certain agencies to promote packages.
(j)  Failing to sufficiently make clear the links within a vertical chain.
(k)  Arranging for vertically linked agents to have preferential access to the viewdata system, particularly during key selling periods.

***Travel agency*** (citing Thomson, Airtours, Thomas Cook and AT Mays):

(a)  Obtaining differential commission rates from different operators not justified by costs or quality of service.
(b)  Refusing to rack the brochures of certain operators.
(c)  De-racking, or threatening to do so, certain operators' brochures.
(d)  Using directional/switch selling to favour holidays of a linked operator.

(e)   Using staff incentives to favour certain linked operators.
(f)   Passing to vertically-linked operators commercial information about other operators to provide a competitive advantage.
(g)   Marketing packages such that the component prices (especially travel insurance) are not transparent.
(h)   Making discounts on certain packages conditional on the purchase of the agent's own travel insurance.
(i)   Failing to sufficiently make clear the links within a vertical chain.

Note that the Commission did not accuse all of those cited groups of all of the alleged restrictive practices; rather they noted that the businesses were involved in one or more of those practices listed.

Having discussed these issues in detail with the companies cited in the provisional findings, the Commission decided to seek the views of various industry bodies (including ABTA, AITO, ARTAC, FTO and NAITA) on three only of the 20 alleged practices noted above, as follows:

(a)   Tying of travel insurance to the purchase of packages by operators and agents, particularly where a discount is offered.
(b)   The imposition by tour operators of restrictive terms on certain travel agents, in particular terms for no-less-favourable package promotion.
(c)   The failure to make sufficiently clear to consumers that vertically integrated groups exist.

After this stage of the consultation process the Commission reached the following conclusion:

> 'Given our views on vertical integration (these being that the MMC did not find sufficient grounds for condemning vertical integration as a whole), we believe that it would be unjustified and inappropriate to address any of the adverse effects we have identified with drastic structural remedies such as divestment. We recommend that the insurance tie and "most favoured customer" clauses should be prohibited. As regards the lack of transparency of ownership links, we recommend a package of measures intended to ensure that the ownership links between the major high street agents and the principal tour operators are made clear to customers.'

Response to the MMC findings can perhaps be summarised in two camps – relief on the part of the majors, and a common view in the industry that the generally lenient stance adopted by the MMC would lead to further concentration in the industry with many medium-sized companies being taken over by the industry giants.

The industry has certainly seen this happening with a number of deals announced since the report was issued, including a number of European acquisitions.

In summary therefore, while the MMC has gone some way to alleviating fears of an increasingly monopolistic UK travel industry many smaller operators and agents still fear that their ability to compete on an even playing field with the majors has been reduced by the stance adopted. Two quotes reported in *Travel Trade Gazette* at the time well illustrate the polarity of opinion.

Thomas Cook's commercial director, Simon Vincent, said:

> 'It is positive in that the market is very competitive and that consumers get good value. But we are disappointed about the unbundling of insurance and discounts',

while the Travel Trust Association (TTA) operations director, Todd Carpenter, noted:

> 'It is only a half-measure. I do not believe it will amount to savings for the consumer. Ultimately, some small operators which provide the consumer with high-quality service, choice and value for money will disappear.'

The message for the adviser to any of these smaller concerns is obvious – with the industry becoming a seller's market in terms of disposals at high values to the multiples, in assisting your clients in achieving managed growth and in professionalising the finance and other functions in place you can add real value to clients before any potential approach comes.

Having discussed in some detail the findings of the important MMC report into the package holiday industry, the implications this has in terms of certain perceived restrictive practices, and the possible direction that the industry may take, in the second half of this chapter we now consider those issues which directors of travel businesses must be aware of in protecting themselves when things go wrong.

This section looks at the definitions of insolvency, offences which directors and shadow directors may be considered to have committed, and pointers as to actions to minimise directors' risks.

## 6.6   Insolvency implications and responsibilities of directors

It is well established that a director has a duty to act in the best interests of the company. The best interests of the company should reflect the interests of the shareholders and also the employees. However, when a company becomes insolvent or if insolvency becomes a possibility, directors will have a responsibility to consider the best interests of the company's creditors.

This is particularly important for officers of companies involved in the travel industry. Travel agencies can be plunged into an insolvent position overnight following the non-payment of a debt by a major business house client. Likewise, tour operators may suffer a setback or series of setbacks which deplete its assets or introduce claims against it which may severely damage its balance sheet. In particular, war, civil, economic or political unrest or exchange rate differentials could kill off demand for a tour operator's product within a relatively short period of time. In such circumstances, the onus is clearly on the directors to take appropriate action to service the best interests of creditors.

By acknowledging the warning signs quickly, directors will go some way to protecting themselves from potential claims of mismanagement or misconduct. In addition, timely diagnosis and action may also lead to the preservation of some or all of the business as a going concern or to a going concern sale of the business and assets. The key advice is that when trading difficulties, budgets, cash flows, forecasts and other factors point to a potentially insolvent situation, directors must seek assistance from either accountants, solicitors, insolvency practitioners or other recognised professionals. Directors must fully appreciate that their actions in the lead up to formal insolvency may come under a rather accusing microscope if creditors' interests have not been adequately considered and protected.

## 6.7    Definition of insolvency

The two basic tests of insolvency are:

- When a company is unable to pay its debts as they fall due.
- When the value of the liabilities (also taking into account contingent and prospective liabilities) exceed the value of the assets.

In considering the duties of directors, references to insolvency generally relate to a company being placed into insolvent liquidation. Broadly speaking, the directors of insolvent companies are often perceived as the 'bad guys'. There *may* be an undercurrent of wrongdoing even if the directors have acted reasonably or if the failure was due to factors beyond managerial control. A liquidator, who is obliged to take the wishes of creditors into account, *may* be required to exercise the remedies available under the Insolvency Act 1986 (IA 1986) which could impose financial penalty upon directors of insolvent companies or, in the worst cases, imprisonment.

## 6.8    Shadow director

It is not uncommon in companies operating in the travel industry to have employees (as opposed to directors) performing key managerial and decision-making roles. This may be by virtue of having absent or part-time directors or in situations where the key personnel have assumed perceived or actual authority.

The IA 1986 introduced a new concept of a 'shadow director'. A shadow director is 'a person in accordance with whose instructions the directors are accustomed to act'. While the definition is designed to catch individuals who have previously acted as directors of insolvent companies and wish to escape detection in subsequent business ventures, senior employees of travel businesses could similarly be liable to attack by a liquidator if, on the balance of information available, they performed an influential role in the management of the failed business.

A professional adviser will not normally be deemed to be a shadow director. While the directors may accept the advice tendered, the adviser is not usually instructed to act in a managerial capacity. The position could, however, be different if an adviser imposes an overriding influence in the management of a company. The distinction between a shadow director and an adviser is a matter to be determined based upon the facts.

A shadow director could conceivably extend to a parent company or bank. This subject matter is far too broad (and contentious) to be considered further here.

In summary therefore, the important thing to note is that the penalties arising following formal insolvency may extend beyond those individuals who are named as directors.

## 6.9    Offences under the Insolvency Act 1986

A quick glance at IA 1986 highlights the following offences where directors of companies that have been placed into insolvent liquidation may face financial penalty, or worse:

● Section 212 – misfeasance or breach of fiduciary or other duty in relation to the company.
● Section 213 – fraudulent trading.
● Section 214 – wrongful trading.
● Sections 216 and 217 – restriction on re-use of company name.

It should be remembered that the above provisions are not exercisable unless a company has been placed into insolvent liquidation. Contrast that, however, with an insolvency practitioner's duty to file conduct reports on directors with the Department of Trade and Industry which is an obligation that extends beyond voluntary liquidation and applies to administrative receivership and administration. (The provisions of the Company Directors Disqualification Act 1986 (CDDA 1986) are considered later in this chapter.)

### 6.9.1 Misfeasance/Breach of duty

A liquidator may bring proceedings under s212 IA 1986 for any breach of duty relating to the company. The section not only applies to officers of a company but also any person who is or has been concerned with, or who has taken part in, the promotion, formation or management of the company.

The section is intended to cover any breach of duty and proceedings may be commenced by a liquidator, the official receiver or any creditor or shareholder of the subject company. A guilty party will be required to repay or restore any misapplied assets.

Quantification of a director's liability may be difficult to prove but in a liquidation, the court may restrict a claim to the amount required to pay the company's debts. In such circumstances, a director is unlikely to be able to set off any debt due to him by the company.

### 6.9.2 Fraudulent trading

The court may, upon the application of a liquidator, declare that any parties who were *knowingly* parties to their carrying on of the business for a fraudulent purpose are liable to make such contribution to the company's assets as the court thinks fit. The key issue is that s213 IA 1986 requires blatant dishonesty coupled with an active participation in the business. Conceivably, any proven cases of fraud could lead to criminal liability (and perhaps, imprisonment) and, as such, require an extremely high level of proof. With this in mind, it is more likely that a travel agency or tour operator which does not, for example, take sufficient steps to safeguard customer deposits, may face action under s214, i.e., wrongful trading. The required level of proof under this section is tilted slightly in favour of the plaintiff.

### 6.9.3 Wrongful trading

The concept of wrongful trading, introduced by s214 IA 1986, is broader in its approach and quite often leads to a comparison between a director's actual conduct and the court's perception of proper and reasonable conduct. If found guilty the court may order that the director or directors should make a contribution to the company's assets.

Wrongful trading proceedings may seek to prove that conduct was negligent (as opposed to dishonest). The section focuses on the actions of a director, former director or shadow director in the period prior to insolvent winding up where actions were taken at a time when the directors knew or ought to have known that there was no prospect of the company avoiding insolvent liquidation. A court may accept pleas of mitigation if it can be established that the directors took every reasonable step with a view to minimising the potential loss to the company's creditors.

It can be seen therefore, that directors who misapply or fail to protect customer deposits before the company is placed into insolvent liquidation are more likely to face proceedings under this section rather than ss212 or 213. The emphasis is on what the directors should have done given that they were aware, or ought to have been aware, that the company could not trade out of its difficulties and was effectively 'doomed'.

There have been a number of successful cases under the wrongful trading provisions and case law is developing all the time. It is again reiterated that should directors have any suspicion as to current or future insolvency, they must take professional advice at the earliest opportunity.

## 6.10    Restriction on reuse of company names

Under s216 IA 1986 a person who was a director of an insolvent company in the 12 months prior to its liquidation cannot, within a period of five years after the date of liquidation, be a director or take part in the management or be directly or indirectly involved with a company using a similar name. A prohibited company name is one which is the same as used by the liquidated company in the 12-month period prior to its liquidation or is a name which is so similar as to suggest an association with that company.

Contraventions of this section can lead to criminal action, being imprisonment and/or a fine. Trading names used by limited companies are treated in exactly the same way.

The only way a person contravening the provisions of s216 can avoid committing an offence by association with a company or business using a prohibited name is either to obtain prior leave of the court under s216(3) or under one of the excepted cases detailed in the Insolvency Rules 1986.

### 6.10.1    Rule 4.228

This applies when a successor company acquires the business of an insolvent company following a sale effected by an insolvency practitioner. In these circumstances, the successor company can give notice to creditors, within 28 days of completion, stating the name and registered number of the insolvent company and the circumstances in which the business and assets have been bought. The notice should also give details of the new or acquired name the successor company wishes to use.

If a director of the successor company was, in turn, a director of the insolvent company, the notice may also make disclosure of this fact. By making the creditors of the failed company aware of their previous involvement in 'oldco' and future involvement in 'newco' the director(s) may not require leave of the court under s216.

## 6.10.2 Rule 4.229

This rule applies to a person who has acted as a director of a company which has gone into liquidation (A) and also acts as a director of another company (B) with the same, or similar sounding name. To prevent contravention of s216, that person may within seven days of the date of the insolvent company going into liquidation, apply to court for leave to continue to use the name of (B).

## 6.10.3 Rule 4.230

Under this rule, leave under s216 is not required if a company with a potentially prohibited name has been trading in its own right for 12 months prior to the liquidation of the insolvent company and is not dormant. This means that legitimate trading companies (e.g., a group) will be allowed to continue and directors will not be prohibited from being involved with the management of that company. However, it does go some way to preventing the 'phoenix in waiting'.

The difference between Rule 4.229 and 4.230 is effectively that the former requires an application to court while the latter does not. An application to court will clarify matters and may be preferable if there is any doubt. It is important to note the criminal sanction which could apply if the matter is not handled correctly. Section 217 also introduces personal liability for 'all of the relevant debts of a company' for contravention of s216. Therefore, a successor company with some form of common management that uses a prohibited name could render such common management personally liable for 'relevant debts' in the event of the successor's insolvency.

In the travel industry in particular there will often be transfers of businesses and assets following insolvency which will include the goodwill and name or trading name of a company. It would not be unusual for such a name to have greater value than the physical assets. Should there be any doubt as to the legal position either as regards an 'arm's length' purchaser or a management buy-out – get legal advice!

# 6.11 Preferences

We should not leave IA 1986 without some reference to ss239 and 240 – 'preferences'.

Before IA 1986 came into force, a preference needed to have some degree of dishonesty. Indeed, it was referred to as a fraudulent preference. The current provisions are framed in a way so that a desire to prefer must be present rather than a dominant intention to perpetrate a fraud.

The preference must be given to a creditor, surety or guarantor of a company which subsequently goes into liquidation. It must have the effect of putting that party into a position which in the event of the company going into insolvent liquidation will be better than the position the party would have been in if that thing (i.e., a repayment of a loan) had not been done (s239(4)(b)).

The period within which preferences may be attackable by a subsequently appointed liquidator are two years prior to winding up in the case of transactions involving connected parties and six months prior to winding up for other transactions.

This is one area where travel agents or tour operators can inadvertently fall foul of IA legislation. For example, travel agents will often have to meet at least one major outgoing in any month, i.e., the monthly BSP payment to IATA. If, in any month, an agent is unable to meet this liability (and the bankers will not extend existing facilities) there is often a temptation to call upon an external source for a loan to settle the liability. The intention is usually to repay the loan as soon as funds become available (sometimes within a few days). Travel agents may have such informal arrangements with family members or group companies and the transactions may at first glance appear to be innocent.

However, should the agency subsequently go into insolvent liquidation, a liquidator may consider that such loan repayments were preferences and the party repaid is liable to repay the preferred amount to the insolvent estate. The liquidator (who will presumably be supported by the unpaid creditors of the insolvent company) will assert that there was a desire to prefer the lender at the expense of other creditors. The fact that the loan was necessary in the first place could well be construed as an admission of insolvency.

Any party that is called upon to make a short-term loan to an agency or to an operator must fully appreciate that in the event of the borrower subsequently becoming insolvent, it may face litigation for the recovery of the loans repaid to it. Such litigation can be time consuming and costly. Given that the court only needs to be satisfied that there was a 'desire to prefer' such a lender is likely to be very much on the defensive.

## 6.12 Director's disqualification

Running parallel with IA 1986 is CDDA 1986. Under the Act, the court must disqualify a person (director) who is or has been a director of a company which has become insolvent if it is satisfied that his conduct makes him unfit to be concerned in the management of a company. The underlying rationale of the Act is that limited liability is a privilege and as such it should not be abused. There is a strong sense of protecting the public and in this regard the past conduct of a director provides persuasive evidence as to the possible risk the public may face in the future.

The CDDA 1986 sets out a number of criteria to which the court must have regard.

- *Section 2*
  Conviction for an indictable offence. An element of negligence or dishonesty is needed.

- *Section 3*
  Persistent breaches of companies legislation. This will relate to failure to complete and submit returns, accounts, notices or other documents required to be filed with Companies House.

- *Section 4*
  Fraud in a winding up. While this is largely self-explanatory, it should be noted that the disqualification may take effect even though the director may not actually be convicted of an offence.

- *Section 6*
  This relates to an 'unfit' director. If the court is satisfied that the conduct of a director of an insolvent company is 'unfit', it must make a disqualification order. An insolvent company extends to a company in insolvent liquidation, a company which has had an administrative receiver appointed over it by a secured creditor and, lastly, where an administration order has been made. The court will need to be satisfied that the director's conduct shows him to be unfit to be concerned in the management of a limited liability company. This is the most common ground for which disqualification orders are sought.

- *Section 8*
  This applies following investigation by company inspectors and it is concluded that disqualification orders are in the best interests of the public.

- *Section 10*
  Disqualification for fraudulent or wrongful trading. This is self-explanatory having been briefly considered above.

An undischarged bankrupt is disqualified from holding office as a director unless there is specific authority given by the court (s11 CDDA 1986).

## 6.13   Procedure for disqualification

The most frequent route to a disqualification order will be following a report submitted by an insolvency practitioner or the official receiver in a compulsory winding up to a specialist unit within the DTI. The practitioner, i.e., a liquidator, administrator or administrative receiver, is obliged to submit a report on directors' conduct (this includes anyone who has acted as a director or shadow director in the three years prior to the date of formal insolvency) within six months of the appointment. Applications for disqualification orders are normally barred following the expiration of two years from the date of insolvency and, therefore, the DTI has a relatively short period of time, not only to make a decision on whether a case is a suitable candidate for disqualification proceedings, but also to get the supporting evidence in place for the proceedings to be commenced.

An adverse report submitted by an insolvency practitioner is taken very seriously by the courts. Usually the DTI would not make an application for disqualification unless it is reasonably sure that there is a case to answer and that the application has good prospects of achieving disqualification. In practice, many applications are defended and, indeed, some are defended successfully.

If the DTI achieve a successful action, the court may make a disqualification order for a minimum period of two years up to a maximum period of 15 years. The DTI also maintains a register of disqualified persons which is open for public inspection. Here, a director with a track record of several company failures is likely to be deemed as a menace to the public and would be likely to be a suitable candidate for disqualification.

As a disqualified director, that person may not act as a director or be concerned (whether directly or indirectly) in the promotion, formation or management of a company for the duration of the order. Any person who continues to act in breach of a disqualification order may face imprisonment, a fine or personal responsibility for the debts of the company, incurred while the disqualified person was involved in the conduct of that business.

# 6.14 Insolvency implications: what should directors do?

It is no longer a defence for directors to act in a belief (which subsequently proves to be ill-founded) that the company can trade out of financial or operational difficulties. While it is recognised that a decision whether to continue trading or to cease trading is normally an extremely difficult one to make, there are a few simple guidelines, which, if implemented, could assist in the decision-making process:

(a) directors of a company must maintain up-to-date and accurate financial information;
(b) directors should seek professional advice at the earliest opportunity should formal insolvency become a real or even distant possibility;
(c) it is usually better to enter into formal insolvency sooner rather than later as indecision or delay could potentially increase the liabilities to creditors which in turn could result in the directors being fully or partially responsible for the losses incurred by creditors by virtue of the delay.

Communication between directors is important and formal board meetings should be encouraged. The board may be willing to seek advice from the company's retained advisers but may be reluctant to call in an independent insolvency practitioner. Such a delay could be detrimental to the company's interests as it may make possible restructuring or refinancing options more difficult, or impossible, to achieve.

A 'rescue culture' is prevalent at the current time and an insolvency practitioner should be asked to advise upon the available rescue (or turnaround) options, such as administration orders, for the preservation of the business as a going concern or company voluntary arrangements whereby the company is allowed to continue its business with the creditors agreeing to accept something other than payment in full.

Even if insolvency is unavoidable, swift action could lead to a beneficial sale of the business and assets within the insolvency. This will maximise realisations for creditors, protect some or all of the existing jobs and minimise disruption to customers which, in the travel industry, is a major benefit.

# Chapter 7 – Commercial considerations for tour operators

## 7.1 Introduction

The key commercial considerations for tour operators can be broken down into three distinct areas: sources of income, costs associated with generating income and identifying and managing the risks related to the income source.

This chapter will look in detail at these three areas giving an insight into the commercial decisions that face tour operators and the accounting and auditing issues that may be associated with those decisions.

## 7.2 Sources of income

### 7.2.1 Selling holidays

This is, of course, the reason why the owner has set up their tour operating business.

New tour operators are primarily looking to sell to either one location (e.g., Greece) or one type of holiday (e.g., pony-trekking). As tour operators grow then more destinations/types of holiday are added to their selling programme.

Alternatively they could just sell charter/scheduled airline seats leaving the customer to arrange his accommodation.

To be in a position to sell holidays the tour operator must firstly source the separate components of the holiday. For example, to be able to sell a holiday to Greece the tour operator will need to contract for the accommodation, the flights to Greece and the transfer from the airport to the accommodation. The aggregate cost of these components will form the basis for the selling price to be charged to the customer.

Ultimately it is this decision as to which holidays in terms of both type and destination the tour operator will offer and the market's reaction to that decision that will lead to the company's success or failure.

## 7.2.2   Forfeit of deposits/Cancellation charges

For various reasons people who book holidays do not always travel. Depending when the customer makes the decision not to travel, he will either forfeit any deposit he has paid for the holiday or incur cancellation charges. Cancellation charges are typically based on a percentage of the sales price of the holiday.

The commercial decision for the tour operator is to devise a timescale before the holiday departure date against which to levy such cancellation charges and the quantum of these.

The industry norm is that any cancellation more than six weeks before departure only causes the deposit paid to be forfeited.

A cancellation also presents the tour operator with an opportunity to resell that holiday. However near to its departure date the tour operator should make every effort to resell the holiday, even below cost, because any proceeds from that sale have a direct impact on the operator's profit.

Along with forfeited deposits and cancellation charges the tour operator should consider what fee, if any, it charges customers for making changes to their holiday arrangements.

## 7.2.3   Bank interest

Tour operators should usually be cash positive. This is a consequence of the normal cash flow cycle in the industry set out in Example 7.1.

---

**Example 7.1**   *Tour operating cash profile*

Sale of holiday for £300, direct costs £250, 10 per cent deposit payable on booking. This assumes the sale is made directly by the operator and therefore no commission is payable to a travel agent.

| Timescale | Action | £ | Running total £ |
|---|---|---|---|
| Booking | Deposit paid | + 30 | + 30 |
| 6 weeks before departure date | Balance paid | + 270 | + 300 |
| 4 weeks before departure date | Tour operator pays for flight | – 150 | + 150 |
| 4 weeks after departure date | Tour operator pays for accommodation | – 100 | + 50 |

---

As can be seen from Example 7.1 the tour operator will hold cash which, although it is required to pay for contracted debts, will be held over a period during which the tour operator can earn significant amounts of interest.

The tour operator must consider how to manage this excess cash to earn the maximum amount of interest while holding enough in accessible accounts to settle debts as they fall due.

As a consequence, successful tour operators typically have a strong treasury management function. This identifies likely amounts receivable and payable on a daily basis and where best to place surplus cash.

The recent advent of on-line banking has also helped tour operators in managing their cash to their best advantage and the availability and charges for such a facility can play a substantial role in the choice of banker by tour operators.

## 7.2.4 Insurance

Although the linking of travel insurance and holiday discounts has been outlawed by the Government from 16 November 1998 (see the MMC report in Chapter 6) and the availability of holiday insurance outside of the travel industry has continued to grow, insurance can still be a significant income source for the tour operator.

The tour operator must first decide whether to offer travel insurance at all. If it does not then it could miss out on passengers who just want to book a holiday and any necessary extras, such as insurance, in one go rather than shopping around.

If the tour operator does decide to offer travel insurance it must then approach insurance companies to contract for insurance cover which it considers is appropriate for its holidays at the lowest cost. It must then decide what mark-up to charge customers on this insurance.

## 7.2.5 Holiday extras

As with insurance, holiday extras such as car hire, excursions, wedding ceremonies, etc., can provide a significant income source.

If the tour operator does decide to offer such extras then typically it will have to enter into contracts with local suppliers in the resort and again decide on the mark-up to be passed on to the customer.

Unlike insurance, these services are controlled and monies received in the resort, hence it is harder for the tour operator to control their quality. More importantly, perhaps, ensuring that the correct income is recorded and collected can be problematic.

The usual practice is to have a holiday representative based in the resort. From their dealings with customers they should be able to identify any problems with quality and will typically control the collection and banking of any income (e.g., from excursions) taken in the resort. Typically the tour operator will have opened local bank accounts to handle these transactions.

### 7.2.6 Profit on foreign currency movements

In dealing with suppliers based at the resort, typically those providing accommodation, the tour operator is likely to contract in local currency rather than sterling.

This situation will lead to the tour operator making book profits or losses due to exchange movements occurring between when the supplier invoice was posted and when it was paid.

In **7.4** we discuss how the tour operator can protect against significant currency losses by hedging.

### 7.2.7 Airport charge rebates

As the UK airports compete against each other for throughput of passengers they can offer incentives to tour operators for providing holidays which depart from their airport.

These incentives typically take the form of rebates against the airport landing tax charges and are either based on a set figure per passenger or year on year growth in passenger numbers .

These figures are usually invoiced by the tour operator at the end of each season and the airport authorities generally require auditors' certification as to the number of passengers declared on that invoice.

Such rebates, however, are more likely to be offered only to larger tour operators. Smaller tour operators should still approach the airport about such rebates, particularly those which may be able to offer significant volumes at regional airports.

## 7.3 Costs associated with generating income

### 7.3.1 Accommodation

The relationship a tour operator builds with its accommodation suppliers can be crucial to its survival. If the hotelier loses confidence in the tour operator's ability to sell his accommodation he may well resell that accommodation. This can lead to double bookings and no availability of alternative accommodation. Such problems can soon put a tour operator out of business.

The key commercial consideration for the tour operator is therefore to find the standard of accommodation for which it considers is appropriate for its perceived customer base. Once identified, the tour operator must contract effectively for that accommodation so that its cost is in line with the expected holiday price.

The tour operator also needs to consider whether to contract for a block of accommodation or individual rooms based on occupancy. It is likely that in the early stages of dealing the accommodation supplier will be more comfortable in contracting for blocks of accommodation so that the cost of any empty rooms can be passed on to the tour operator. The holiday representative in the resort can play a vital role in monitoring the relationship with the hotel on behalf of the tour operator.

The tour operator should always have in mind that without accommodation it has no product to sell.

### 7.3.2  Transport

As with accommodation, without transport arrangements the tour operator has no product to sell.

The decision for the independent tour operator as to which transport supplier to use is usually a compromise between price and quality.

The tour operator must consider the quality of the transportation and its cost and whether that meets the expectations of perceived customer base and the price those customers are prepared to pay for that service.

Larger tour operators quite often have their own in-house supplier of transport (i.e., a fellow group company) to ensure that they have fewer worries about obtaining transport than an independent tour operator.

The tour operator should also not forget the secondary element of transportation, i.e., from the airport/port to the accommodation. As with accommodation the holiday representative can play a vital role for the tour operator in ensuring that any problems are quickly addressed and resolved.

### 7.3.3  Brochures

Despite the emergence of direct selling media such as teletext, the Internet and digital television the brochure is still the predominant source from which holiday bookings are derived.

The first consideration is therefore whether the holiday being sold requires a brochure to sell it.

If the decision is made that a brochure is required then another early consideration is whether it can be produced in-house or by an outside supplier.

The format of the brochure (i.e., description and pictures of resort, accommodation, other artwork) is the next decision. The costing of the holiday must be calculated (see **7.3.1** and **7.3.2** above) and from that the sales price of the holiday in order that it can be entered into the brochure. Although the tour operator can state in its booking conditions that the brochure price is only valid at the date of publication, it is the brochure price that is going to be one of the major influences which attracts its target customers.

Once the tour operator is satisfied with the brochure they need to consider how many to print, which printer to use and brochure distribution to travel agents.

The overriding strategic decision is when to launch the brochure and if and when a second edition/supplemental brochure should be issued. This decision needs to be based on when the tour operator perceives its target customer base is likely to be looking for a holiday to buy.

## 7.3.4 Advertising and promotion

As with most advertising and promotional activity the tour operator is aiming either to increase awareness of its name and its product or to directly increase sales.

The tour operator's perception of the advertising medium to which its target customer base will respond will determine the type of advertising and promotional activity to be undertaken.

In effect the tour operator needs to do a cost/benefit analysis on each advertising medium.

Promotions and discounts typically occur either at brochure launch or close to departure dates.

Activity at the brochure launch is intended to generate early bookings allowing the tour operator to finalise its accommodation and transport commitments more easily. It also generates immediate cash thus providing surplus funds on which interest can be earned (see **7.2.3** above). The decision for the tour operator is how much of its product it should offer at promotional rates and how long the promotion should run for.

Activity close to departure date usually occurs when the tour operator is looking to offload holidays it has been unable to sell at full price. The judgement for the tour operator is how much discount needs to be offered to sell that holiday. This decision should be reviewed almost on a daily basis as receiving £50 for a holiday costing £200 is better than receiving nothing at all.

Alternatively the tour operator can look at selling the accommodation and the transport separately to other tour operators.

Teletext, at the present time, is used principally as a means of accessing the late bookings market, i.e., the holiday is close to its departure date.

To utilise this market the operator could look to having its own teletext page to sell directly to customers. Otherwise its could offer attractive commission rates to the travel agents that have teletext pages so that its holidays appear on those pages.

Another selling strategy which applies throughout the selling cycle are tie-ups with third-party organisations. For example, a credit card company could enclose a flyer with its statements which offers a discount on the stated operator's holiday if paid for by using that credit card.

### 7.3.5 *Ex gratias* and compensation

However hard the tour operator strives to deliver the perfect product at the right price things do go wrong and customers complain about them. This leads to the tour operator having to make voluntary *ex gratia* payments and settling compensation claims.

The commercial consideration for the tour operator is the monetary level of these *ex gratia* payments and the circumstances in which it will refuse to offer any. From a customer service viewpoint the monetary level of the *ex gratia* payment should clearly seek to reflect the level of customer dissatisfaction.

The judgement to make on refusing *ex gratia* claims is whether it will lead to formal action being taken against the tour operator.

When making these decisions the tour operator should always consider whether it needs significant repeat custom to survive. The more reliant it is on repeat business the more biased its *ex gratia* payments policy must be towards the customer.

### 7.3.6 Bonding

As described in Chapter 2, to act as a tour operator, where the holiday involves a flight, requires bonding with the CAA. There is therefore no commercial decision as to whether to incur these costs or not. It is a matter of talking to bond providers (banks, insurance companies) to arrange sufficient bonding at the lowest cost.

The tour operator can, however, decide whether or not to be a member of ABTA and therefore whether or not to incur those bonding costs. However, ABTA membership is taken as the predominant 'guarantee' of quality in the eyes of the public. The tour operator is therefore likely to take up membership of ABTA to convey that it is a company of substance to its target customer base.

### 7.3.7   Holiday representatives

As we have already mentioned the use of holiday representatives in the resort can be vital to a tour operator's relationship with the local suppliers.

The decision for the tour operator is how many representatives it requires to handle its customers, and then whether they should be employees of the operator or whether the services of a specialist repping company should be employed.

If it is decided to use a repping company the tour operator is again faced with controlling services supplied at the resort from its head office.

### 7.3.8   Sales team

The tour operator will need sales administration staff, customer support staff and, if selling direct, telesales staff to deal with the bookings.

The cost/benefit decision the tour operator has to make is how many people it should employ to maintain customer satisfaction and service at their predetermined level.

This can lead to a 'hire and fire them' attitude to support staff and the use of seasonal workers (e.g., school leavers). The introduction of the minimum wage is likely to have an effect on tour operators' attitudes to staff numbers.

The most difficult judgement for the tour operator is determining whether an extra telesales employee will generate bookings to cover his salary.

### 7.3.9   Information technology (IT)

The need for accurate and timely information is, as with most industries, very important. The tour operator is, however, reliant on that information for deciding its strategy and then communicating that to travel agents and other sales media.

There are plenty of specialist travel IT suppliers, the decision for the tour operator being which system they require, the initial cost and perhaps even more importantly its adaptability/support offered if the tour operator's requirements change.

## 7.4 Identifying and managing the risks related to the income source

We start by looking at some general risks which will affect tour operators whichever market they are selling to.

Firstly there is the nature of the market the tour operator is in. Then there are decisions with regard to the structure of the tour operator's company(ies). Finally how the tour operator ensures that costs and revenues are correctly matched in its accounts.

We then look at the risks directly associated with the points raised in **7.2** and **7.3** above.

### 7.4.1   Nature of the market

Generally the less specialised the holiday package the lower the likely gross margin on that package. This leads to tour operators striving for a high volume of customers to generate sufficient gross profit to cover their overheads.

Being forced by the market to operate at a low gross margins results in the operator's profitability being very sensitive to the numbers of holidays sold. In trying to address this risk the operator will monitor its 'load factors'. 'Load factors' are a percentage calculation of actual sales versus contracted capacity.

The operator should have allowed for some level of unutilised transport and accommodation in its costings and therefore its sales price strategy. By looking at its actual achieved load factor versus what it had budgeted for the operator can quickly determine exactly where it is making or losing money.

### 7.4.2   Structure

*Year end*
The tour operating year splits into two seasons, winter and summer, which typically run from 1 November to 30 April and 1 May to 31 October respectively.

Typically tour operators choose either of the two season ends, i.e., 30 April or 31 October, as their year end. For most tour operators one of the seasons will be significantly more profitable than the other, e.g., a tour operator selling ski holidays will have a better winter season, whereas a tour operator selling holidays to, say, Tunisia will have a better summer season.

The risk to the tour operator is whether the extra attention given to the administrative and accounting functions subsequent to a year end will have a harmful impact on the selling activity for the subsequent season.

The choice of year end can also significantly affect the look of the balance sheet, although only at a gross assets and liabilities level rather than the net position. This is due to the likely differences between the levels of bookings taken at each season end.

For example, take a tour operator selling holidays to Tunisia.

At the end of the summer season, 31 October, it is unlikely to have had significant bookings because its next major holiday month is May of the following year. Consequently the balance sheet will show low cash levels but also low creditors for deposits on future holidays.

At the end of the winter season, 30 April, it is likely to have had significant bookings with holidays due to depart in the next few months. Consequently the balance sheet will have high cash levels but also high creditors for deposits on future holidays.

*Off-peak business*
As stated above, most tour operators will have one season where trading is better than the other. It is the management of this off-peak business that will have a significant impact on the long-term success of the tour operator.

This risk comes down to two decisions:

(a) Can a product and customer base be found to fit into the off-peak season? For example, the tour operator sells ski holidays in winter and then mountain walking holidays to the same resort in summer.
(b) While still being able to sell for the peak season, how can costs be kept to a minimum? This will usually be based on a judgement of the balance between staff numbers and customer service.

*Tour Operators' Margin Scheme (TOMS) subsidiary*
From 1 January 1996, to bring UK VAT legislation in line with the EU, transport costs between EU countries have been treated as standard-rated for TOMS calculations.

When this amendment was proposed there were numerous complaints that this would lead to a higher VAT charge for tour operators. Customs & Excise set out three main ways in which tour operators could structure their transport contracts so that they paid no more VAT than under the existing rules. The three ways are:

(a) Amending contractual arrangements with transport suppliers so that the tour operator is acting as an agent for them.
(b) Setting up a new wholly owned subsidiary company which will buy the transport and resell it to the tour operator.
(c) Ensure that supplies of transport are treated as 'in-house' supplies, i.e., by owning the transport provider, or that the transport supplier is in the same VAT group.

The simplest of the above is (b), a TOMS subsidiary.

The tour operator should therefore consider whether any of its transport costs are for travel between EU Member States and if so whether the level of VAT charged on that travel is less than the cost of setting up and running a subsidiary company. The costs to consider are direct ones such as audit cost, filing fees and indirect costs such as division of corporation tax profit limits between two rather than one company. If the tour operator is selling exclusively EU holidays then it will inevitably be cheaper for it to set up a TOMS subsidiary.

TOMS is dealt with in detail within Chapter 16.

*Directors' personal guarantees*
Since 1 November 1997 directors of tour operators holding an ATOL have either had to provide personal guarantees against overtrading (i.e., selling more airline seats than they have licence for) or provide the CAA with a bigger bond to cover this risk.

The directors must therefore consider whether the risk and cost of these personal guarantees being called upon is cheaper than providing extra bonding. It may also be possible for them to insure against the guarantee being called.

*Shareholder capital structure*
ABTA requires new members to have minimum paid up share capital of £50,000. The shareholder capital structure of a tour operator above that level is more a matter of commercial judgement.

When a tour operator is profitable, providing it meets the net asset criteria of ABTA and the CAA, it can either leave shareholder capital at the minimum level or increase it by whatever means it sees fit, i.e., preference shares, ordinary shares, shareholder loans. When it is not profitable, however, and fails the net asset criteria then the regulatory bodies can seek to influence how the shareholders structure the refinancing of the company.

Refinancing is usually a choice between further share capital and subordinated loans. Subordinated loans will typically be the better option for the shareholder as when the company returns to profitability these loans can start to be repaid which may not be possible with share capital. The tour operator must seek to identify, as soon as possible, when it is at risk of not meeting the regulatory bodies' financial criteria and putting into place refinancing that suits it rather than leaving itself open to imposed refinancing by the regulatory bodies.

In practice, the operator usually has six months after its year end to rectify the position, i.e., before accounts are required to be sent to the relevant regulatory authority.

### 7.4.3   Matching costs and revenues

*End of season*
As mentioned in **7.4.2** tour operators typically have their accounting year end at the end of a season. This will mean the cycle of operation whereby transport takes outgoing customers to the resort and returning customers back from the resort (rotations) comes to an end. This can lead to the incorrect matching of costs and revenues, as explained below.

Most tour operators account for turnover by reference to departure dates, i.e., if a holiday starts on 5 April this is when the sales value of the holiday is posted in their accounts. This holiday value will also typically be based on the whole holiday including the marked-up cost of the return flight.

This is not of particular concern in the middle of a season but at the year end the following will occur: customers will have departed before the year end and the revenue posted for the whole of the holiday, but the cost of their return flight will be incurred and posted to the accounting records in the next accounting year.

The tour operator must therefore capture the information of how many passengers are actually in the resort at the year end and then devise a calculation for the cost that needs to be accrued in this year's figures so that costs and revenues are correctly matched.

Another consideration for the tour operator which could influence its pricing policy is that the plane that flies out to bring its customers home at the end of the season will fly out with few or no passengers on board. The provision mentioned above is therefore often called the 'empty leg' provision.

*Deferred expenditure*

During the current year the tour operator will incur expenditure the benefits of which will not accrue until subsequent accounting periods. Typical examples are brochure costs, advertising campaigns, trade shows and computer system developments.

The risk to the tour operator lies in not identifying these costs and carrying them forward to the correct revenue period or conversely in carrying these costs forward when no benefit will arise in the future.

With regard to brochure, advertising and exhibition costs it is usually quite clear as to what season's products the tour operator is selling. Developments to the computer system and the timescale of the benefits derived from such developments are much more a matter of judgement. This will often involve a discussion with auditors as to how best to apply the matching and prudence concepts of accounting.

*Deferred income*

Invariably the tour operator will be taking bookings and receiving deposits and final balances in one accounting period which relate to holidays that do not depart until the following period. If the tour operator does not correctly recognise this income then its results can be greatly distorted.

The usual source for the deferred income figure is the reservation system which typically will be able to group bookings and related receipts into the month of departure. The reliability of this figure is therefore highly dependent on the accuracy of the reservation system and its interrelationship to the financial systems.

## 7.4.4 Selling

*Receipt before ticketing*

As set out at Example 7.1 in **7.2.3** the customer typically pays the balance of the holiday value six weeks before departure. Following the payment of the balance the travel documents including the plane tickets are sent to the customer.

This should mean that nobody travels on a tour operator's holiday unless he has paid. Therefore, you would expect that a tour operator has no bad debt risk. However, the tour operator's relationship with travel agents means that this is not the case.

Unless the customer has booked directly with the tour operator, he actually pays monies due to a travel agent, which then subsequently pays the tour operator, depending on agreed credit terms. Depending upon the agreement between the tour operator and the travel agent the settlement of the holiday value could occur after departure date.

The tour operator must therefore manage the risk of potential bad debts from failed travel agents against giving travel agents credit terms to encourage them to sell their holidays.

*Sales team rewards*

As we discussed in **7.3.8** tour operators usually seek to have seasonal levels of sales team staffing to try to match expected booking peaks.

Once the numbers in the sales team have been decided, the tour operator has to consider how to reward them in order that they are encouraged to take as many bookings as possible at the highest price possible.

The commercial risk lies in achieving the correct balance between salary and commission levels which encourage the sales team to strive for the goal set out above.

Arising from that decision the tour operator has two further considerations – the impact of cancellations on commission calculations and matching commission costs against revenue derived from the bookings taken. The tour operator should always be investigating why and when holiday cancellations occur (if only to determine cancellation fees). It should then determine whether commission payments to sales staff should be reduced, usually retrospectively, for cancellations or not. Obviously if they are deducted then it saves the tour operator money but this may stop sales staff taking bookings when there seems to be a risk of cancellation. Conversely the tour operator must be aware of the potential for bogus bookings made for commission-earning purposes, these bookings then being subsequently cancelled from the reservation system.

Depending on the pattern of the tour operator's bookings the commission earned by sales staff could be matched in the accounts against the date of the holiday on which it was earned. However, as this is a quite complex task it is not usually undertaken.

*Flexibility of sales price*

More than six weeks before departure a tour operator's sales price is usually stable with any amendments being agreed at high levels of authority (e.g., sales director) and formally communicated to all selling media. As it gets nearer to departure then the sales price decision for unsold holidays becomes a day-by-day judgement with rapid communication required to update all selling outlets. Tour operators with direct selling departments may allow their sales team staff to make pricing decisions themselves.

The risk for the tour operator to manage is whether the sales team starts selling at say £50 whereas the demand for the holiday would allow it to be sold at £75.

The tour operator needs to decide whether the sales team staff will work within specified variance limits outside which they must obtain authorisation. This, however, may lead to lost sales. Alternatively it could give the sales team freedom to agree any price to seek to sell all holidays.

### Brochure racking

As described in **7.3.3** the tour operator can spend a great deal of time and money in producing brochures to stimulate sales. This time and money may be all for nothing if travel agents are not prepared to carry these brochures on their racks.

The tour operator must target those travel agents which it thinks its potential customers are likely to visit and then decide how to encourage those travel agents to display its brochure. A simple incentive is increased commission on holidays sold. This could either be on a sale-by-sale basis or based on target figures for each season.

If the tour operator cannot find a travel agent that will offer its products to its satisfaction then it may have to consider whether it should set up or acquire a travel agent for its own use.

## 7.4.5   Direct costs

### Overcapacity versus panic buying

Tour operators will usually fully contract transport and accommodation for their planned level of demand and we have discussed the implications if they are not reaching their planned sales levels.

When products begin to sell above planned levels the tour operator must make some more key decisions. For example, if it has already sold its current capacity to a destination departing on a particular date and it is apparent that it is able to continue taking more bookings, does it seek to buy the exact number of additional flights/accommodation or does it contract for a block of seats/rooms and look to sell that additional capacity? The risk is failing to balance having too much spare flights/accommodation – 'overcapacity' – and having to agree premium rate contracts to fulfil holiday obligations – 'panic buying'.

### Scheduled or charter air travel

In deciding which customer base it is targeting the tour operator must consider whether to buy scheduled or charter air travel.

As an airline is obliged to operate its scheduled flights the tour operator can sell on the basis that the flight details will not change. The cost, however, is usually significantly higher than an equivalent charter flight and therefore the tour operator has to try to pass this on to the customer. The tour operator is also likely to have a limited choice of airlines it can use.

Charter flights are available from a wider choice of airline and are typically cheaper than their scheduled alternative (if it exists). Charter flights, however, can be amended by the principal charterer (see below) if it sees fit, which can lead to poorer customer service. The risk for the tour operator is having either scheduled flights which increase the holiday price above that which its target customers are prepared to pay or charter flights which may be either of such low quality or are cancelled and rescheduled so many times that the customer will never purchase that product again.

*Whole/Part buying of charter airline seats*
If, the tour operator has decided to buy charter airline seats then its next decision is whether to charter all or part of the plane.

Whole plane charters give the tour operator freedom to change flight details if necessary and are likely to be cheaper per seat than just buying blocks of seats. The tour operator will of course have to seek to fill the whole plane with its customers or, if it cannot, selling the remaining seats to other tour operators. This policy can easily lead to overcapacity problems as described above.

Part plane charters obviously reduce the number of holidays to be sold travelling on that flight for the tour operator to reach its allocation. The tour operator can have problems where its allocation is much less than another tour operator which could then amend flight details which the secondary tour operator just has to follow.

This policy can lead to panic buying as described above.

The risk to manage is having a whole plane charter which travels with too many unsold seats hence incurring a loss on that flight or having to buy extra seats at a price that cannot be fully recovered from the customer.

*Advance contracting*
As well as producing brochures and carrying out advertising and promotions for next year's holidays the tour operator should be continually looking at its ongoing contracts for transport and accommodation.

This could well lead to the tour operator having to commit itself to transport and in particular accommodation a number of years in advance. A consequence of this is that significant deposits may be requested by hoteliers to secure future accommodation.

Where such sums are paid relating to periods more than one year in advance then the operator's accounts should reflect these sums as 'debtors due after more than one year'. This can therefore have implications when the various regulatory bodies review the accounts, as such amounts are usually ignored in the assessment of the current working capital position.

The risk is easy to define but very difficult to mitigate fully. That risk being having a contract for transport/accommodation that no customer wants to use or not being able to buy the transport/accommodation you want and either having a different quality product to sell or no product at all.

*Currency cost hedging*

As discussed in **7.2.6** the tour operator is likely to have significant obligations in foreign currencies. These obligations will give rise to exchange profits or losses as the exchange rates move.

To hedge against exchange rate losses (this also will restrict any profits) the tour operator can take out forward currency contracts with banks. See Example 7.2.

---

**Example 7.2**   *Currency hedging*

The tour operator expects to incur $1.6m accommodation costs in May and the terms with the supplier mean that payment is due in June. The tour operator takes out a contract to buy $1.6m in June at $1.50/£.

| Exchange rates | May $1.6/£ | June $1.3/£ |
|---|---|---|
| *Without hedging* | | £ |
| Invoice | $1.6m @ $1.6/£ | 1,000,000 |
| Paid | $1.6m @ $1.3/£ | 1,230,769 |
| Loss on exchange | | 230,769 |
| | | |
| *With hedging* | | |
| Invoice | $1.6m @ $1.6/£ | 1,000,000 |
| Paid to bank | $1.6m @ £1.5/£ | 1,066.667 |
| Loss on exchange | | 66,667 |

The decision for the tour operator is whether it believes sterling will weaken (exchange losses) or strengthen (exchange gains) and how much of that exchange risk it should hedge against, and hedging costs.

---

*IT support*

As discussed in **7.3.9** IT is vital to a tour operator's success. A tour operator must therefore ensure that it has either the internal or external support to ensure that any IT problems do not significantly impact upon the business.

As with most contingency decisions this is a judgement between the cost and benefits of becoming fully operational within a certain timeframe from an IT problem.

# Chapter 8 – Commercial consideration for travel agents

## 8.1  Background

Travel agents are the retailers of the travel industry, acting as intermediary between tour operators and airlines on the one hand and the consumer on the other. They provide market information to the consumer in order to meet travel requirements and a retail point of sale.

The early 1950s saw a trend in an increasing number of travel agencies. From a membership of less than 100 in 1950, ABTA membership had swelled to almost 3,000 in 1990. The industry, however, was one of the most badly affected by the recession in the early 1990s, so that by 1995 the membership of ABTA had fallen to around 2,200.

In the 1960s many travel agencies sprang up outside the control of ABTA, resulting in the public not being able to take advantage of the consumer protection schemes afforded by ABTA membership. At that time, numerous agents were forced to close down or merely disappeared overnight and the travel agency industry developed a relatively poor image. Today, most UK travel agents are members of ABTA. By joining this voluntary association, the travel agent is insured against financial failure, thereby providing consumer protection. This protection encourages the public to use the services of ABTA registered travel agents, since they can then be assured of peace of mind in the event of the agent's insolvency. While alternative bonding arrangements are available, e.g., the Travel Trust Association (TTA), ABTA remains the principal provider in respect of non-licensable turnover.

Since the 1950s the industry has polarised towards a few large players. One of the most celebrated is the Thomas Cook Group, which was established by Thomas Cook in 1841. He started in business by offering short excursions, the first one being a 12-mile return trip for the cost of a shilling. He soon expanded, however, to providing trips to Wales, Scotland and Ireland. Then in 1851 he took 150,000 people to the Great Exhibition in London and started to prove himself a worthy entrepreneur – the Richard Branson of his day! His acumen led him to expand into new areas. He wrote a guide book and produced a newspaper to promote his tours. In the 1850s and 1860s he started trips to several countries in Europe and in 1874 launched his *circular note*, which was the forerunner of the traveller's cheque.

Business development continued with international expansion in the 1880s. In those early years Thomas Cook and Son had no real competitor, until in 1928 it was sold to the continental Wagons-Lits group which had by then become the only real international rival. It subsequently became part of the nationalised British Railways and then in 1972, as the world's largest travel group, it was sold by the British Government to a consortium of major UK companies. In 1977, Midland Bank bought out the other members of the consortium to become the sole owner.

Today Thomas Cook is a wholly-owned subsidiary of Westdeutsche Landesbank Girozentrale and continues to prosper by facing change head-on. The latest challenges are no exception with its key to success being the ability to blend the old with the new, as evidenced by the company being the first UK travel retailer to open a transactional web site.

The consolidation of the UK travel industry has continued through the 1990s with several recent deals resulting, by 1997, in almost one half of the UK travel agency market lying in the hands of the following three agents.

## 8.1.1   Thomas Cook Group Limited

By 1997, Thomas Cook was the third largest agency with 10 per cent of the UK market, even though it owns only 6 per cent of the nation's travel agency outlets. Over recent years, it has acquired the tour operator Sunworld, the airline Airworld and the city-break specialist Time Off.

## 8.1.2   Going Places (part of the Airtours Group)

Going Places has approximately 15 per cent of the UK market with 700 shops and the teletext service, Late Escapes. It was formed when Airtours acquired the Pickfords Travel Agent sites in 1992 and the Hogg Robinson outlets the following year. Over the last few years it has also expanded its foreign exchange operations.

## 8.1.3   Lunn Poly (part of the Thomson Travel Group)

The Lunn Poly Agency was formed in 1964 through the combination of two businesses which had started in the late 19th century. It subsequently became the UK's largest retail agency chain with almost 25 per cent of the market share.

In recent years it has maintained its UK market leadership with a programme of rapid store openings and now has over 800 outlets. It has also developed its own tailor-made point-of-sale computer system and, in 1995, launched a foreign exchange and traveller's cheque service, which now competes with the long-established one offered by Thomas Cook.

The other half of the market is divided among a further 7,000 or so travel agents. The above reflects the continuing concentration of the travel industry which was assisted by the recent Monopolies and Mergers Commission (MMC) report on the industry which, as noted in Chapter 6, did not force vertically integrated groups to sell or dramatically reduce their agency operations.

Smaller agents had complained that the large integrated groups were squeezing them out through uncompetitive practices; however, the MMC decided that this integrated structure was 'broadly competitive', while acknowledging that the large groups often used their in-house travel agents to promote their own holidays.

It was this industry clearance, after a year-long investigation, which encouraged Thomson Travel (owned by a Canadian group) to float on the London Stock Exchange earlier this year since it could then be confident that it would not have to sell its Lunn Poly chain.

Within the travel industry generally, the three large groups owning the above-mentioned three large travel agents are joined by First Choice as the big four. However, First Choice is the only company in the big four which does not own a travel agency and there is a strong possibility that it may be looking to link up with an agency chain.

## 8.2   Operation

The types of consumer buying from a travel agent can be divided between private holidays and business travel. Since many companies need to send their staff to conduct business in overseas locations, the travel agent provides a useful method of coordinating the various necessities of air travel, hotel accommodation, transport to and from both the departure and the arrival airport. The travel agent can provide the coordination on behalf of the customer in an efficient and cost-conscious manner which generally cannot be matched by the business companies themselves.

In order to compete with the large groupings of agents and reduce their vulnerability in an uncertain market, some independent small travel agents choose to become franchisees. This gives the advantage of ownership together with the involvement with a large chain of agents gaining the benefit of an established brand name and operational advice from the franchisor.

In the modern world, booking holidays from teletext and the Internet has developed, but travel agents have two main advantages. Firstly, they provide the 'human touch' in the service rendered to the public and, secondly, in the independent advice, enhanced by the educational visits undertaken by an agent's staff so that they can advise customers by drawing upon personal experience gained while visiting the holiday location. It will be interesting to see how agents adapt to the ever-increasing sophistication of direct bookings – it is likely that the weaker agents will find these competitive pressures very hard.

Since membership of ABTA imposes a code of conduct on its members, a minority of travel agents still choose to remain unregulated and therefore cannot benefit from the advantages of ABTA membership. Due to the vetting procedures for membership, other parties can be confident as to the suitability and financial stability of the travel agent. This is ensured by stringent rules imposed by ABTA, e.g., the requirement that every member shall keep books of accounts that properly record:

- all sums received and expended by the member with adequate documentation as to the origin of the income or expense;
- all sales and purchases of goods and services; and
- all assets and liabilities.

Members are further required to prepare balance sheets showing a true and fair view of the state of affairs of the member firm and a profit and loss account for the period ending on the date of the balance sheet.

In order to verify the above, ABTA places reliance on the statutory audit report produced for all *incorporated* businesses, so that it is only for *unincorporated* members that auditors are required to submit an additional annual report to ABTA confirming that proper books of account have been maintained, and that the profit and loss account and balance sheet show a true and fair view.

However, for *all* members, auditors are required to confirm they have examined the turnover certificate supplied by the member firm, and that in their opinion the figures included in the certificate are in accordance with the member's books and records. These reporting requirements have been considered in detail in Chapter 3.

Travel agents would normally ask for a deposit for holidays booked and would have to pay an equivalent deposit to the tour operator. As an incentive, agents occasionally offer a no deposit transaction, but this would be at the discretion of the agent and would have to be met from the agent's own cash flow.

The commission earned by a travel agent on the sale of a travel product (a ticket or a holiday) is not borne by the consumer, but instead by the airline or the tour operator. In this way, since the travel agent is paid by the vendor, it is similar to an estate agent, with the purchaser (the member of the public) paying no more for the travel product than if he was to buy direct from an airline or a tour operator.

Since the 1950s, agents have attempted to increase the commission rates they receive but, depending on the type of travel or tour, these have remained in the 7 per cent to 11 per cent range. The basic margin on sales is therefore quite small and sales volume needs to be at a high level in order to cover the business's main fixed costs of salaries and shop establishment expenses. There are now moves by tour operators to radically shake up their relationship with agents. Airtours, for example, has warned that 10 per cent commission rates are 'no longer sacrosanct'.

Unijet has urged agents to improve brochure sales conversion rates so that there is a better return to the operator for the high costs of printing glossy colour brochures. Since Unijet only achieves, on average, one sale for every 14 brochures distributed, it warns that basic commission rates will have to be reviewed for agents failing to convert brochure supplies into firm bookings. In fact, Airtours has indicated that it may in future pay a scale of commission dependent on the level of conversion.

Agents may also be asked to perform brochure stock control which will help to prevent a repeat of the situation which occurred in January 1998 with many agents running out of key brochures.

In addition to these basic commissions, the agent will earn two types of override commissions:

- Firstly, the agent can produce a steady stream of income by providing a certain amount of window space or shelf space to a certain airline or tour operator which is therefore not dependent on the agent making any sales.
- Secondly, further commission can be earned which *is* dependent on sales and is based on the *increase* in the volume of sales earned from particular airline or tour operator, when compared with a previous period.

By necessity, the agent has intensive discussions each year with all providers to negotiate as high a level of override as possible, which can amount to more than 20 per cent.

Finally, the agent can also earn commission from the sale of insurance for the specialised travel insurance often sold as part of the full agency package.

Some agents have now been urged to charge customers a fee for services so as to reduce their reliance on commissions at rates dictated by the operators. This suggestion has created heated debates between agents and operators, the latter have pointed out that agents which introduce disproportionate fees could expect to see commission rates drop. However, it is felt by the operators that the charging of fees to the consumer will enhance the level and quality of service provided by agents.

Clearly we are witnessing some fairly radical changes in the relationship between operators/airlines and independent agents, driven at least in part by the threat of direct sales to customers via the Internet and digital television and the competitive pressures introduced by a concentrated market. The next few years will demand that independent agents act flexibly and rapidly in response to changing market conditions. We could see that those who are unable to respond in this way may well be forced out of the marketplace.

# Chapter 9 – Airline operation

## 9.1 Methods of acquiring aircraft

As part of its business plan each airline will have a strategy determining the method or methods it uses to acquire aircraft. Such a strategy will be determined by considerations such as the market sector it is in, the availability of capital and the capital cost of the aircraft.

The choice of aircraft type will not be considered in this chapter although it is essentially a function of the market sector and the type of operation the airline envisages. It is true to say that concentration on as few types as possible brings economies in areas such as spares holdings and crew training if the airline can operate types in a particular aircraft 'family'. However, having decided on the appropriate aircraft type(s) the airline can acquire them by:

- outright purchase;
- loan, hire purchase or finance lease; or
- an operating lease agreement.

### 9.1.1 Outright purchase

Outright purchase is uncommon because airlines are capital intensive. For example, a start-up would be unlikely to want to tie up a substantial proportion of its available capital in an asset with a long life span. In view of the relatively low returns on the capital employed which is generated by the airlines and the other calls on capital it is also relatively uncommon for established airlines to acquire aircraft for cash. It is not simply a case of buying the aircraft and engines but also the need to acquire buyer-furnished equipment, spares and invest money in crew training which places demands on the available cash resources and capital.

The above scenario is, however, likely to be less relevant to second-hand aircraft where the capital cost will be lower.

With new aircraft and engines the availability of delivery slots is a key consideration and this is to an extent determined by the stage of boom or bust in the aircraft ordering cycle in the world economy. When demand for new aircraft is strong, secured delivery slots are valuable and have been traded in the past.

In addition to having operational use of the aircraft the benefits of ownership may include:

- manufacturer incentives to buy their product;
- an asset which has a residual value; and
- an asset which can be refinanced to generate capital should the need arise, subject to tax considerations.

Some of the disadvantages of ownership include:

- the need to place deposits and make stage payments to the manufacturer;
- a lack of flexibility if market changes make an aircraft type less attractive; and
- the commitment of a substantial part of the company's capital to an asset with a long life span.

## 9.1.2   Loan, hire purchase or finance lease

These are all ways of securing the benefits of 'ownership' set out above while spreading the financial burden of paying for the aircraft over a period that approximates to its anticipated useful life. Notwithstanding their different legal form they fall to be accounted for in a similar way as they give the airline similar risks and rewards although their taxation treatment is different, a subject which is covered in **15.6.4**.

The cost of these methods of acquiring an aircraft is determined by prevailing market interest rates and the level of risk perceived by the provider of the finance. As part of its treasury management strategy the airline will decide whether it wants to enter into a fixed or variable interest rate agreement. If variable rate is chosen the airline can use financial instruments such as rate swaps or buying forward to manage its interest rate exposure. The provider of finance will assess his risk and hence his interest rate margin in terms of:

- the level of security offered by the aircraft;
- the percentage of the cost of the aircraft that is to be financed;
- the airline's ability to service its debts;
- any additional security that can be provided by the borrower; and
- the borrowing history of the company/directors.

As most aircraft are traded in US dollars there is also the potential for the risk of foreign exchange movements to complicate the picture although the providers of finance have avoided this problem in recent times by deciding to make funds for aircraft purchases available in US dollars. This practice passes the foreign exchange risk on to the airline and there is an additional accounting complication for an airline which prepares its financial statements in currencies other than US dollars. In the UK the provisions of SSAP 21 *Leases and Hire Purchase Contracts* would normally mean that the aircraft cost be translated into sterling at the exchange rate prevailing at date of acquisition whereas the outstanding loan balance is retranslated at each year end with any exchange differences being taken to the profit and loss account. However, a number of airlines including British Airways, who have substantial US dollar income, avoid the potentially large distortions in reported profits that might result from significant foreign exchange differences by accounting for such transactions as a foreign currency 'branch' within the provisions of SSAP 21. Using this method both the asset and loan are retranslated at each year end with the exchange differences taken into reserve. Notwithstanding this an airline can 'hedge' its exposure to foreign currencies by the use of forward contracts.

Having eliminated the foreign exchange risk the providers of finance will thus assess risk in terms of the security provided by the asset and borrower. It is logical to expect that the highest rates are charged to poor credit risks who wish to finance substantially all of the cost of the aircraft. In such circumstances the provision of other security such as a guarantee from a third party is likely to reduce the interest rate charged although there will inevitably be a cost associated with the provision of other security which needs to be taken into account.

The choice between loan, hire purchase and finance lease is determined by:

- the varying rates of interest applicable to each;
- the taxation strategy of the airline; and
- the choice of the most advantageous financial structure.

### 9.1.3   Operating lease arrangements

An operating lease gives the flexibility that the other methods of acquisition may not as it can be for a relatively short period of time. As such it is ideal for a start up or for an established airline which wants to trial a new aircraft type, for example. In view of the buying power of the major operating lessors such a lease may be the only way that an airline can 'acquire' certain aircraft types. It is also true that an airline with a weak balance sheet may only be able to obtain aircraft by way of operating leases.

Once again the lease rental will reflect the level of risk perceived by the lessor and supply and demand in the marketplace. The lease can be structured in different ways including rentals for the airframe and engines plus contributions to maintenance funds for major checks based on hours flown and numbers of rotations. Rentals tend to be denominated in US dollars and treasury management considerations to cover forward exposures are again relevant.

Given the short-term nature of the initial lease period it is clearly desirable for the airline to be able to extend the lease on a defined basis and rate. This is particularly relevant if a particular aircraft type becomes desirable and therefore in short supply at a time that an airline wishes to expand. However, if the airline decides to enter into a long-term operating lease this reduces flexibility if market changes make an aircraft type less attractive.

## 9.2   Audit considerations

The key to auditing this aspect of airline operations is a thorough review of the legal paperwork associated with the acquisition of the aircraft. For a new aircraft there will usually be a substantial 'bible' of agreements recording the arrangements between the manufacturer and the airline, the airline and the providers of finance and so on. By virtue of its simpler nature the agreements associated with an operating lease tend to be much more limited, often comprising just a lease agreement.

The interpretation of contents of the legal agreements will determine the accounting treatment followed by the airline concerned, subject of course to the provisions of Accounting Standards.

## 9.3   Capacity management

Although charter and scheduled airlines may employ different techniques their objective in managing capacity is the same: to maximise contribution per flight or series of flights operated. In view of the high fixed costs of an aircraft it is clearly desirable to fly it as much as possible although there is also the trade off between direct operating costs and the revenue generated from a flight to be considered.

### 9.3.1   Charter operations

The optimum technique for the maximisation of contribution will be determined by the customer base of the airline. The income of airlines such as Britannia, which forms part of a vertically integrated group where it is considered the 'transport division', is determined by the 'feed' from the in-house tour operator. On the assumption that a price for the operation of a series of flights has been agreed then the airline does not bear the risk if the tour operator fails to sell all seats on the aircraft. However, the techniques used by charter airlines which serve a variety of tour operators will include:

- whole plane charters;
- split plane charters; and
- freesale arrangements.

Whole plane charters involve the sale of a series of flights to one customer which may be either a tour or seat-only operator, seat broker or consolidator. The advantage to the airline is that its income is predetermined by the contract and the administration is therefore simplified as all invoicing is to one customer.

Where the number of seats required by the customer is insufficient for a whole plane charter then the airline will seek to combine the requirements of several operators which wish to fly passengers to the same destination. This technique gives the customer access to seats which it might either not be able to get or would have to buy at scheduled rates. Although the administration costs to the airline of having a number of customers are higher it may have to employ this technique because it has insufficient in-house 'feed' from a tour or seat-only operator or no links with an operator at all. The attraction to the airline is higher utilisation of its aircraft and contribution to fixed costs.

Freesale arrangements include giving tour or seat operators the ability to sell more than their fixed entitlement of seats on a particular flight thereby responding to increases in demand. The airline will have obtained an acceptable contribution from the sale of the committed seats and also stands to benefit from the success of the tour-only operators in selling more holidays than anticipated, although the administration costs of the more complex arrangements are inevitably higher.

### Audit considerations

Other than ensuring proper matching of costs and revenues at the airline's year end the accounting treatment of whole and split plane charters is straightforward. The complications arise when operators sell more than their fixed seat entitlement and there are delays in the airline becoming aware of the situation. Taken to the extreme, in the past this has led to overbooking and tarnished the image of the industry. The only way to be sure whose passengers are carried on a flight is to count the ticket coupons, then to compare them to the contracted entitlements and raise the appropriate invoices on the operators. Unfortunately there is inevitably a time delay in this process and consideration will need to be given to the recoverability of the debts. The auditor should, if this type of sales technique is part of the normal operation of the airline, review the procedures for controlling this source of revenue.

## 9.3.2   Scheduled operations

The techniques used by scheduled airlines to maximise contribution on each flight are often more complex and involve the use of sophisticated software programs. These techniques include:

- Frequent flyer or loyalty schemes.
- Different classes of accommodation.
- Advertising of low fares which have limited availability.
- Flexible pricing to reflect levels of demand and proximity of departure date.

Frequent flyer schemes are designed to tie a passenger in to the airline as they give 'points' or 'miles' to scheme members which can be applied to discounted or free flights in future. Such schemes are attractive to regular travellers and are designed to ensure that they remain loyal to the airline thereby increasing contribution. For example, the 'Airmiles' scheme provides both a loyal and an additional source of passengers for British Airways.

Careful use of differential pricing between 'first', 'business' and 'economy' class can also maximise contribution for the airline. The degree of success will depend on the passenger mix between business and pleasure as well as the route and flight timing.

Use of 'headline' low prices to attract passengers is a popular tool of many airlines. Low cost operators often only have a limited number of seats available at the advertised prices which are sold on a first-come first-served basis with more expensive seats then available to passengers. British Airways, for example, uses the tactic of running periodic special price sales of seats to stimulate demand and increase contribution at times of the year when the load factor is expected to be low.

Sophisticated software programs are used by airlines to vary prices according to demand. Using seat sales trends and historic data the airline can vary prices both up and down so as to maximise contribution as the date of departure approaches.

### Audit considerations

The terms of the various contribution maximisation schemes will need to be examined and tested. Where prices are varied by computer software then the integrity of the controls over the system and operation of the system should be tested by computer-assisted audit techniques to ensure that the airline receives the correct income from a flight. Where an airline operates a frequent flyer or loyalty scheme consideration will need to be given to the accounting treatment of the accrued liability under the scheme and the recognition of the associated costs.

### 9.3.3 Other capacity management issues

These include:

- planned maintenance; and
- sub-leasing.

The timing of maintenance should be planned to cause minimal disruption to the airline's operation. Airlines with large fleets find it easier to spread planned maintenance more evenly over the year whereas charter operators prefer to have their aircraft overhauled in the winter when demand is lower.

Sub-leasing is a way of varying the size of the airline's fleet to match the levels of demand. For instance, a UK charter airline may seek to sub-lease its aircraft overseas during the winter so as to maximise contribution in that period. Similarly, a UK charter airline may sub-lease extra aircraft in to cope with demand in the busy summer months.

## 9.4 Maintenance

The question of whether an airline should have its own in-house maintenance capability or make use of the services of a third-party provider of maintenance is the subject of much debate. At one extreme there is a school of thought that argues that an airline should concentrate on what it does best and outsource maintenance to a third-party specialist, whereas others would argue for further vertical integration and bring maintenance into the in-house supply chain. As ever, the choice is a function of a number of interrelated factors including:

- the amount of capital available;
- the size of the airline's fleet;
- the nature of the operation;
- how much of the capacity of the maintenance facility the airline will use; and
- the relative costs of in-house and third-party maintenance.

### 9.4.1 Available capital

The likely return on capital employed will have a significant bearing on whether the airline chooses to use any spare capital it may have, or decides to seek additional capital, to establish its own maintenance facility. As one would expect the costs of establishing a maintenance facility for an expensive asset, such as a fleet of aircraft, is itself capital intensive. In addition to acquiring use of hangar space there is a need for costly tooling, equipment and aircraft spares to support the operation. Furthermore, skilled engineers and the administration necessary to run an efficient maintenance operation all add to the cost. For these reasons start up and smaller airlines usually make use of third parties to provide their maintenance support. Dependent on the terms of the contract with the maintenance provider, such airline operators can 'pay by the flying hour' for their maintenance thus enabling them to control and monitor this expenditure or pay on a check-by-check basis plus a charge for line maintenance.

### 9.4.2  Fleet size

Once the number of aircraft in an airline's fleet reaches a certain level it may become more economical to bring the maintenance facility in-house. This strategy tends to be followed by the larger airlines, including the national flag carriers the scheduled operations of which require large fleets of aircraft. In these circumstances the airline can benefit from economies of scale and more direct control over its maintenance. The airline may also now choose to acquire its own pool of spares which can be used to support its operation and, possibly, that of other airlines. In recent years there have been disputes between airlines and maintenance providers over the quality of the latter's work when it has impacted adversely on the operation of the airline. Clearly, one way to remove this issue is for the airline to take maintenance in-house once its operations have reached a particular size.

### 9.4.3  Nature of operation

In view of the amounts of capital tied up in a maintenance operation and the associated overhead costs it is desirable for there to be a steady work flow for the maintenance operation. This is easier to achieve with a scheduled airline as maintenance can be spread over the whole year without disrupting the operation of the airline too much.

Other than line maintenance, which is necessary to keep the aircraft operational in the busy season, the fundamental challenge for maintaining charter aircraft is to arrange for the major planned maintenance checks to occur in the quieter winter season. The extent of the winter season bunching of maintenance can be mitigated by the creation of space capacity in the fleet and/or the use of a back-up aircraft so as to enable aircraft to be withdrawn for major checks. An airline's strategy in this area will be determined by analysis of the economics of the different economics although it should be easier to plan major maintenance when the fleet reached a minimum size. However, if the charter airline has its own maintenance facility it will need to find work during the summer season so as to make a contribution towards the overhead costs.

### 9.4.4 Capacity of maintenance facility

In an ideal world the maintenance facility would match the size of its airline counterpart and allow for variation as market conditions change. Surplus capacity could be made available to third parties and vice versa. The precise strategy will be determined by availability of and likely return on capital.

### 9.4.5 Relative costs

Generally speaking these are determined by the availability of maintenance facilities in the airline's home or near home market. At present there is an over-supply of maintenance facilities in Europe which has tended to drive down rates and make it more attractive for airlines to outsource their maintenance. This was a contributory factor to the recent decision taken by Aer Lingus to dispose of its unprofitable maintenance arm, Team.

### 9.4.6 Audit considerations

These focus around an in-depth review of the contractual arrangements between the airline and its maintenance provider. Where both are members of the same group of companies the accounting should be straightforward although consideration should be given to any possible mismatch of costs and revenues. The accounting for flying hour contracts, where additional charges may be levied on the airline when costs exceed those budgeted, is an example of where a detailed understanding of the overhaul process is required to ensure an appropriate accounting treatment.

## 9.5 Vertical integration

The major UK tour operators have employed a strategy of vertical integration as they have expanded their operations. They own travel agencies and charter airlines as well as their tour operation activities so as to keep as much of the supply chain in-house as possible.

The advantages of such a strategy include:

- an ability to ensure high load factors for the airline;
- close matching between aircraft types and the volumes/destinations generated by the tour operator;
- high aircraft utilisation and hence economies of scale;
- cost savings on, for example, commissions payable to third parties;
- control over airline quality and consistent brand image associated with the inclusive tour product;
- simplified administration; and
- use of third parties to satisfy peaks in demand thereby reducing the size of the airline's fleet to match core demand only.

The Monopolies and Mergers Commission (MMC) report of December 1997 highlighted the strategies employed by the major tour operators. Thomson Travel Group said that Britannia Airways 'was not set up to supply third parties, and that it operated effectively as Thomson's transport division'. Airtours plc had a similar strategy although the airlines of the smaller tour operators are set up to fly passengers for third parties as well as the operators themselves with Caledonian, for example, selling about 30 per cent of its capacity to Inspirations plc in 1995/96. The independent tour operators argued that they found it difficult to secure seats at desirable times at competitive rates and that where they had secured seats on an aircraft of one of the major tour operators it was their customers who were moved to another flight if overbooking occurred. Against this the MMC found that the smaller tour operators could find aircraft seats from airlines such as Monarch Airlines or obtain seat allocations from consolidators.

In summary, it can be concluded that once a tour operator reaches a certain size it is cost-effective for it to have its own airline for the reasons listed above. As the industry continues to polarise, Thomson and Airtours become even larger international groups and the scope for further economies of scale by increased aircraft utilisation must inevitably strengthen their market position. Against this the smaller tour operators will continue to have access to aircraft seats provided by independent airlines.

### 9.5.1 Audit considerations

A full understanding of the trading arrangements within the vertically integrated group is the key to auditing this area. Where, for example, contracts for aircraft seats straddle the end of an accounting period cut off needs to be checked carefully to ensure proper matching of costs and revenues throughout the group.

## 9.6 Alliances

For many years the major world airlines have been cooperating by means of alliances of various sorts with the aim of increasing market share and achieving greater economies of scale. The alliances take a number of forms including:

- equity ownership;
- joint buying and maintenance;
- reservation systems; and
- franchising.

### 9.6.1 Equity ownership

This can encompass a full or partial ownership of equity in the alliance partner or, in some cases, cross-ownership of each partner's equity.

113

Whatever the legal structure, the objective is to ensure coordination between the commercial activities of the alliance partners. This coordination may involve synchronisation of flight schedules and removal or reduction of the number of competing flights operated by partners on the same route. Passengers can therefore benefit from booking through services which involve improved frequencies and reduced waiting times for connecting flights, while the airline's administration can be simplified. Equity ownership clearly facilitates greater, if not total, control over the activities of the alliance partners so as to ensure quality control and economies of scale for the enlarged grouping.

### 9.6.2   Joint buying and maintenance

Certain airlines have limited the scope of their cooperation to these areas which can of themselves yield significant benefits. The joint buying power of the alliance brings the opportunity to negotiate larger discounts from aircraft manufacturers and suppliers. Taken one step further, if the partners decide to standardise their fleets then additional economies can result. In terms of maintenance, it may enable individual units to concentrate on particular aircraft types thereby rationalising costs and improving efficiency.

### 9.6.3   Reservation systems

The main global computer reservation systems include Amadeus, Galileo, Sabre and Worldspan and are substantially owned by the major world airlines. Each system favours the flights operated by its owners and therefore the benefits of feeding into the networks of the partners in the respective systems follow.

### 9.6.4   Franchising

This method of extending the network of the franchisor is used by a number of major airlines including British Airways. The attraction is that the passenger experiences an apparently seamless transfer between flights operated by franchisor and franchisee as the aircraft of both parties are in the same livery and equipped to a given standard. From the franchisee's perspective it is able to feed into and from the much larger network of the franchisor and can also benefit from the greater buying power associated with the grouping. In contrast, where it would be uneconomic for the franchisor to extend its own network, because the load factors are expected to be lower and smaller aircraft types are required, it is able to benefit from the lower costs associated with the franchisee's 'leaner' operation.

### 9.6.5 Audit considerations

A thorough review of the alliance agreements and their application will be necessary. For example, the formula for the allocation of revenue between the alliance partners will be embodied in the agreements between them and these will need to be reviewed and the systems tested to ensure that they are carried out in practice. Similar principles will apply to all aspects of the areas of cooperation.

# Chapter 10 – Reservation and ticketing systems

## 10.1 Introduction

There is, apart from the creeping centralisation of power in the industry, perhaps no more topical subject within the travel industry than the rapid advance towards direct booking by passengers of flight and package arrangements.

The traditional structure of the industry has been one where competing tour operators would sell holiday packages through competing high-street travel agents rewarding the agent for his efforts by way of sales commission. In the traditional scenario the benefits to the tour operator and the agent are obvious. The operator is given access to the buying public without the necessity to establish retail chains, and the agent is able to increase commissions by increasing sales. The buying public are able to shop around the various local travel agencies to compare product offerings and the level of package information known to the sales representatives.

While vertical integration in the travel industry has changed the customer-agent-operator relationship (with the largest agents and operators linked through ownership and therefore product offering) the buying pattern has remained essentially unchanged since the post-war travel boom.

So how then have holiday packages and flight arrangements been sold and what systems have been in place?

## 10.2 The traditional customer, agent, operator arrangement

As noted above, until recently almost all holiday and flight arrangements would be made by travellers using the high-street travel agent as the retail point of sale.

The customer may be buying a package holiday, a scheduled airline ticket, rail ferry or coach tickets, and may additionally take out travel insurance, buy currency, make a hire car booking. In each of these circumstances the agent will need to access information from the service provider's computerised booking system, and while such reservation systems all have the same ambition (to sell the service) there are different computer links for each different form of travel arrangement. In particular, there are a number of competing airline ticket reservation systems and many different tour operating systems available.

Agents would have available computerised reservation systems linked to the tour operators and airlines (for scheduled travel arrangements) and booking clerks would use what are termed 'viewdata' systems to identify tour package and flight availability.

It is important to distinguish between those systems operated by the airlines to sell scheduled flights and those of tour operators to sell packages with chartered air transport. Obviously, as packages put together by tour operators will generally be on the basis that the operator has already reserved seats on chartered flights (either in respect of all the seats available or shared with other operators) when booking, the agent will not need to access airline reservation systems. If the traveller seeks the additional services noted above, there will be further reservation systems to encounter.

Having enquired via the respective system as to holiday availability, the agent will make the booking on behalf of the client directly via the viewdata screens. An important practical concern is that no two computer reservation systems (CRSs) will be alike, and agents will require training on the use of individual systems.

The booking for holiday arrangements will have been made via an operator's booking system, though traditionally these systems have not been fully integrated with tour operator's financial systems. Although systems integration has improved over time, and typically an operator's reservation system will be integrated with the sales ledger, and possibly with other bolt-on ledgers (most probably the purchase ledger), there will still be the need to post onto the financial accounting nominal ledger by way of journal.

Considerations arise from a commercial point of view and a control perspective.

**Commercial point of view**

(a) Every sale made by an operator, or airline, requires the involvement of a travel agent. Commercially the service providers must match the commission cost of agents (typically between 10 and 15 per cent but increasingly on an incentive basis) against the agents' ability to sell products to the public. While agents have traditionally performed a very valuable role in providing informed, user-friendly advice to the general public there is certainly a trend towards direct selling by the principal service providers (tour operators, airlines and rail, coach and ferry companies) and the advent of Internet booking described below can only accelerate this trend despite service providers' persistent claims to the contrary.

(b) Ensuring that booking clerks are trained on the various systems is an obvious cost of travel whether these costs are shared by the service providers and agents, or are passed on to the public.

(c) One of the more recent innovations in increasing efficiency of viewdata reservation systems has been that of system 'transparency'. The term is commonly found in the sales literature of reservation system companies and means that one system will operate effectively through another, i.e., in the same format, and reducing system-specific training.

**Control perspective**

(a) With less than fully integrated back and front office systems the accountant must ensure that the systems' interfaces are operating correctly, i.e., that all sales are correctly entered into the accounting system and that the information contained within the two systems reconciles.

(b) Such reconciliations have great importance not only for the accuracy of the financial accounts but are also critical where information for regulatory returns is extracted from the reservation system. For example, if returns of passenger numbers are made on information extracted from the reservation system the accountant and auditor will need to ensure that, when certifying returned amounts, these have been adequately reconciled between the respective systems.

While tour operators will run bespoke or off-the-shelf reservation systems, and there are a number of these available in the UK, the industry adviser is well advised to be conversant with a number of the more common reservation systems such as FSS and Anite.

In terms of airline reservation systems, or global distribution systems (GDSs), as these are commonly called, the industry is dominated by a small number of international systems including Galileo, Sabre, Amadeus and Worldspan.

We set out below a brief summary of the leading GDS companies.

## 10.3   Galileo

Galileo was formed in 1987 by an international consortium including British Airways, KLM and United. Other consortium members are Swissair, USAir, Alitalia and United Airlines.

More than 60 airlines can be accessed via the system and, with an estimated 75 per cent of the UK market, Galileo is clearly the UK market leader. Through links with other viewdata systems bookings can be made in respect of ferries, rail transport and other service providers.

## 10.4   Sabre

Sabre is owned by the holding company of American Airlines and was the first UK competitor to Galileo.

It has an estimated 10 per cent share of the UK market and 30 per cent worldwide. Access is also available to car hire, hotel, rail and ferry companies.

## 10.5   Amadeus

A consortium venture by Air France, Lufthansa, SAS and Iberia, Amadeus was launched in the UK in 1991.

Like Sabre, Amadeus has an approximate UK market share of 10 per cent but has significantly stronger worldwide representation.

## 10.6   Worldspan

Introduced in 1990 following the bringing together of the former Pars and DATAS II systems owned by, amongst others, Delta and Northwest, the Worldspan system is Galileo's major UK rival. As with the other systems access is available to an array of other travel providers.

## 10.7   Current developments

Many in the travel industry believe that Internet bookings will in the near future signal the end of viewdata bookings and critically will see increasing direct bookings between customers and principal service providers.

Internet bookings, or 'intranet' bookings (such systems being a managed Internet link between computers within a company or group of companies that have authorised access), became a reality as recently as 1997, and there has recently been massive investment on the part of airlines and tour operators to bring the technology to fruition.

At present airlines and operators are working with agents (via the intranet route) to introduce Internet bookings, but the technology does of course raise questions in the longer term about the volume of bookings which may occur directly from the customer to the service provider. One recent survey by Jupiter Communications estimated that on-line travel revenues could reach over £4 billion over the next five years, clearly indicating a massively growing market.

The attitude of the large UK operators to Internet technology has been interesting. Since the largest operators already have distribution channels through their own agencies, they do not, publicly at least, see Internet sales in any way replacing sales via travel agents, but rather (in the words of a Thomas Cook executive) 'the Internet compliments our existing network and telephone ordering service'. While this may or may not prove to be the case, certainly the largest operators are all preparing themselves for full-scale direct bookings via the Internet.

# Chapter 11 – The euro and its impact on the travel industry

## 11.1   Introduction

Regardless of the individual's view of the respective pros and cons of Britain joining the euro project and to a large extent regardless of whether the Government leads us into early or late entry, the fact remains that for businesses of every size, international or not, the introduction of a single European currency will have significant and immediate implications. If anything, the UK travel industry will feel the impact of the euro even faster than most other sectors.

In this chapter we set out a brief summary of the euro timetable and how it is likely to impact on UK travel businesses, as well as noting some of the systems implications which arise directly out of the launch of the single currency.

While even the French franc and the German mark will be with us until 30 June 2002, in many respects the key date in the demise of 11 'local' European currencies is 1 January 1999 when irrevocable fixing of the 11 exchange rates occurs 12 years after the inception of the euro which commenced when the Hannover Summit appointed the Delors committee to consider monetary integration.

Looking forward, the key timetable is as follows.

## 11.2   1 January 1999

On 1 January 1999 the exchange rates for the 11 euro currencies are locked 'forever'. From this date currency fluctuations between those Member States will be impossible (unless the catastrophic scenario of a financial disaster forcing, say, Italy to devalue during the transition period occurs) and while the euro as currency will not exist, in business to business transactions between European countries the euro will quickly develop as the stated currency of preference.

For businesses in those Member States which have opted into the first wave of membership, as they have fixed exchange rates against each other, and as they will in any event have adopted the euro in full by 1 July 2002, it is very likely that euro accounting will commence from 1 January 1999 and accelerate rapidly thereafter. This has very significant consequences for UK companies whether or not we join the single currency.

## 11.3   1 January 2002

From this date euro notes and coins will be circulated alongside local currencies. Prices will have to be expressed in both local currency and euros but in practice this will have happened a long time before. The author actually spotted a menu in a French restaurant priced in francs and euros as early as July 1998, and French bank statements have shown balances in euro-equivalent for more than two years now.

## 11.4   1 July 2002

The single currency rules as local currencies are withdrawn from this date.

## 11.5   The implications for UK firms

Notwithstanding that the Government has deferred joining the first wave of euro entries, UK businesses will have to face up to the need to account in euros as well as sterling, either under force from suppliers, or to maintain competitive edge.

### 11.5.1   Euro accounting under compunction

Many large multinationals, and not only those which operate out of the first-wave Member States, will very soon demand that their suppliers render invoices in euro denominations. If the supplier cannot, it is likely that alternative supply sources will be sought.

A good example of this type of reaction is that of multinationals located (but not necessarily headquartered) in the UK, such as Rover Group, which has a stated rapid transition programme under parental guidance from BMW and will expect UK suppliers to invoice in euros and accept payment in euros.

What implication does this have for the UK company? Well there are actually quite a lot of implications, even if these have been largely overlooked by UK businesses. For a start the company may have to commence invoicing in foreign currency and may receive payment in foreign currency. There is no particular problem with the latter point (apart of course from currency losses and uncertainty parity between the euro and sterling), but invoicing in euros leads quite easily to the need to maintain euro and sterling ledgers and invoice systems.

Given that these issues arise even if Britain permanently defers membership of the European Monetary Union (EMU), then there are obviously issues which accountants in practice and in industry need to address now, quite apart from the significant impact the single currency may have on trading performance and competitiveness of UK companies.

## 11.5.2   Euro accounting to maintain competitive edge

Prices within the group of 11 euro states will become immediately transparent once stated in euros and, since this is already happening, consumers will be able more easily to purchase goods and services across national borders. Because such cross-border barriers to trade are removed, every company operating from a euro state will have access to a potentially much larger market.

Those companies which are able to react rapidly to change and opportunity will see instantly larger business opportunities, while those which are not face being driven out of the market. Since that statement is made of companies which operate from euro states, it will be obvious that UK companies, even before any decision on entry into the single currency is made, will, by virtue of the need to compete be forced to price products and services in euros when selling into the 11 euro states.

For travel companies the implications are obvious. With cross-border selling of packages destined to increase, and it seems clear that this will be the case despite the logistical difficulties of transporting customers from different outbound airports to their destination, UK operators will soon have to consider pricing packages in euros if they are ever to take advantage of the potentially massive European market.

## 11.6   Immediate issues for the financial director and auditor

Accepting all of the above, it seems fairly inevitable that, whether or not we as a country join the single currency, businesses which trade with businesses in any of the 11 euro states, or which have customers in the UK which have unilaterally taken the decision to euro account, or those which seek to sell into the enhanced European market, will have no choice but to implement systems to allow euro accounting, especially where an international group includes companies in EMU member countries. As the business will also need to consider the opportunities and threats arising from the single currency, it may well be advisable to consider other changes to the system which will give the company strategic advantage at the same time.

If the business believes that the UK's membership of the single currency is only a matter of time, then it would be as well for *any* system enhancements to be put in place as from now to enable euro accounting.

The alternative view would be that the single currency will fail and that, with weaker economies being picked off one by one, the separate European currencies will return, much battered. However, adopting this view has many risks, not the least being that a soaraway euro will render uncompetitive those UK firms which are not flexible enough to react to the single currency.

It is imperative for the future competitiveness of UK travel businesses that preparations for the onset of the single currency are not considered as a finance department project, left to the finance department to ensure that the accounting ledgers and systems are able to operate in an environment of euro accounting and not considered at a broader, core business level. Businesses should be considering:

(a)  How compliant are accounting systems to euro or dual currency accounting operation at present? Given that many companies will be considering year 2000 compliance in any event, it is just as well to address this issue at the same time.

(b)  How they are going to react to the potential threat to competitiveness from 1 January 1999.

    (i)  Recognising that on continental Europe cross-border selling will inevitably increase, and perhaps rapidly so, how should core business strategy be formed to deal with competitors who may take a great lead in consolidating the European market before the UK, if ever, joins the single currency?
One reaction may be to consider European acquisitions now to enable the UK company to gain a foothold into the single currency market.

    (ii)  When, if at all, should the UK business commence dual pricing? It should be noted of course that while businesses from the 11 Member States will probably move rapidly to full euro accounting, UK businesses will be forced to dual price and, with sterling fluctuating against the euro, currency risks as well as system and administration costs will be comparatively higher for UK businesses.

    (iii)  Will UK operators be at a competitive disadvantage against European competitors when reserving hotel accommodation and other local services in Europe?

(c)  Recognising that UK membership of the single currency is not going to be the trigger for commencing staff training, businesses should consider staff needs immediately.

(d)   UK businesses need also to immediately consider the commercial operation of treasury management systems and banking support available to them.

In summary, the advent of the single European currency will have possibly dramatic consequences for all UK businesses, and the UK travel sector needs quickly to address these issues.

It would be a grave error to wait and see if we as a country join the euro system. International trade means that if that is the reaction of UK businesses then competitiveness may well be eroded before we are able to recognise it, and possibly at great cost to the UK economy.

# Chapter 12 – Accounting policies

## 12.1   Introduction

This chapter examines the accounting policies of travel companies which relate to their particular line of business – the travel industry. We have obviously not commented on generally applicable policies to any business – such as for example, pension costs.

For the purposes of this chapter we have surveyed the accounts of around 50 UK companies. These include a cross-section of tour operators, travel agents and airline operators (and some companies which operate in two or more of these areas) and range from large quoted companies to smaller private firms.

## 12.2   Tour operators

### 12.2.1   Income and cost recognition

The most important accounting policy for any tour operator is the timing of income and cost recognition. This principally relates to:

(a)   at which point in the process of a client booking a holiday income and associated costs are recognised; and
(b)   in which season brochure and marketing costs and other related costs are recognised.

There are also issues of disclosure in describing the nature of turnover. For example should the accounting policy reflect how trade discounts are accounted for? Should there be any breakdown of the variety of sources of turnover?

*Point of income and costs recognition relating to holidays*
Revenue is normally recognised at the point in time that the holiday or travel arrangement takes place.

For example First Choice states, within the accounting policy on turnover:

> 'Revenue is recognised on the date of departure and related costs of holidays and flights are charged to the profit and loss account on the same basis.'

It also has a separate note for 'Client money received in advance':

> 'Client money received at the balance sheet date relating to holidays commencing and flights departing after the year end is included in creditors.'

In our survey of accounts this is not always clearly stated, and sometimes left out altogether. One useful accounting policy states that turnover is:

> 'income received in respect of passengers whose tours have been finalised at the balance sheet date.' (Destination Group Ltd)

Presumably in this example income is being recognised on the completion of the holiday.

### Point of cost recognition relating to brochures and marketing
In the accounts we have surveyed accounting policies on cost recognition are stated more often than those on income recognition.

With tour operators there are heavy costs attributable to brochure production and related marketing activity. These costs are usually either related to the time when the costs were incurred, e.g., when the brochures were produced, or the holiday season to which they relate, depending on what is most prudent for the company.

Here is an example of each kind:

(a)   As a separate accounting policy on 'Marketing Costs':

> 'Brochure and other marketing costs are charged to the profit and loss account in the season to which they relate.' (First Choice Holidays Plc)

(b)   As a separate accounting policy on 'Marketing expenditure and brochure costs':

> 'Marketing expenditure and brochure costs are written off as incurred.' (British Airways Holidays Ltd)

Another company states in more detail the nature of its marketing costs:

> 'All costs incurred in brochure production and distribution, advertising, promotions, exhibitions and market research which relate to the subsequent year's holidays are prepaid and charged in the year to which they relate.' (CIT Holidays Ltd)

### Description of turnover and disclosure issues
In accounting policies describing turnover, cost of sales and other areas which refer to the nature of the company's business there are some issues of disclosure.

*Accounting policies*

Issues described in some of the accounts included in our survey cover:

- VAT (Tour Operators' Margin Scheme)
- Geography
- Commissions
- Trade discounts
- Range of services provided.

Most companies in our survey describe turnover by reference to (or a restatement of) their principal activity already described in the report and accounts, with an extra reference to the exclusion of VAT.

For example:

> 'Turnover, which relates to continuing activities only, represents total invoiced sales in the United Kingdom, excluding VAT, in respect of tours and travel services for which the company acts as principal.' (CIT Holidays Ltd)

(Turnover is either described as a general accounting policy, or at the note relating to turnover.)

In this above example the geographical nature of the sale is referred to by reference to the area of the point of sale; in this case, the UK. Sometimes turnover is also broken down into destination areas, e.g., by continent.

Other businesses list their principle sources of income. In particular this may be the case if the company operates as both a tour operator and as a travel agency. For example a company which falls into this category states:

> 'Group turnover represents the amounts (excluding value added tax) derived from the sale of scheduled airline tickets, hotel accommodation, the sales of overseas tours and package tours.' (Gold Medal Travel Group Plc)

Sometimes the figures for turnover, profit and net assets are disclosed for these segments. However, in our survey, the majority of companies did not give a breakdown of areas of activity or by geography.

Other tour operators break down their description of turnover to take in other issues. The following examples refer to both commission and trade discounts:

> 'Turnover represents gross handling income, commissions receivable and gross income from tour operations.' (Creative Tours Ltd)

> 'Turnover comprises the invoiced value of goods and services and commissions receivable net of discounts and excluding value added tax.' (Transolar Holdings Ltd)

128

Some companies are much more specific, e.g., giving the following description of cost of sales:

'Cost of sales comprises hotel costs, flight costs, transfer costs, travel agent's commissions and VAT on margin.' (CIT Holidays Ltd)

## 12.3 Travel agents

Like tour operators, the point of recognition of income and costs is the most important accounting policy which needs to be stated for travel agents.

### 12.3.1 Income and cost recognition

The point where income is recognised needs to be stated clearly. Because most income from travel agents is commission-based, the period of income recognition for travel agents is usually after the cancellation date has passed and when all monies have been received from the customer.

One example of such a policy is:

'Commissions on holiday bookings and insurance policies and the charge for discounts given are recognised when the final balance of moneys from the customer is due.' (Callers-Pegasus Travel Service Ltd)

Here is a note used by one company changing from one policy to another:

'In previous periods, turnover has been recognised upon the receipt of moneys from clients, however with effect from 1 January 1996 turnover has been recognised at the point of booking confirmation. The revised policy provides a better matching of administrative expenditure with the sales generated by the activity and therefore gives a more fair representation of results. It is also in line with the group accounting policy.' (Travelworld (Northern) Ltd)

Sometimes there may be a different policy on point of income recognition for commission received for different types of sales. The following example differentiates between travel bookings and insurance policies:

'Turnover represents the net commissions earned, as travel agents, excluding VAT. These commissions are recognised for each element of the holiday as full payment is received and for insurance sales, when the policy comes into force.' (Lunn Poly Ltd)

Some travel agents have special arrangement for deposits up to the point where moneys received from the customer might be recognised as income. For example one company which holds deposits in a trust fund while customers are still able to cancel their bookings, states:

*Accounting policies*

> 'Transactions relating to customer travel bookings are recognised in the accounts at such time as payments are received from customers and deposited to the trust accounts. (See Note 11.) This treatment reflects the fact that customers retain the right to change or cancel their travel bookings at any time up to the date of payment.' (Trailfinders Ltd)

> 'Transactions relating to customer bookings are reflected in turnover when there is reasonable certainty that such transactions will be completed.' (Trailfinders Ltd)

This is expanded on in a note relating to 'Moneys held on trust':

> 'The amounts held on trust are represented by bank balances. Amounts held on trust are only available to settle liabilities arising from the customers' travel arrangements and related services and the company's profit margin thereon. Interest arising from the funds held on trust belongs to the company.' (Trailfinders Ltd)

### Point of costs recognition relating to brochures and marketing

Like tour operators, travel agents can match marketing costs either to the season to which they relate in accordance with SSAP 2 or write off the costs as they are incurred, if a more prudent approach is required. Much the same policy given by tour operators can be applied to travel agents also.

Here is an example given by a leading travel agent as a separate note on 'Deferred revenue expenditure':

> 'Expenditure incurred during the year, which relates to the following year's advertising campaign, has been carried forward. This is in order to match the income derived from the advertising campaign with expenditure incurred on it.' (Lunn Poly Ltd)

Some of the examples given for tour operators in **12.2** also apply for travel agents.

### Definition of turnover

Turnover for travel agents can be defined in two ways:

- as the gross sales value of services sold; and
- as total commissions received by the agent.

In describing turnover another issue emerges in the disclosure of the variety of travel services performed by the agent. Commission will be made not only from the sale of holidays, air tickets and tickets for other transportation but also on currency transactions, insurance policies and other related travel services. The two examples below refer to these different aspects, while others in our survey refer to activities perhaps less associated with the travel agent, e.g., photo processing.

130

Here is a separate accounting policy on 'turnover' which defines it as total sales:

> 'Turnover represents the sales value of air tickets, travel insurance, hotel bookings and related services, including non-refundable deposits, and excluding value added tax.' (Travelbag Plc)

While some of the agents in our survey define turnover as total sales, others recognise it as commission received on sales.

The accounting policy of this leading travel agent clearly defines turnover from its tour operations as total sales, but its travel agency activities as commission:

> 'Turnover comprises commissions on travel arrangements, sales in respect of tour operations, traveller's cheque and foreign exchange commissions and margins on sales of currencies.' (Thomas Cook Group Ltd)

Although total sales will include the level of commission received by the agent, some policies define turnover by separating total sales and commission received:

> 'Turnover represents the total value of sales and commissions receivable for goods sold and services rendered, excluding value added tax and trade discounts in the normal course of business.' (STA Travel Ltd)

In our survey at least one company had switched from one policy of turnover recognition to the other:

> 'Turnover, excluding value added tax, represents sales, net of rebates and discounts, earned during the year. Turnover now includes gross sales of business travel transactions. In previous years only commission and fees were reported. Comparatives have accordingly been restated.' (Hogg Robinson Plc)

## 12.3.2 Stocks

Some travel agents in our survey give some breakdown for stock which includes tickets waiting to be sold. It may be represented as an accounting policy in this way:

> 'Stocks represent tickets, publications and sundry items held for resale and are stated at the lower of cost and net realisable value.' (STA Travel Ltd)

Or

> 'Stocks of tickets, travel cards and guides are valued at the lower of cost and net realisable value.' (USIT Britain Ltd)

Within the notes themselves no breakdown between the type of stock is generally given. For example in one instance the sole item listed as stock is 'tickets, cards and guides for resales'.

One agent distinguishes stocks of brochures which are related to the next holiday season:

> 'Prepaid stocks of brochures which will be distributed free are included at cost in prepayments.' (Travelbag Plc)

## 12.4 Airline operators

Many of the issues which need to be considered for the accounting policies of airline operators are different to those of travel agents and tour operators, in particular relating to the holding of aircraft as tangible fixed assets. In this section we consider the major issues.

### 12.4.1 Definition of turnover: point of income and costs recognition

Like tour operators and travel agents, the point of income and cost recognition is an important accounting policy for airlines, particularly if a significant number of seats are sold directly by the airline operator. Other issues regarding the sale of tickets, e.g., the destination of revenue from ticket sales not yet taken at the year end, can also be covered.

Most of the airlines in our survey did not cover these issues in any great detail. Here are the policies of the ones who did.

*Turnover*

> 'Passenger ticket and cargo waybill sales, net of discounts, are recorded as current liabilities in the "sales in advance of carriage" account until recognised as revenue when the transportation service is provided. Commission costs are recognised at the same time as the revenue to which they relate and are charged to cost of sales. Unused tickets are recognised as revenue on a systematic basis. Other revenue is recognised at the time the service is provided.' (British Airways Plc)

*Airline operations*

> 'Represents the value of tickets flown in the year, together with the amounts (excluding value added tax) derived from the provision of services to customers during the year'. (Jersey European Airways (UK) Ltd)

> 'Turnover is stated net of commission and comprises revenue from passenger ticket sales and freight arising from flights during the period. Revenue relating

132

to flights after the accounting date, together with any commission thereon, is carried forward as deferred income'. (Virgin Atlantic Airways Ltd)

## 12.4.2 Segmental reporting of turnover

Some disclosure of business segmentation is touched upon in descriptions of turnover within the general accounting policies section of the notes to the accounts. For example:

'Turnover represents flown revenue from scheduled services, charter, freight and other activities net of value added tax.' (Maersk Air Ltd)

However, most segmental issues are covered specifically in the notes relating to turnover.

The segmental reporting of turnover falls into two main categories:

- segmentation by business activity; and
- segmentation by geography.

### Segmentation by business activity
Within the accounts covered within our survey there are not many that have general accounting policies (usually appearing as Note 1) which relate to business segmentation. The actual segmentation itself usually appears as the actual breakdown of turnover without explanation.

For example British Airways refers to this in its general accounting policies as:

'*Business segments*: The directors regard all Group activities as relating to the airline business.'

However, British Airways does actually break down its 'traffic revenue' in the specific note covering the turnover into 'Scheduled services – passenger', 'Scheduled services – freight and mail' and 'Non-scheduled services – other revenue (including aircraft maintenance, package holidays and other airline services).'

Other airlines give a different emphasis, while some give no breakdown at all. Here are two examples:

Passenger scheduled services, charter and leasing, aircraft handling services, cargo services, bar sales, other. (British Midland Plc)

Scheduled operations, other flying revenue, charter operations, in-flight sales and other income. (GB Airways Ltd)

### *Segmentation by geography*

For geographical breakdowns British Airways gives a detailed accounting policy covering geographical segmentation with reference to destination and origin, as well as the location of net assets:

*'b: Geographical segments*

> (i) *Turnover by destination*: The analysis of turnover by destination is based on the following criteria:
>
> *Schedule and non-scheduled service*: Turnover from domestic services within the United Kingdom is attributed to the United Kingdom. Turnover from inbound and outbound services between the United Kingdom and overseas points is attributed to the geographical area in which the relevant overseas point lies.
>
> *Other revenue:* Revenue from the sale of package holidays is attributed to the geographical area in which the holiday is taken, while revenue from aircraft maintenance and other miscellaneous services is attributed on the basis of where the customer resides.
>
> (ii) *Turnover by origin*: The analysis of turnover by origin is derived by allocating revenue to the area in which the sale was made. Operating profit resulting from turnover generated in each geographical area according to origin of sale is not disclosed as it is neither practical nor meaningful to allocate the Group's operating expenditure on this basis.
>
> (iii) *Geographical analysis of net assets*: The major revenue-earning assets of the Group are comprised of aircraft fleets, the majority of which are registered in the United Kingdom. Since the Group's aircraft fleets are employed flexibly across its world-wide route network, there is no suitable basis of allocating such assets and related liabilities to geographical segments.'

Other airlines clarify the definition of turnover relating to the UK. The first is in the section covering general accounting policies, and the second is a footnote following geographical segmentation:

> 'Most sales are made within the UK to UK customers.' (Britannia Airways Ltd)
>
> 'Turnover within the British Isles comprises revenue from domestic flights. Turnover between the British Isles and other areas comprises revenue from inbound and outbound flights between the British Isles and other areas.' (British Midland Plc)

## 12.4.3 Tangible fixed assets

The accounting policies relating to tangible fixed assets are unique for airline operators because of the aircraft and related equipment they own or lease. In various policies relating to valuation, depreciation and leasing of tangible fixed assets the following groups of equipment are mentioned in the accounts we have surveyed:

- Aircraft
- Aircraft held on leases
- Rotables
- Consumables
- Flight simulator
- Cabin interiors
- In-flight equipment.

Below we examine polices published relating to:

- Cost and valuation of tangible fixed assets
- Leasing arrangements
- Cost and valuation of rotables and consumables
- Depreciation.

### Cost and valuation of tangible fixed assets

Accounting policies on the cost or valuation of aircraft often refer to the different arrangements of how the aircraft might be owned or leased, especially if this affects the calculation of cost or valuation. Usually policies do not refer separately to the aircraft and its engine and they are valued together.

Within these policies the treatment of different airline equipment is sometimes given. Chiefly this includes:

- aircraft rotables (equipment which must be serviced after a certain period of usage under CAA requirements); and
- aircraft consumables (aircraft parts with a non-renewable life).

With an airline that has a large fleet like British Airways the accounting policy on the cost or valuation of the fleet reflects the different ownership patterns of the fleet. Their accounting policy addresses:

- General policy that all aircraft are stated at cost.
- Policy on aircraft not in current use.
- Special cases (in this case Concorde).
- Aircraft financed in foreign currency and arrangements for translation into sterling.

### Cost or valuation

'All aircraft are stated at cost, net of manufacturer's credits, with the exception of a small number that are stated at 31 March 1988 valuations, with subsequent expenditure stated at cost. The Concorde fleet remains at nil book value. Aircraft not in current use are included at estimated net realisable value. Aircraft which are financed in foreign currency, either by loans, finance leases or hire purchase agreements, are regarded together with the related liabilities as a separate group of assets and liabilities and accounted for in foreign currency. The amounts in foreign currency are translated into Sterling at rates ruling at the balance sheet date and the net differences arising from the translation of aircraft costs and related foreign currency loans are taken to reserves. The cost of all other aircraft is fixed in sterling at rates ruling at the date of purchase.' (British Airways Plc)

### Leasing arrangements

As stated in SSAP 21 *Leases and Hire Purchase Contracts*, assets held under finance leases will be treated as if they have been purchased. Assets held under operating leases are charged on a straight-line basis, and to the profit and loss – not to the balance sheet. In addition some disclosure is required of the amount charged in the year and how much the lessee is committed to annually at the year end.

One of the airlines in our survey stated the difference between finance leases and operating leases in its accounting policies:

'Hire purchase and lease agreements:

Assets acquired under finance leases and hire purchase agreements are treated as being owned and a liability equivalent to the cost is recognised. The finance costs are charged to the profit and loss account over the period of the lease in proportion to the balance outstanding.

Operating leases are charged to the profit and loss account on a straight-line basis.' (Maersk Air Ltd)

British Airways, again reflecting its large fleet, also gives attention to leasing arrangements, distinguishing between finance and operating leases. The accounting policy detailed below covers:

- Criteria for treatment of assets held under finance leases or hire purchase arrangements.
- Definition of the cost, obligations and interest element of these lease payments.
- Destination of payments for operating leases (e.g., the balance sheet).
- Arrangements for terminating and extending operating leases.

### Leased and hire purchased assets

'Where assets are financed through finance leases or hire purchase arrangements, under which substantially all the risks and rewards of ownership are transferred to the Group, the assets are treated as if they had been purchased outright. The amount included in the cost of tangible fixed assets represents the aggregate of the capital elements payable during the lease or hire purchase term. The corresponding obligation, reduced by the appropriate proportion of lease or hire purchase payments made, is included in creditors. The amount included in the cost of tangible fixed assets is depreciated on the basis described in the preceding paragraphs and the interest element of lease or hire purchase payments made is included in interest payable in the profit and loss account. Payments under all other lease arrangements, known as operating leases, are charged to the profit and loss account in equal annual amounts over the period of the lease. In respect of aircraft, operating lease arrangements allow the Group to terminate the leases after a limited initial period, normally five to seven years, without further material financial obligations. In certain cases the Group is entitled to extend the initial lease period on pre-determined terms; such leases are described as extendible operating leases.'

Other airlines give varying degrees of detail in policy or disclosure about their leasing arrangements and the way this relates to cost or valuation of assets.

For example as a part of the notes on tangible assets:

'The aircraft and engines cost include £xxx (1996 – £xxx) in respect of assets which are subject to hire purchase and finance lease contracts.' (Monarch Holdings Plc)

Another adds the following to its note about tangible fixed assets:

'Included within leased assets are one aircraft and two engines. The aircraft and one engine are held under finance leases, the terms of which give the Group the right to participate in the final sales proceeds. The other engine is held under a hire purchase contract.' (First Choice Holidays Plc)

Commitments to next year's operating leases and finance leases are given in some accounts as separate notes. (SSAP 21 states that commitments to operating leases should be issued as separate notes.)

One airline has a note headed 'Obligations under operating leases' giving separate figures for 'Aircraft & Plant' and 'Land and Buildings' (Britannia Airways Ltd)

Another airline mentions its commitments under finance leases and hire purchase contracts as follows:

'The future net minimum lease payments to which the Group and Company is committed as at 30 April 1997 under finance lease and hire purchase contract obligations incurred in the acquisition of aircraft, engines, spares and other equipment are as follows' (Virgin Atlantic Airways Ltd)

It should also be noted that some airlines include any modifications and maintenance to their aircraft held under operating leases as a separate item in tangible fixed assets. For example one set of accounts expresses this as 'modifications to leased aircraft on operating leases'.

137

### Cost and valuation of rotables and consumables

One of the airline operators in our survey had separate notes about the valuation of aircraft rotables and consumables which gives useful definitions for both:

> '*Aircraft rotable*: These comprise aircraft parts which have a renewable time/usage life which upon expiry are required by the Civil Aviation Authority to be serviced by approved engineers. Such parts are valued at a directors' valuation based on a proportion of manufacturer's list price.
>
> *Aircraft consumable*: These comprise aircraft parts having a non-renewable life. These are valued at the lower of cost or net realisable value for each separately identified batch purchased.' (Jersey European Airways (UK) Ltd)

Most references to rotables and consumbables are in the policies on depreciation, or actual breakdowns of the tangible fixed assets. When the actual tangible fixed assets are broken down the consumables and rotables are sometimes included with another asset:

> 'Rotable aircraft parts are shown within plant, equipment and motor vehicles at directors' valuation to reflect current market values. The net book value of £1,542,000 *(1996: £nil)* does not differ materially from that which would be shown under historic cost.' (Jersey European Airways (UK) Ltd)

Variably in other notes rotables and consumables are:

- included as a separate asset themselves (Monarch Airlines Plc);
- treated as 'rotable spares and ancillary equipment' (Virgin Atlantic Airways Ltd);
- included with aircraft 'aircraft and rotable spares' (Maersk Air Ltd).

It should also be noted that aircraft consumables or spare aircraft consumables are sometimes included within stock where appropriate (for example if the airline is involved in leasing aircraft on operating leases to another airline, or perhaps a subsidiary).

### Depreciation of tangible fixed assets

The depreciation of tangible fixed assets is obviously an important accounting policy in auditing airline operators.

In most cases the accounting policy on depreciation includes a general section stating that tangible fixed assets are depreciated on a straight-line basis. Then a list of specific depreciation rates or the number of years of expected economic life for the various different assets are given. Within this list will be specific examples from the list above.

Here are two fairly typical examples:

'*Depreciation*': Tangible fixed assets are depreciated on a straight-line basis, at rates calculated to write off the cost or valuation, less estimated residual value, of each asset over its expected useful economic life.

The years used are as follows:

| | |
|---|---|
| Freehold Properties | 50 years |
| Short leasehold properties | Lease period |
| Finance lease aircraft and equipment | Lease period to residual value |
| Aircraft spares and equipment | 12 years |
| Computer equipment | 3 years |
| Other assets | 4 years' |

(First Choice Holidays Plc)

'*Depreciation*'

Aircraft and technical spares are depreciated using a straight-line basis calculated to write down their cost to the current estimated residual values on the anticipated date of withdrawal from service or disposal. These estimates are reviewed regularly and adjusted as appropriate.

The current estimates of economic life are as follows:

| Aircraft type | Economic life |
|---|---|
| Boeing 737 – 500 | 19 years from date of construction |
| Rotables | 5 to 15 years |
| ATP spares | Period to 31 July 2002 |
| BAe 146 aircraft and spares | Period to 30 June 2005 |
| Shorts 360 Spares | Period to 31 March 1999 |
| Islanders | 13 years |
| Boeing 737 Simulator | 15 years |

All other plant and equipment is depreciated on a straight line basis over 5 years except handling equipment, motor vehicles and certain computer equipment which are 7, 4 and 3 years respectively.' (British Midland Plc)

Some airlines mention specific arrangements surrounding the lease period:

'Aircraft and engines – straight line over 10-12 years to a residual value of 45% or 40% of cost. Subsequent to the primary lease period aircraft are depreciated over 10 years to a residual value of 10% of cost.' (Monarch Holdings Plc)

Others specify a different policy between aircraft and cabin interiors:

'*(ii) Depreciation*: Fleet assets owned, or held on finance leases or hire purchase arrangements, are depreciated at rates calculated to write down the cost or valuation to the estimated residual value at the end of the planned operational lives. Cabin interiors, including those required for brand changes and relaunches, are depreciated over the lower of five years and the remaining life of the aircraft at the date of such modification. Residual values and operational lives are reviewed annually.' (British Airways Plc)

### 12.4.4  Aircraft maintenance costs

Aircraft and engine maintenance costs come under two categories:

- those incurred on a routine basis; and
- heavier maintenance and overhauls calculated on a flight hour basis.

The accounts in our survey generally write off routine maintenance costs to the profit and loss as they are incurred.

For the heavier maintenance and overhaul costs for the aircraft and its engine an estimate is made over a number of years so these costs can then be spread over the lifetime of the aircraft so it is in optimum condition. These particular costs are then taken to the profit and loss in a particular given year on a flight-hour basis.

The following two examples of accounting policies are fairly representative:

> 'Routine maintenance costs including annual airframe checks are written off to the profit and loss account as incurred. Heavy maintenance and engine overhaul costs are provided for in the profit and loss account on a flight hour basis.' (Virgin Atlantic Airways Ltd)

> 'Dependent upon the provisions of the financing or lease arrangements engine overhaul costs are usually either accrued or amortised on the basis of hours flown. Other engine and airframe maintenance costs are in the main written off as incurred.' (Monarch Holdings Plc)

The following accounting policy deals with heavier maintenance costs and how these are anticipated in much greater detail and does not mention routine maintenance. It also mentions the importance of the full overhaul cycle of the aircraft:

> '*Aircraft maintenance costs*: Provision is made in respect of maintenance, overhaul and repair costs of airframes, engines and rotable spares based on the total anticipated costs over the useful economic life of the assets calculated by reference to costs experienced and published manufacturers' data. The charge to the profit and loss account is calculated by reference to the number of hours flown or by reference to the length of the full overhaul cycle. Costs incurred are charged against the provision.' (First Choice Holidays Plc)

### 12.4.5  Deferred expenditure

Some airlines defer certain heavy expenditure when either new routes or aircraft are being introduced. Two of the companies in our survey mentioned this in their accounting policies.

Under the accounting policy heading 'Development expenditure':

'Certain development expenditure, relating primarily to the setting up of new routes and introducing additional aircraft to the fleet, is deferred and written off over five years or the length of the underlying aircraft lease.' (Virgin Atlantic Airways Ltd)

The other example gives the period of deferrence for each different area:

'Expenditure on new operations and aircraft introductory costs are charged over the following periods:

Introductory costs on aircraft fleet additions – within two years of commencement of passenger carrying services

New routes – within one year of commencement of passenger carrying services

Pilot training – within five years of commencement of flying.' (British Midland Plc)

However, at least one company in our survey charged set-up costs for new routes to the profit and loss as incurred:

'**New route promotion and set-up costs:**

Costs relating to the set-up and promotion of new routes are charged to the profit and loss account as incurred.' (GB Airways Ltd)

## 12.4.6 Frequent flyer programme

Many airlines operate loyalty and incentive programmes usually based around earning extra flights for those who travel regularly with the same airline.

In our survey two of the airlines have established accounting policies about their frequent flyer programmes as they form part of the cost of sales.

The first is British Airways Plc:

'The Group operates two principal frequent flyer programmes. The main Airline schemes are run through the "Executive Club" and "Frequent Traveller" programmes where frequent travellers may accumulate mileage credits which entitle them to a choice of various awards, including free travel. The main United Kingdom scheme is run under the brand name of "Airmiles" and principally involves the selling of miles of travel to United Kingdom companies to use for promotional incentives. The incremental direct cost of providing free travel in exchange for redemption of miles earned by members of the Group's Executive Club, Frequent Traveller programmes and Airmiles scheme is accrued as members of these schemes accumulate mileage. Costs accrued include incremental passenger service charges and security, fuel, catering, and lost baggage insurance: these costs are charged to cost of sales.'

The second is Virgin Atlantic Airways Ltd:

'The estimated incremental cost of providing free travel and other rewards in exchange for redemption of miles earned by members of the Virgin Freeway frequent flyer scheme is accrued at the expected redemption rates as members of this scheme accumulate mileage.'

### 12.4.7 Stocks

Some airline operators list stocks where the breakdown or description is particularly apt to the business of an airline operator. In particular there are references to aircraft consumables. Where this is the case it may be because aircraft are being leased to other airlines on an operating lease basis, or to another company within that group.

Here are four examples of the breakdowns of stocks from the accounts in our survey:

- 'Raw materials, consumables and work in progress' (stated as a sole item) (British Airways Plc).
- 'Work in progress', 'Aircraft rotables', 'Aircraft consumables' (Jersey European Airways (UK) Ltd).
- 'Aircraft consumable spares', 'Finished goods and goods for resale', 'Uniforms' (Virgin Atlantic Airways Ltd).
- 'In-flight sale goods', 'Catering equipment', 'Tickets and stationery', 'Engineering and spare seats' (GB Airways Ltd).

## 12.5   Foreign exchange contracts

Most tour operators, travel agents and airlines have similar accounting policies on foreign exchange conversions. These policies fall into three main categories:

- Translation of transactions in foreign currencies and of assets and liabilities in foreign currencies.
- Translation of profits and losses from overseas subsidiaries.
- Forward currency contracts.

### 12.5.1   Translation of assets and liabilities in foreign currencies

Policies on translations of assets and liabilities in foreign currencies and the destination of any gains or losses made on this translation are not that different to how they might be treated in any set of accounts.

The policy can cover:

- Rates of exchange used to translate transactions in foreign currencies.
- Rates of exchange used to translate monetary assets and liabilities in foreign currencies.
- Destination of gains or losses made from changes in exchange rates.

For example, under a separate accounting policy marked 'foreign curren-cies' the following covers all these three main areas:

'Transactions denominated in foreign currencies are recorded in sterling at the exchange rates as of the date of the transaction. Monetary assets and lia-bilities denominated in foreign currencies at the year end are reported at the rates of exchange prevailing at the year end. Any gain or loss arising from a change in exchange rates subsequent to the date of the transaction is included as an exchange gain or loss in the profit and loss account.' (STA Travel Ltd)

Airline operators in our survey generally have similar accounting policies to the above, but they may mention, in addition, the exclusion of differences arising in exchange rates relating to payments towards aircraft on operating leases:

'Monetary assets and liabilities denominated in foreign currencies have been translated into sterling at the rates of exchange ruling at the balance sheet date or, where forward cover has been taken, at the forward rate. Differences aris-ing from changes in exchange rates are included in trading profits except for those which relate to advance payments for aircraft subsequently subject to operating leases. These exchange differences are amortised over the initial lease periods.' (Britannia Airways Ltd)

## 12.5.2   Profits and losses from overseas subsidiaries

Travel businesses are perhaps more likely to have overseas subsidiaries than some other industries.

Accounting policies relating to profits and losses of overseas subsidiaries, should cover:

● Rate of exchange used for translation of overseas subsidiary profits or losses.
● Destination for differences arising from the translation.

While exchange rates used can differ slightly, as in the two examples below, the destination for differences arising from the translation tends to be taken to the reserves:

'The profit and losses on the overseas subsidiary undertakings and the group's net investments are translated at closing rates of exchange. Differences arising on translation are added to or deducted from reserves.' (Trailfinders Ltd)

'The results of overseas operations are translated at the average rates of exchange during the year and their balance sheet at the rate prevailing at the balance sheet date. Exchange differences arising on translation of the opening net assets and results of overseas operations are dealt with through reserves.' (MTG (UK) Ltd)

One airline operator comments on arrangements relating to fleet assets held under foreign branch arrangements:

> 'Assets and liabilities denominated in foreign currencies are translated into sterling at the rates of exchange ruling at the end of the accounting period or where applicable at a hedged rate. Exchange differences arising through the translation of certain foreign currency borrowings and related fleet assets which are designated as foreign branches are taken to reserves.' (Virgin Atlantic Airways Ltd)

### 12.5.3   Forward currency contracts

In general the accounting polices of the firms in our survey do not cover the issue of forward currency contracts. Where they do they usually refer to the rate of exchange used:

> 'Forward contracts entered into as foreign exchange dealers and foreign currency assets and liabilities are valued at the rate of exchange ruling on the balance sheet date.' (Thomas Cook Group Ltd)

More often specific details of forward contracts are given in the contingent liabilities section of the notes to the accounts. This example is more detailed than most:

> 'The company has given guarantees and indemnities at 28th February 1998 amounting to £1,312,721 (1997: £820,543).
>
> At the balance sheet date the group and the company had commitments under foreign exchange currency contracts on which the total sterling equivalent outstanding amounted to £2,316,308. It is anticipated that the foreign currency so purchased will be utilised for the servicing of travel transactions during the following year.
>
> The group and company had also entered into forward currency option contracts on which the total sterling equivalent outstanding amounted to £3,764,295. It is anticipated that the foreign currency so purchased will be utilised for the servicing of travel transactions during the following year.
>
> The group and company had also entered into forward currency option contracts on which the total sterling equivalent outstanding amounted to £3,784,295. Of this amount, £946,074 has become committed since the year end.' (Trailfinders Ltd)

Similar information is also sometimes given in a separate note of 'commitments'.

## 12.6   Travel industry bonds and guarantees

Travel businesses may lodge bonds and guarantees with the airlines, train and coach operators they deal with, as well as the regulators.

These are generally recorded in the contingent liabilities section of the notes to the accounts. In our survey of accounts these are supplied in varying degrees of detail.

One example gives overall details of the amount of contingent liabilities:

> 'The company has issued bonds and guarantees for £1,234,000 (1996: £736,000) securing the company's indebtedness to certain airlines and trade bodies arising from normal trading activities.' (Travelbag Plc)

One travel agent gives details within a note headed 'Secured assets', referring to the security of the fixed charge to some of its properties:

> 'Note 21: Secured assets
>
> The Association of British Travel Agents (ABTA) require its members to provide an annual bond to secure the monies and benefits of their clients in the event of the failure of the member. This bond is provided by the company's bankers and amounts to £1,338,903 commencing from 30 November 1995.
>
> In order to obtain this bond, the company has granted a fixed charge over three of its freehold properties in favour of Barclays Bank Plc, as part security. The aggregate realisable value of the properties concerned is estimated to be £665,000.
>
> These financial statements include the company's full liabilities to its creditors, and consequently this bonding arrangement is not considered to constitute its contingent liability.' (Althams Travel Services Ltd)

# Chapter 13 – Statutory audit considerations

## 13.1 Introduction

When preparing or auditing the financial statements of a travel business the accountant must consider those requirements imposed under the Companies Act and Financial Reporting Standards as well as those imposed by the Civil Aviation Authority (CAA) or trade associations to which the business may report.

This and the following chapter examine auditing considerations imposed under these general and specific regulations.

Within this chapter we consider general audit matters supporting the statutory audit report to the members of any incorporated travel business. While many of the audit techniques recommended to support the statutory audit to the members will also assist in the preparation of audit returns to the industry regulators, those specific audit requirements are considered in detail in Chapter 14.

It is also worth noting at this point that the industry regulators do of course rely on the audited financial statements of a travel business as well as those specific returns required variously by the CAA, ABTA and the other bodies and an audit approach which marries general and specific audit requirements applicable to each business considered individually will also result in efficient audit techniques.

The adoption of efficient techniques will of course result in cost efficiencies both to the auditor and the client, and minimisation of audit errors.

## 13.2 Understanding the client business and its reporting requirements

It is a simple mistake for the audit firm to draft audit programmes designed to support the statutory audit opinion to the members and then to 'tag on' specific tests to support, for example CAA returns, as an afterthought. Such an approach can never be efficient and can easily lead to audit errors.

A clear understanding of the client business, the requirements imposed under general and specific reporting requirements, and how these can most efficiently be achieved is the key to successful audit planning.

At the planning stage the following steps should be carried out:

**(a) Consider the legal status of the business and requirements imposed under constitutional arrangements**

- *Is the business incorporated or un-incorporated?*
  In practice most travel businesses, and certainly tour operators and airlines, will be incorporated businesses and will therefore (with exceptions for small business falling within the exemption limits) require a statutory audit under the Companies Act.

  Additionally, ABTA requires all member firms, incorporated and unincorporated, to produce audited accounts, and CAA have similar provisions.

- *Are there other reporting requirements imposed under the constitution of the business?*
  Auditors may be required to provide valuation certificates and commonly, in joint-venture arrangements, to certify profit allocations for example.

Having made this fairly straightforward analysis of reporting requirements the auditor will be in a position to ascertain the required form of the audit report and any 'constitutional' reports. Nothing special so far, and certainly an approach which should be adopted for all businesses – not only those involved in the travel sector.

**(b) Consider those requirements imposed either (under statute) by the CAA or by accreditation/membership of industry bodies**

- Identify by discussion with the client which bodies are likely to require returns. For travel businesses this is generally a fairly straightforward task as business documents will be emblazoned with an ATOL badge, the IATA logo, etc., as appropriate to the business.
- Identify which levels of licence/membership are appropriate to the business.

While it may not be obvious, the level of work required by the auditor of a fully-bonded ATOL holder may well be different to that appropriate to holders of lower level licences.

**(c) Examine the reporting requirements attaching to each individual travel industry licence/membership**

**(d) Consider to what extent these specific reporting requirements can be achieved by the statutory audit to the members**

It may well be the case that what may seem like a specific test requirement is actually a restatement of a matter covered by the statutory audit.

For example, auditors of ABTA members are required to certify compliance with Article 14 of ABTA's Articles of Association. A careful look at Article 14 will show that this is no more than a restatement of ss221 and 226 Companies Act 1985 requiring businesses to keep proper books of account, and to prepare a balance sheet profit and loss account presenting a true and fair view of the state of affairs of the business. Therefore, as long as the statutory audit to the members does not identify non-compliance with the Companies Act 1985 then compliance with ABTA's Article 14 is automatically achieved.

**(e)  Consider all of those requirements imposed on the auditor over and above work carried out to support the statutory audit to the members**

These requirements are considered in detail in Chapter 14. A simple example to illustrate the point, though, is the required level of testing of the composition of a tour operator's turnover.

Under statutory accounting disclosure requirements the statutory financial statements of a business must disclose turnover analysed between its major component elements. The statutory audit report requires that the financial statements are true and fair.

The disclosure of sales mix need not be between licensed and non-licensed business – it more than likely will be between destination countries or continents, services, or perhaps by customer origin.

CAA and ABTA reporting requirements do though require the auditors to report at the level of detail. Clearly, to comply with industry regulations the auditor will have to broaden the scope of his audit. Ideally, of course, audit tests to support the industry-specific returns will be carried out concurrently with the statutory audit.

**(f)  Consider the timing of reporting requirements and the periods covered by the various reports**

- *Timing of reporting requirements*

  - Incorporated business must file financial statements with Companies House within either seven months for a plc (public limited company) or 10 months for other companies of the accounting reporting date.

  - IATA accredited agents must though file these statutory financial statements with IATA within six months of the accounting reporting date.

  - CAA returns and ABTA returns must be submitted as set out in Chapters 2 and 3.

It is necessary therefore to establish the critical dates for reporting –

148

setting these out within the audit planning documentation is a useful discipline.

- *Periods covered by the various reports*
  Returns of licensable turnover to the CAA may well be non-coterminous with statutory accounting periods. When planning the statutory audit it is just as well to know that additional periods may need to be considered, and possibly additional cut-off tests planned.

Having gone through this planning process the auditor and client will have a clear understanding of:

- the level of reporting detail required to satisfy general and industry-specific reporting requirements;
- the level of audit work required over and above that necessary to support the statutory audit report to the members; and
- the timescale imposed upon reporting deadlines.

The importance of the approach set out above really cannot be overstated; the key to travel industry auditing and reporting (apart, of course, from a detailed knowledge of the industry) is careful planning.

Working in cooperation with the client finance department to achieve a focused and targeted work programme will lead to efficiencies for both auditor and client. The uniformed auditor and unsophisticated client are probably replicating effort, missing key areas, and exposing both parties to risk. Furthermore, of course, by following the approach set out above it will become apparent that much of the additional reporting imposed by industry regulators can be dealt with by integrating it within the audit of the statutory report to members.

## 13.3   Supporting the statutory audit report to members

Having set out an approach to auditing travel businesses the remainder of this chapter deals specifically with those considerations essential to support the statutory report to the members.

Like all industries, the timing of income and cost recognition is key to financial reporting in the travel sector and, once again, a complete understanding of the various business operations undertaken by the entity is the key to successful auditing.

An understanding of the fundamental business elements of travel operation is the starting point. Appreciating that things may not also appear as they seem is the next step.

We have already defined 'agency' and 'tour operating' and airline operation has been considered in Chapter 9. It should be apparent that there are
distinct bases of income recognition attaching to the various forms of travel
activity. Moreover, it may well be that a travel business combines more than
one form of business operation – perhaps a travel agent may put together a
number of its own packages, or a tour operator may on-sell as agent packages put together by other operators.

Having broken down the business into its constituent business elements,
and having recognised the reporting requirements appertaining to each of
these, the auditor should adopt a 'modular' approach to each business
activity, recognising of course that once the modules are put together an
audit appreciation of the reporting entry as a whole is obtained.

## 13.4   Risk-based auditing

While auditing firms will generally apply their own approaches to the audit
of any business, modern audit procedures widely adopted among the larger
or more progressive practices will almost certainly be based on a 'risk-
based' approach. To put such an approach into context, it is worthwhile setting out what will in most instances be the end product to an incorported
company audit – that is the standard audit report to members.

> **Example 13.1**
>
> *To the shareholders of XYZ Limited*
>
> We have audited the financial statements on pages x to y which have been pre-
> pared under the accounting policies set out on page z.
>
> *Respective responsibilities of directors and auditors*
>
> As described on page X the company's directors are responsible for the prepa-
> ration of the financial statements. It is our responsibility to form an indepen-
> dent opinion, based on our audit, on those statements and to report our
> opinion to you.
>
> *Basis of opinion*
>
> We conducted our audit in accordance with Auditing Standards issued by the
> Auditing Practices Board. An audit includes examination, on a test basis, of evi-
> dence relevant to the amounts and disclosures in the financial statements. It
> also includes an assessment of the significant estimates and judgements made
> by the directors in the preparation of the financial statements, and of whether
> the accounting policies are appropriate to the company's circumstances, con-
> sistently applied and adequately disclosed.
>
> We planned and performed our audit so as to obtain all the information and
> explanations which we considered necessary in order to provide us with suffi-

cient evidence to give reasonable assurance that the financial statements are free from material misstatement, whether caused by fraud or other irregularity or error. In forming our opinion we also evaluated the overall adequacy of the presentation of information in the financial statements.

*Opinion*

In our opinion the financial statements give a true and fair view of the state of the company's affairs as at 31 Month 1999 and of its profit for the year ended and have been properly prepared in accordance with the Companies Act 1985.

**BDO STOY HAYWARD**

*Chartered Accountants and Registered Auditors*

London

The auditor's key tasks are therefore to conclude that the financial statements:

- have been prepared in compliance with the Companies Act 1985 and applicable Accounting and Auditing Standards; and
- that the balance sheet, profit and loss account, cash flow statement and ancillary statements show a true and fair view.

The risk-based approach relies on a thorough understanding of the client business – not only of the finance function but also the business environment and internal control framework in which the business operates. This approach seeks to record, in some detail, not only how the business has recorded its income and expenses, and assets and liabilities, but to explain why the financial statements look like they do – why a certain profit (or loss) has been recorded, and why the balance sheet appears as it does.

Having carried out an analysis of the business – breaking down operations into their consistent elements where appropriate, the auditor can then identify those areas within the client business where there is a higher than normal risk of error, and concentrate work in those areas.

For travel businesses, such a risk-based approach sits well with the approach set out above to plan, control and record the statutory audit to the members and those additional requirements imposed by the industry regulators.

While every business should be considered as an individual reporting entity, those areas most commonly considered critical to the audit function of the three forms of travel operation covered by this book are set out below.

## 13.5  Travel agency

In its true form travel agency is no more than the provision of holiday or other travel arrangements under which the travel agents acts on behalf of tour operators and other principal service providers in providing a retail point of sale to the buying public.

Having already noted that the timing of income and cost recognition is key to the audit of travel businesses, the fundamental audit concern is then to ascertain at what stage in the provision of the travel arrangements should the agent recognise income.

Consider the following circumstances:

(a)  A customer has paid a deposit to an agent for travel arrangements taking place some time in the future. The balance on the travel arrangements is not due for some time – probably a matter of weeks before travel.

(b)  A customer has paid the initial deposit and has now settled the remainder of the travel cost with the agent. The agent may or may not have settled up with the travel provider.

(c)  A customer has paid all monies due and has commenced his holiday, but not returned.

(d)  A customer has paid all monies due and successfully (i.e., without claims arising) completed the travel arrangements.

At which stage should income be recognised by the travel agent? Is it important whether monies have been received by the agent or passed over to the service provider?

The general accounting concept of prudence applies: income should only be recognised when it is prudent to do so. In the circumstances of travel agency, this will normally only be after the cancellation date has passed and all amounts have been received by the agent. Monies due to the service provider will be recognised as prepayments until this date. Care must be taken to ensure that the accounting policy is correctly adopted as some agencies adopt a different approach (see Chapter 12).

### 13.5.1  Commission income

Travel agents will earn commission income from a number of different sources:

- from tour operators on the sale of holiday packages;
- from airlines on the sale of flights;
- from coach and rail operators;

- on currency transactions; and
- on the sale of travel insurance.

While each arrangement between a service provider and an agent needs to be considered individually, there are industry norms, e.g., tour operators will typically pay between 10 per cent and 15 per cent to agents, and airlines will pay between 7.5 per cent and 9 per cent according to the flight destination. Incentive arrangements are increasingly common between operators/airlines and agents, and a thorough knowledge of the specific client circumstances is essential.

The auditor should seek to test the fair statement of income by adopting the following work programme:

(a) Ascertain each distinct source of income which the agent receives – not only to the level noted above, but also between, for example, tour operators where different commission levels may arise.
(b) By discussion with management, and where appropriate for material income sources by reference to correspondence between the parties, ascertain appropriate commission levels and incentive arrangements in place.
(c) Ascertain for each material form of income the stage in the transaction with the customer at which the agent has 'earned' the commission.
(d) Evaluate client systems for recording and processing commission income.
    (i) Record and evaluate document flows in the audit trail – from client enquiries through to processing onto ledgers.
    (ii) Carry out test checks to ensure that income is correctly recorded. For example, are different sources of commission income correctly recorded as such within the financial records?
(e) Test timing of income recognition around the end of the client's accounting date. In particular, having evaluated the stage in any sales transaction at which the agent can be said to have earned commission income, ensure that not only are client systems capable of correct recording but that a number of sales before and after the year end have actually been correctly recorded in the financial records of the business.
(f) Evaluate client systems for recording and matching cash, cheques, and credit card receipts to sales.

## 13.6   The Billing and Settlement Plan (BSP)

The Billing and Settlement Plan (BSP; formerly Bank Settlement Plan) scheme operates for IATA accredited agents and allows them to sell airline tickets with a credit period of 17 days from the end of the trading month, as noted in Chapter 4. The auditor should document the client systems, review client reconciliations, and agree the balance sheet creditor to the post-year end payment.

# 13.7 Tour operating

Tour operators, acting as principals in the provision of package tour arrangements, recognise income in a very different manner than that described for travel agents. In such circumstances, the fundamental accounting concepts of accruals, consistency and prudence apply, in addition of course to the assumption that the business is a going concern.

## 13.7.1 Income and cost recognition

Application of the four fundamental accounting concepts will dictate that income and costs will be recognised at the time that a tour programme takes place.

To illustrate the point, consider an operation which has a reporting date of 31 October and has by the year end incurred costs in respect of its summer tour programme for the following year. Following recent trends, it may well be that not only have brochure costs been incurred, but that the brochure has been issued and some sales made. How then should the costs and income be recognised in the financial statements to 31 October?

Following the concept of prudence it should be obvious that income should not be recognised at 31 October – the service to be provided (i.e., the holiday package) will not be completed until the next summer, and the monies received (generally in the form of a customer deposit) should be accounted for at 31 October within the balance sheet as accruals and deferred income.

Matching the programme costs with the income, these should be accounted for at 31 October as prepayments. At the time of the tour programme in the next summer, both amounts are transferred to the profit and loss account, and any profit or loss recognised.

When auditing a tour operator system for income recognition the following work programme will apply:

(a) Identify the operator's stated accounting policy with regard to income recognition.
(b) Record and evaluate management systems for the recording and processing of cash payments/receipts as well as systems for identifying income and cost recognition.

154

(c)   Investigate the nature of the operator's package provision
    (i)   Identify all direct costs incurred with respect to a tour pro-
        gramme and identify the relevant time at which such costs are
        incurred by the operator. Brochure costs have already been noted
        above as costs which may well be incurred in one accounting
        period for recognition (i.e., in the profit and loss account) in the
        next accounting period. Other costs which may be contracted for
        well in advance of the package taking place are:
        – Hotel deposits. Operators may well pay deposits to secure ser-
          vices for a number of future seasons – perhaps for several years
          hence. It will be necessary for the auditor to evaluate deposits
          paid between those now recognisable, and between those
          within one year, and greater than one year, and disclose
          accordingly.
        – Where an operator makes payments to villas or hotels to
          upgrade facilities (such as the building of a swimming pool at
          a 'tied' villa) the auditor will need to decide over which
          future period the payments should be spread. When the villa
          has been successfully utilised by the operator and the villa
          owner is contracted for a number of years it is this period
          over which payments will normally be spread. If the payment
          is in the form of a loan rather than an outright contribution
          to costs, the auditor will need to assess recovery of amounts
          advanced.
(d)   At all times consider not only the carry forward of costs and income
    to match the timing of the package, but also the future profitability
    of the programme. For example, if an operator has incurred substan-
    tial (presumably unbudgeted) costs in respect of a programme, and
    at the reporting date it is apparent that losses will result on the pro-
    gramme, careful consideration will be necessary as to recognising
    these at an early stage, potentially in earlier financial years. Such a
    judgement is obviously subjective and the auditor's skill in under-
    standing the industry and his client's business will certainly be
    required in tackling an intransigent finance director seeking to defer
    losses!

It will be apparent from the above analysis that the key to successful auditing of a tour operator is in recognising that the timing of payments and
receipts may well be very different from the timing of recognition of these
within the profit and loss account. A clear understanding of how each tour
programme operates and the implications this will have for income and
cost recognition is therefore of paramount importance.

**Example 13.2**   *Income and cost recognition*

In 1999 a tour operator develops a new tour programme for launch in the summer of 2000. The operator has a financial reporting year end of 31 October and envisaging a successful programme enters into the following arrangements:

(i)   In March 1999 the operator contracts with a number of hotels and villas in the tour location as follows:
  - Hotel A: Payment of £60,000 deposit to secure a number of rooms for the summer seasons in 2000, 2001 and 2002. The deposit is not specifically allocated by contract between the three years, but is deductible against bookings made equally over the three seasons.
  - Hotel B: Not considered to be as attractive a proposition as hotel A, and contracted only for the first season (in 2000) with a deposit of £10,000 paid by the operator.
  - The owner of three villas: while the villas are considered an intrinsic part of the programme, one requires immediate repair work for which the operator contributes £15,000 to the villa owner's costs. The operator signs a five-year deal, but makes no deposit payment to secure the accommodation, and there are no penalty clauses for cancellation by either party.

(ii)  During the summer of 1999 the operator employs a destination manager on a £20,000 per annum remuneration package commencing 1 May 1999, and allocates a director to oversee the operation.

(iii) Brochure developments costs, lay out and design costs of £10,000 have been spent by 31 October 1999. The balance of printing costs of £5,000 are incurred in November 1999.

(iv)  The brochure is launched in January 2000 and the season runs from Easter to 15 October in each year. Annual revenue of £200,000 is received.

(v)   The operator deals directly with the public, and only small agency commission costs are incurred – say £5,000 per annum.

(vi)  Assume that annual costs (brochure, etc.) and revenue remain constant over time, and that the following annual accommodation costs arise:

|         | £      |
|---------|--------|
| Hotel A | 60,000 |
| Hotel B | 25,000 |
| Villas  | 10,000 |

| Year 1 *(to 31 October 1999)* | *Profit and loss account* | *Balance sheet* |
|---|---|---|
| (1) Payment to hotel A | | £50,000 prepayment |
| (2) Deposit payment to hotel B | | £10,000 prepayment |
| (3) Contribution to villa repairs | | £15,000 prepayment |
| (4) Salary costs (£20,000/2) | | £10,000 prepayment |
| (5) Brochure costs | | £10,000 prepayment |

**Year 2 (to 31 October 2000)**

| | | | |
|---|---|---|---|
| (1) | Deposit payment to hotel A | £20,000 expense | £40,000 prepayment |
| | Room costs hotel A | £40,000 expense | |
| | (£60,000 less deposit £20,000) | | |
| (2) | Deposit payment to hotel B | £10,000 expense | |
| | Room costs hotel B | £15,000 expense | |
| | (£25,000 less deposit £10,000) | | |
| (3) | Contribution to villa repairs | £3,000 expense | £12,000 prepayment |
| | (£15,000/5) | | |
| (4) | Salary costs | £20,000 expense | £10,000 prepayment |
| (5) | Brochure costs | £15,000 expense | £10,000 prepayment |
| (6) | Agent's commission | £5,000 expense | |
| (7) | Annual revenue | £200,000 income | |

In each future year prepaid deposits will be released to profit and loss account to match against income.

Management must assess whether:

- At each year end whether prepayments can justifiably be carried forward. For example, if in year three it is decided to change villas, the carried cost of the contribution to villa repairs should be written off in full.
- At each year end continued programme operation will take place. If the answer is no, then there is no justification for carrying forward any prepaid expenses.

# 13.8 Resort expenditure

Tour operators will in almost every case employ local representatives in resorts to deal with customers and liaise with and act on behalf of the operator with service providers such as hotels, airlines and transport companies.

The local representative will report either directly to head office, or may report to an area or country supervisor.

The operator will probably choose to open local currency accounts in the resort, and will fund resort expenditure including in many cases the local representatives' salary costs by regular drawdowns from the local accounts. Therefore, at any point in time during the season the local operation will operate effectively as a branch of the head office, with cash and bank balances, incurring expenses and receiving income (generally in the form of day excursion receipts).

There will be an obvious need for systems of financial control which enable central management to ensure that:

- local resort expenses and income are recorded in a correct and timely manner and that financial information is relayed to head office quickly and accurately; and
- monies advanced are used for business purposes and are adequately safeguarded.

It is likely that the tour operator will have adopted at least basic internal control procedures to address the control of resort expenditure ranging from simple comparative analysis to full-scale internal audit.

The auditor should then:

(a) *Review and record client systems for the control of resort income and expenditure*
These systems will generally include many of the following controls:
   - regular cash and bank reconciliations to ensure that monies transferred from head office accounts to the local currency account are fully accounted for in terms of amounts held and supported by receipted income and expenditure;
   - weekly or monthly submissions of financial information to head office for processing onto head office ledgers. With the availability of e-mail via the Internet it is useful to have local accounts mailed electronically with hard copies following;
   - substantive checks of expenditure to supporting documentation, including review of expense type and approval procedures; and
   - analytical review procedures comparing income and expenditure resort by resort and against budgets and comparative performance. Care should be taken in reviewing such procedures, especially where a potentially underperforming local representative has been in resort for more than one season. From a control perspective it may well be worth moving representatives around resorts, albeit at the loss of expert local knowledge when dealing with clients.
(b) *Carry out limited audit tests to ensure proper operation of the control system in place*
The auditor's role when testing resort income and expenditure will in many ways be that of a review of the existing internal control procedures, together with limited substantive testing of income and expense amounts and allocation.

Finally, while resort income and expenditure may not be greatly significant to the financial statements of a tour operator; it is often an area taking a disproportionate amount of management time. It is certainly an area where the expert adviser can add value to the audit process in proposing system enhancements.

## 13.9  Accounting for foreign currency transactions

The auditor faces two issues in respect of foreign currencies:

(a)  the present situation facing operators who will transact in a number of currencies and who therefore have a number of profit and loss account transactions in foreign currencies and balances held as deposits and cash; and
(b)  the future situation facing all businesses, and travel businesses earlier than most, when the euro is adopted throughout the EU.

The present situation is in theory very simple. Client accounting systems must be capable of ensuring compliance with SSAP 20 *Foreign Currency Translation*, and the auditor's role will be to test this compliance.

The situation surrounding the euro is explained in more detail in Chapter 11.

## 13.10  Airlines

Airlines are faced with similar issues as travel agents and tour operators with regard to income and expenditure recognition, foreign exchange, etc. They are, however, faced with the distinctive issues with regard to purchase of aircraft, flight capacity management, maintenance costs and vertically integrated and alliance groups. These areas have been explored in detail and audit considerations highlighted in Chapter 9.

## 13.11  Audit programmes

In this section we have not set out to prepare audit programmes that are considered to be all encompassing or suitable to be applied in every circumstance. The following audit programmes focus on areas of specific interest to a tour operator, airline and travel agent respectively. The auditor should design programmes appropriate to the individual client's business which give sufficient audit assurance for him to carry out his statutory and regulatory responsibilities. These audit programmes do not cover standard tests applicable to businesses in general.

### 13.11.1  Travel agents

(a)  Review procedures for storage, issuing, recording and processing of tickets including reconciliation of airline tickets to BSP statements and to supplier statements for other tickets.

159

(b) Test in total commission rates received.

(c) Test cash received and match sample to tickets issued.

(d) Ascertain procedures for storage, issuing, recording and processing of travellers cheques and other currency transactions.

(e) Review payment schedules for receipts from customers, considering low payment deposits, and payment profiles to tour operators and ensure cut off is correct.

### 13.11.2   Tour operators

(a) Ascertain the client's systems for recording and processing transactions and evaluate the systems in place with consideration to reporting requirements.

(b) Test a sample of ledger postings and ensure that sales have been correctly categorised and that cut off, on a monthly basis, has been correctly applied for reporting purposes.

(c) Review and sample test cut-off procedures at the year end and ensure that the accounting policy has been correctly adopted in the following areas:

    (i) Costs incurred in respect of future packages, e.g., brochures and advance accommodation contracts.

    (ii) Empty-leg provisions – ensure the accounting policy has been correctly and consistently adopted, e.g., where customers still on resort, and income recognised on departure; ensure all costs in respect of those holidays, including the cost of bringing those customers home, have been accounted for. Specifically:

        – review long haul/short haul empty-leg provisions;

        – ensure flights with less than capacity are included; and

        – ensure average seat rate provisions are reasonable based on airline invoices.

    (iii) Review pre-year end bookings for post-year end departures and ensure accrued income is correctly accounted for.

(d) Review contracts with travel agents and check that incentive commissions payable at the year end are reasonable.

(e) Test treatment of foreign exchange calculations.

(f) Accounting for resort expenditure and consideration of control systems in place.

(g) Review detailed calculations of Tour Operators' Margin Scheme (TOMS).

### 13.11.3   Airlines

(a) Engine overhauls.

    (i) Test multiple of engine overhauls.

    (ii) Review purchase orders which qualify to be a prepayment and vouch to invoice.

(iii) Test sample of amortisation charges by reference to invoices, hours flown and verify amortisation is not over a period longer than the lease.

(b) Review crew training costs and ensure treatment is in accordance with the accounting policy.

(c) Review schedule of fuel and oil in advance, vouch to a sample of invoices and obtain explanations of debit balances.

(d) Review recoverability of insurance claims outstanding at the year end.

(e) Obtain a schedule of aircraft deposits at the year end and verify a sample to third-party certificates. Also obtain last year's schedule and review movements.

(f) Test airline's system of recording flights which have been operated and no third-party costs, e.g., catering and navigation, received thereby verifying the accrual.

(g) Test block check accrual.

(h) Review legal documentation on the acquisition of aircraft, verifying the treatment of the lease classification.

# Chapter 14 – Auditing client returns to the regulatory bodies

## 14.1 Introduction

The growth of the travel industry has moved the industry into a position of being highly regulated. This has significant implications for the auditor over and above the statutory audit requirements discussed in Chapter 13. As noted in that chapter it is essential that the auditor gives due consideration in planning his audit to the reporting requirements of the regulatory bodies. This will help ensure that the audit process is carried out in an efficient manner and that auditing the regulatory returns is not simply an after thought.

In this chapter the travel industry 'regulatory bodies' (the regulators) considered in detail are the Civil Aviation Authority (CAA) (see also Chapter 2), the Association of British Travel Agents (ABTA) (see also Chapter 3) and the International Air Transport Association (IATA) (see also Chapter 4). Other industry bodies (see Chapter 5) and their reporting requirements must also be considered, where applicable, by the auditor in planning his work.

It is worth noting that ABTA and IATA are trade associations and do not have the direct backing of statute, although, as noted in Chapter 3, the Package Travel, Package Holidays and Package Tours Regulations 1992 provide this status indirectly. For these bodies their regulatory role comes through the enforcement of their trade association membership rules rather than directly through any statutory powers.

The associations' unusual position of being trade associations, principally in existence to help their members, combined with the task of regulating the industry, must also be fully understood by the auditor in assessing the audit work to be carried out and the reasons for the degree of reliance placed on this work.

The auditor, in performing his work, must consider Auditing Standards and Guidelines. Although, no specific guidelines currently exist for the travel industry, the growth in the sector could well lead to this being a next step. The auditor should, however, look to the standards and guidelines that exist for other regulated industries. In particular he should consider

162

sectors such as the financial services and insurance sectors where guidance is available.

## 14.2    Reporting to the regulators

The additional reports required by the regulators primarily focus on three key areas: turnover certification, the net asset position of the company and the quality of the books and records. As noted in Chapter 13, the quality of the books and records is an area that should be considered as part of normal audit procedures and therefore is not covered in any further detail in this chapter.

## 14.3    Turnover certification

All three regulators need to evaluate how each business segment is generating turnover. Turnover is a key indicator not only in assessing the type of business but also in assessing the risk of a business failing. With a full understanding of the dynamics of the business the regulator can then determine the level of financial protection required, e.g., its bond. The aim of the CAA and ABTA is to ensure, should financial failure occur, that sufficient coverage exists in the protection requested to repatriate and/or reimburse customers. If insufficient funds exist this will require the regulator to meet these costs; a situation it clearly wants to avoid.

The certificates are concerned with confirming the accuracy of the analysis of turnover between licensable, non-licensable and retail. The distinction between the various types of turnover is critical to not only understanding the business, but also in verifying these returns.

- *Licensable turnover* – broadly speaking this relates to travel arrangements involving air transportation. These activities require an ATOL from the CAA. This turnover will include **all** elements sold as a part of the package, e.g., hotel and air fares.
- *Non-licensable turnover* – this is all other activities carried out by a tour operator as *principal* but not requiring an ATOL.
- *Retail turnover* – this covers turnover of the business where it acts as an agent.

The distinction between licensable and non-licensable is important in distinguishing with which regulator the turnover should be bonded, i.e., licensable with CAA and non-licensable with ABTA. For the regulator this is very important as well. If turnover is incorrectly bonded and a financial failure occurs the level of bond will quite conceivably be insufficient and lead to a financial loss by the individual regulatory body. Overbonding, while not a problem for the regulator, commercially is expensive for the business.

The distinction between acting as principal or agent needs to be clear. The principal puts together packages and is ultimately responsible for the completion of the contract. The agent acts as the intermediary between the principal and the customer, normally for a commission. Should the agent fail, the exposure is limited because in the majority of cases the principal would have been paid and the contract can be fulfilled. Financial failure of the principal generally has greater consequences.

The auditor needs to understand these distinctions and the importance not only to the regulator but also commercially for the business. Different classifications of turnover carry a variety of risks, and therefore cost in terms of the level of bond required.

The auditor's audit of turnover needs to be extended to considering the risks attaching to and resulting from the different categories of turnover and include a review of the control systems in place over the processing of transactions. Confirmation that the company's accountant understands the distinction is also a key control when assessing the inherent risk of the business.

ABTA also require a month by month turnover analysis of non-licensable turnover (Appendix 2 Form Audit 009(S)). This would not normally form part of the auditor's statutory work and therefore requires the additional work by the auditor to enable this document to be signed.

These turnover certificates will be used by the regulators for a variety of purposes including ensuring that the business did not overtrade during the year and providing valuable data in assessing the accuracy of future projections of turnover and the level of bonding required for the next year. It should be obvious that the regulators are placing reliance upon the certified turnover and that auditors are aware of this reliance when issuing their reports. To date there have not been any substantial legal cases which deal with an auditor's liability to a travel industry regulator, a company or company's customer where an incorrect report results in inadequate financial protection and subsequent losses. Nevertheless, it seems likely that an auditor could face potential legal action in such a situation.

## 14.4   Net asset position

The regulators' interest in the net asset position of the business as at the year end is another area that requires special consideration by the auditor. The assessment of overall risk relating to the business can only be carried out by combining the turnover projections of the business and assessing the financial stability of the business. The net asset position is viewed differently by the various regulators and these are examined below.

ABTA require an audited statement of net recoverable current assets to be submitted with the financial statements. This is considered in detail in **3.10.2**. As can be seen from the sample form Audit 008, in Appendix 2, confirmation of specific details are required that are not available from the audited financial statements. Work should be directed to confirming the specific details on these forms.

The CAA also monitors the net asset position of the business. The CAA requires there to be a sufficient ratio of free assets in relation to projected turnover. In calculating free assets the CAA specifically excludes various assets such as brochure expenditure. A detailed analysis of the free asset calculation can be seen in **2.2.4**. Although the auditor is not required to specifically sign off on the free asset position of the business for the CAA, a detailed awareness though is essential in understanding the factors which may motivate the directors to misanalyse certain items as this could be critical to the bonding levels of the business.

## 14.5 New businesses

By their very nature new businesses are of increased risk to a regulator. The barriers to entry into the travel market can be perceived as relatively low for an entrepreneur. This creates a high level of competition and therefore the level of failures in this early stage of the business are reasonably high.

ABTA considers a new business to be 'new' for a period of three years. This includes businesses where the ownership has changed, regardless of the trading background of the entity. Therefore the veil of incorporation is non-existent for ABTA's purposes and it looks beyond the legal entity to who owns the business. This is key to ensuring that nobody can short cut the requirements under the Articles that they must demonstrate that they are fit and proper individuals (see **3.5**).

As a result the regulators require a reasonable level of detail from the auditors of the new business. For example ABTA requires the following documents:

- projected profit and loss account and balance sheet to be accompanied by a standard format statement from the member's auditors confirming the projections are on a reasonable basis;
- audited quarterly turnover certificates;
- the standard reports required by all businesses (see earlier paragraphs); and
- audited management accounts for the first six-month period.

This is not only onerous on a new business but relatively high risk work for the auditor, especially in assessing the reasonableness of projections. The level of reliance the regulators will look to put on such reports is, however, clear.

## 14.6   Other returns

Quite often the regulators require a one-off certificate from the auditors, such as confirmation that all passengers have returned. The level of duty of care in performing this work is no less than in any other industry. Due consideration must be given to the implications of signing such a report and the audit process must be fully evidenced.

## 14.7   Duty of care

IATA does not require the submission of additional audited reports or returns, only the statutory audited financial statements. The auditor must consider in planning his work the impact of the financial statements and how these will be perceived by IATA and the other regulators. This will normally form part of the inherent risk analysis.

For example, a bond is only normally required from IATA where a company makes a loss. Commercially this bond can be very expensive to the business. Understanding the factors such as this which could give rise to motivation of the business owners to manipulate the profits is therefore critical in assessing risk.

The duty of care that auditors have to the regulators is quite clear and therefore the risks associated with this must be fully considered as part of the audit process.

## 14.8   Summary

There are risks attached to signing these regulatory reports. Should the business fail and the financial protection in place be insufficient this will result in the regulators suffering a financial loss. In this situation, or any other where a financial loss results, the regulator could consider the auditor to have been negligent and look to recover the loss arising.

Auditors should never simply complete an inherent risk assessment, conclude that company is a going concern and sign the regulators' returns on this basis alone.

# Chapter 15 – UK tax implications

## 15.1    Introduction

This chapter covers the UK taxation implications for travel agency, tour operating and airline operations in the United Kingdom. The areas identified are those which would be of particular relevance to a company operating in these sectors. Given that the majority of people operating in this area do so via a corporate entity, it has been assumed that this is the case in this instance. However, the issues affecting a sole trader or partnership would in the main follow the same rules applicable to an incorporated entity.

## 15.2    Tax implications of accounting policies

As is the case for all companies, the starting point for determining a company's taxable profit is its accounting profit. As a result, the accounting treatment adopted by a company will normally have a direct bearing on its UK corporation taxation liability.

In particular the issue of income recognition is likely to have significant implications as far as the timing of tax liabilities is concerned. Generally the Inland Revenue will accept the method of income recognition adopted by a company when it follows the generally accepted accounting principles set out in the Statements of Standard Accounting Practice and Financial Reporting Standards. These have been addressed in detail in previous chapters.

This is not to say, however, that the Inland Revenue will not seek to satisfy itself that the policy adopted is reasonable and, in more recent times, there has been a trend by the Revenue to question the policies adopted by a company to ensure that they fairly reflect the underlying substance of business transactions. Indeed the Revenue constantly seeking to recruit new staff with a better understanding of financial statements.

In practice it is apparent that one area which is singled out for review is a company's policy of income recognition, particularly with regard to the concepts of prudence and matching. It is clear to see why the Revenue would wish to address this area – by merely adopting a prudent income recognition policy, it is possible to defer the tax liability arising on a profit until such time as it is reflected in the financial statements of the company. In a recent case heard by the Special Commissioners, the Inland Revenue successfully argued that the method by which a transaction had been dealt with in the financial statements should not be followed for tax purposes. As this decision has only recently been reached, the potential effects of this have yet to be seen. Indeed, it may be a decision that is overturned by subsequent case law but is a point to bear in mind when considering the commerciality of the accounting policy to be adopted.

As well as income recognition, the Revenue also looks at the recognition of costs. This encompasses the treatment of brochure costs and also other expenditure such as repair costs. Indeed, in *Johnston* v *Britannia Airways*, the Revenue contested a deduction made in the financial statements for the future overhaul of a jet aircraft. The provision was based on historic data and a formula was applied to compute the amount to be provided. On appeal the deduction was allowed. The Special Commissioners considered that the provision gave a true and fair view of the company's trading position and that as there was no overriding legislation which required the provision to be ignored for profit purposes; it was correct to allow the provision.

This case is often of use when considering the tax treatment of engine maintenance reserves. It is important to show that the provision made is specific and is not just a 'guesstimate'.

Accordingly, the potential tax implications of following a specific accounting policy should not be overlooked. The policies should be capable of being substantiated to the Inland Revenue as being reasonable in the circumstances.

In practice, the Revenue tries to concentrate large companies in specific industries within specific Revenue Districts, e.g., the large business offices in Nottingham and Manchester deal with scheduled and chartered airlines respectively.

## 15.3   Trading status

It will not be a surprise to anybody reading this chapter that a company operating in the UK travel industry is highly likely to be treated as a trading company. As such its income is assessable to corporation tax under Schedule D Case I (being income arising from a trade).

It is possible for companies to operate in more than one area of the travel industry, e.g., run a travel agency and also act as a tour operator. In practice these are treated as one trade: that of travel. It is unlikely that there could be any benefit of seeking to establish that the two activities were separate and should be treated as such for corporation tax purposes. The likelihood is that if one of the segments of the business incurred losses and the other incurred profits, depending on the timing and quantum of the amounts involved, losses could be locked into one of the segments of the business and unavailable for offset against the other in the event that a company treated the trades separately.

The choice of operating on a divisional basis or group basis should be decided, taking account of the commercial considerations. The implications for use of losses for a group of companies is discussed in more detail in **15.4** below. However, this is not the only issue which needs to be considered. Along with the issue of loss utilisation, there are other practical difficulties that can arise with groups of companies. As they are separate entities the issue of transfer pricing will need to be considered unless the companies are UK resident. To the extent that one company within a group provides services to another, the level of recharges will need to be determined. It will be important to ensure that these are set on an arm's-length basis.

As the trade's profits and losses will be built up within different companies, another area which will require more detailed thought will be the distribution of reserves.

The effective rate of corporation tax will change where a group of companies is set up, rather than divisions within a company. This is because the thresholds for corporation tax (currently £300,000 and £1,500,000) are divided by the number of active companies within the group. Where profits are not earned evenly across the board without careful planning, a group may end up paying corporation tax at a higher rate than would otherwise have been the case.

## 15.4   Groups of companies

It may be that, from a commercial view point, it is desirable to carry out the different activities within different companies. These might all be standalone companies; alternatively these may be within the same group. Again, this can result in losses arising in one company which are unable to be offset against a profitable company, resulting in losses carried forward to the future, unavailable for offset against profits made by other companies. It is important to recognise this possibility when using separate entities to carry out activities and indeed to appreciate the effects of this on the companies' respective corporation tax liabilities. Consideration should be given to structuring the companies in such a way to ensure group relief will be available if it is anticipated that such relief will be required.

169

## 15.5   Choice of year end

Another issue which should be addressed by the company is its choice of year end. This is important in so far as it affects the recognition and timing of income and the corresponding tax liability thereon. In the event of a seasonal business, consideration should be given as to whether the company's year end should be prior to any seasonal peaks. If before, this would ensure that profits and income were not unnecessarily brought forward and liable to corporation tax earlier than would otherwise be the case. This should be considered in conjunction with the effect of the company's accounting policy on income recognition, cut-off and also reporting requirements. As an example, assume a company receives the majority of its income and profits in the two months of May and June. Assuming an April year end, the tax on the profits for May and June would not fall due for payment for 21 months. Assuming a June year end, the corporation tax would be liable for payment nine months after the end of the accounting period. Comparing this to the April year end and the two months' differential between April and June the choice of June year end can delay the payment of the corporation tax liability by 10 months.

## 15.6   Areas specific to the travel industry

There are various areas worthy of comment when specifically considering the travel industry. These have been identified as follows:

- Bonding
- Foreign exchange
- Capital allowances
- Operating leases, finance leases and hire purchase agreements
- Deposits
- Brochures and advertising
- Subscriptions
- Sponsorship, conferences and entertaining.

These are not necessarily the only areas which will be of importance but are those that have been identified as applying in the majority of cases to most companies operating in the travel industry.

### 15.6.1   Bonding

As has been discussed earlier in this book, there is a requirement for companies operating in the travel industry to lodge bonds with various industry regulators. As a result of this requirement, some travel companies receive interest income. Others meet the requirement by bonding through banks or insurance companies and, as a result, do not generate such interest.

Generally, for accounts purposes this is reflected within interest receivable in the profit and loss account and not within turnover. Indeed, it is not considered part of the trade in its pure sense. For corporate tax purposes the interest income can arguably be treated as interest arising on a trade advance. Accordingly it effectively is taxed as trading income rather than interest income. This is as distinct from interest earned on core cash which is not a part of a company's working capital. This is treated as a 'non-trading loan relationship credit' and is taxable on an accruals basis under the corporate debt rules which came into effect from 1 April 1996. In fact the title was adopted following the Revenue's decision to rewrite the UK tax legislation in plain English!

Prior to 1 April 1996, the rules were somewhat different. Interest income was assessable to UK tax as Schedule D Case III income on a received basis. Trading losses were generally only available to carry forward for offset against trading profits. This resulted in interest income remaining within the charge to corporation tax. However, buried in the loss relief provisions was s393(8) Income and Corporation Taxes Act 1988, which allowed trading losses brought forward to be offset against interest income where it could be shown that the interest had arisen on monies that formed an integral part of the company's business. This would include working capital and the interest earned on any bonding requirements. It would not cover surplus cash. Accordingly, these rules effectively afforded the same relief as the current rules, albeit the mechanics of achieving the relief are not the same.

Generally, when all the profits of the company are subject to tax both the old and the new rules have no effect on the company's overall tax liability, apart from the presentation of the computation. The distinction of this interest income, however, does have effect when considering utilisation of losses within the company.

If a company incurs a trading loss, this is available to carry forward for offset against future trading profits and, by treating the interest income as trading, this effectively allows trading losses brought forward to be offset against interest income.

## 15.6.2 Foreign exchange gains and losses

Most entities operating in the travel industry will have some exposure to foreign currency, whether this is in the form of having to settle invoices expressed in another currency or, at the other end of the spectrum, whether the company operates a branch or subsidiary in an overseas territory. Accordingly it is common for the rules on foreign exchange to have some impact on any entity in this industry.

171

Exchange gains and losses are calculated on 'monetary assets and liabilities' denominated in a foreign currency and the gain or loss arising is taxed in that accounting period. Monetary assets and liabilities generally include bank balances, loan advances, intercompany borrowings and foreign currency deposits. Gains or losses on funds used for the purposes of a company's trade are taxed or allowed under Schedule D Case I. Gains and losses arising which do not relate to the purpose of the company's trade are taxed or allowed as income as non-trading exchange gains and losses under Schedule D Case III. Schedule D Case III taxes interest income and other profits on loan, financial instrument profits and gains and exchange gains. If these items produce a loss, the loss is a 'non-trading deficit'.

Losses incurred under Schedule D Case III can be set against current year income and gains of the company of any description, against Schedule D Case III 'non-trading credits' arising in the previous year, current year income and gains of other group companies and finally carried forward and offset against either Schedule D Case III income or against investment income (including chargeable gains) in subsequent years.

Where long-term capital assets or liabilities are held (being debts due for settlement more than one year after creation), where the net exchange gains exceed 10 per cent of the profits chargeable to corporation tax before such a deferral claim, the excess may be deferred to the next accounting period. Further provisions apply for subsequent years if the asset or liability continues to be held.

Consideration should be given by a company operating a branch overseas to making use of local currency elections. Under these provisions a company may elect for its Schedule D Case I profits or losses (excluding capital allowances) to be calculated using a foreign currency which is the functional currency of its trade (or part of it). There are various criteria which much be met. The tax adjusted trading profits in the foreign currency are then translated into sterling at the going rate.

There are specific tax rules dealing with foreign exchange gains and losses on borrowings taken out to acquire aircraft which broadly ensure that the accounting treatment may be followed. However, it is more usual for aircraft to be financed by way of operating lease, finance lease or hire purchase (see **15.6.4** below) and the foreign exchange position then becomes much more complex. As a result the tax treatment may not necessarily follow the accounting treatment.

The legislation set out above came into effect for companies on the first day of their accounting period beginning on or after 23 March 1995. To the extent that assets or liabilities in a foreign currency were in existence in an earlier accounting period, transitional provisions apply.

### 15.6.3 Capital allowances

Most travel companies will have some assets which qualify for capital allowances. The most common allowances are those of plant and machinery. Indeed, most companies will have invested in some form of plant and machinery and as such are entitled to claim capital allowances on such assets. Generally, the claim is based on the cost to the company of the assets. For plant and machinery writing-down allowances are afforded at the rate of 25 per cent per annum on a reducing balance basis. In the case of small- and medium-sized companies (using the Companies Act definition), for the period from 2 July 1997 to 1 July 1998, first year allowances of 50 per cent are available and in the period from 2 July 1998 to 30 June 1999, this is reduced to 40 per cent.

An area of the business which may require significant investment is that of computers, particularly given the sometimes complex nature of booking system. Significant sums can be expended on bespoke packages and, even where programs are not tailor-made, the sums can run into thousands of pounds. In practice, hardware is generally capitalised and software is written off to the profit and loss account of the company. To the extent that the computers are capitalised, capital allowances should be available. It is more difficult to argue a revenue deduction for such expenditure when it has been capitalised in the accounts of the company.

An area which should be addressed is the possibility of making short-life asset elections for computers. Given the potential short life of computers, as a result of the speed with which technology advances, it is not unusual to see companies updating their entire systems on a regular basis. To the extent that it is a possibility that a computer will not be in use in the business for a period of more than five years, it is worthwhile electing to put it into a separate pool where its second-hand value is likely to be lower than its tax written-down value. This has the benefit of bringing forward the relief for the balancing allowance (being the difference between the disposal proceeds and the tax written-down value). Otherwise the benefit of the inherent balancing allowance would only slowly be released from the pool over time.

Capital allowances are available on computer licences which are considered to be capital assets. This would be the case if the licence had an enduring nature. Where this is not the case, i.e., payments under the licence are similar to those that would be made under a rental agreement or where the software has a useful economic life of less than two years, a revenue deduction will be available. Generally this is more favourable as the full amount is relieved from tax in the first one or two years. For example, if software with a useful life of just under two years was acquired at a cost of £20,000, and for accountancy purposes it was considered that £15,000 should be written off in the first accounting period the balance in the second, on the basis that this write off in the accounts could be justified to the Inland Revenue, tax relief would also be afforded to the company in the same amounts for those two years.

Where investments are being made into computer hardware and software and there is uncertainty as to the tax treatment which will be applied, reference should be made to the Inland Revenue *Tax Bulletin* issued in November 1993 which sets out its general views as to the treatment of the expenditure.

Another potential area for capital allowance claims, to the extent that it is relevant to the business concerned, is that of aeroplanes. These are not afforded the more generous relief of 25 per cent writing-down allowances. The Government recently revised the allowances for such expenditure to 4 per cent per annum cost. These reduced rates of capital allowances apply to long-life assets, i.e., assets which the Inland Revenue considers have a life of more than 25 years. It is not sufficient to write off an aeroplane's cost over 20 years in the accounts of the company as this will not circumvent these rules. The cost of this change in legislation to companies owning aeroplanes is high given the amounts spent on this category of assets.

Indeed, one stance taken was to treat each part of an aeroplane as a separate asset – the wheels were one asset, the seats another, etc., with a view to creating a significant class of assets with lives of less than 25 years. Although a few items would have lives in excess of 25 years, the idea was to reduce the quantum of assets falling within the category of a life greater than 25 years. Unfortunately the Revenue does not concur with this view on the basis that an aeroplane is one asset and not a combination of smaller assets. However, it does show the eagerness of aircraft owners in seeking to circumvent this new reduced rate of capital allowances. Indeed further research is being undertaken on behalf of the industry to seek to put forward a case to the Inland Revenue concerning the unreasonableness of the reduced rates of capital allowances. In the course of time, it is anticipated that the legislation may be revised to take account of such representations.

### 15.6.4   Operating leases, finance leases and hire purchase agreements

As is common in the case of aircraft, companies will often finance their acquisition of major assets via operating leases, finance leases and hire purchase agreements. The tax treatment of each of these differs, as does the accounting treatment.

An asset which is acquired under an operating lease is not recognised in the financial statements of a company. Payments made under the operating lease are deductible in computing the company's corporation tax profits. They are treated as rental payments. No capital allowances are afforded to the company leasing the asset.

At the other end of the spectrum are hire purchase agreements. These are probably as near to an outright purchase that exists. As a result of this, they are to all extents and purposes treated as such. Capital allowances are afforded to the company which has acquired the asset under a hire purchase agreement and the asset is recognised in the accounts of the company. Rental payments are not allowed as a deduction although the interest element of the agreement will be treated as an expense in the company's profit and loss account and this will be deductible in arriving at taxable profits.

The last type of agreement is the finance lease. This is a lease where the agreement almost equates to outright ownership. An asset acquired under finance lease will be recognised as an asset in the accounts of the company. As long as the finance lease is treated in accordance with Statement of Standard Accounting Practice No 21, the element of depreciation relating to the lease will be allowable as a corporation tax deduction, as long as the lease has been taken out after 11 April 1991. The interest element relating to the lease will also be allowable as a corporation tax deduction. This method of allowing corporation tax relief is considered fair as SSAP 21 results in rental payments being properly spread over the rental period. Where SSAP 21 has not been followed, the method adopted in the financial statements of the company will generally be accepted as long as the rental payments have been properly spread, otherwise appropriate adjustments will be made.

Prior to 11 April 1991, neither depreciation nor interest charges were allowable as corporation tax deductions for finance leases. Instead, relief was given for the rental payments made under the terms of the lease.

## 15.6.5   Deposits

The issue of bonding has been addressed in **15.6.1** above. The issue of deposits, however, needs further comment.

For accountancy purposes, deposits received are not normally recognised as income until such time as the holiday is taken by the customer. This enables the full amount to be received from the customer to be matched with the cost to be incurred by the company. Where a customer has cancelled a holiday and has forfeited a deposit, the deposit will generally be recognised in that accounting period. Deposits recognised as income will be treated as trading income under Schedule D Case I.

### 15.6.6  Brochures and advertising

Generally, this is an area which the Inland Revenue has a tendency to scrutinise. The reason for this is the extent to which brochures and advertising campaigns are considered to be for the long-term benefit of a trade and could be argued to relate to the goodwill and capital of a company rather than the short-term trading of a company. To the extent that monies are expended on producing brochures, from an accounts perspective, it will be necessary to identify the rate of release of the expense to the profit and loss account taking account of the general matching provisions of accounting concepts and the prudence concept. As such this is the starting point for tax purposes subject to the comments made in the general introduction to this chapter. To the extent that the Inland Revenue questions the purpose of the brochures and advertising, it is always of use to have supporting documentation covering the rationale behind the campaign, e.g., possible minutes of directors' meetings stating the objectives of any advertising campaign and the perceived timescale of receiving benefits from it. Furthermore, any minutes of meetings or other documentation concerning the anticipated future revenues of holidays should be retained. It is common for an element of expenditure on brochures to be accrued at the end of an accounting period to reflect the longer-term nature of such expenditure.

### 15.6.7  Subscriptions

Subscriptions paid to ABTA, CAA and any other regulatory bodies and associations of the travel industry are allowed as a tax deduction. This is on the basis that they are incurred 'wholly and exclusively' in the course of the company's trade.

### 15.6.8  Sponsorship, conferences and entertaining

The costs of sponsorship are generally allowable as a corporation tax deduction on the basis that they are a form of advertising and have been undertaken for the benefit of the trade as a whole. Ideally, where large sums are expended on sponsorship, it would be easier to substantiate the tax deduction for the sums where there is documentation supporting the target market of the sponsorship.

Conferences should also be allowable as a corporation tax deduction. This is on the basis that these are normally advertising and marketing events and possibly even have a training element to them.

176

Finally, the costs incurred relating to entertaining are generally not deductible for corporation tax purposes. The only entertainment which is allowable is staff entertainment, at a capped limit.

## 15.7   The overseas dimension

Given the involvement of a travel company with overseas matters, it is not uncommon to find that a company has some presence in an overseas jurisdiction particularly when looking at tour operators. This can take the form of an overseas representative, the use of a foreign branch or, in some circumstances the use of a foreign subsidiary. As a result, it is often important to consider the international tax aspects of running some business operations abroad. First it is necessary to identify exposure to the local taxes in the area in which the business is being operated and secondly to review the terms of any double taxation convention to determine the effects that this has on the taxation of the profits generated.

To the extent that profits are generated overseas by a branch operation and are taxable in the UK, these will fall into charge under Schedule D Case I. In some circumstances this could be Schedule D Case V where it is held the branch is effectively managed and controlled abroad. These foreign profits are subject to corporation tax in the same way as UK profits. If foreign tax has been suffered on these profits, relief is available as either a credit against UK corporation tax liability or as an expense. The credit method of relief is generally followed where the UK company is liable to corporation tax. It is important to note that credit is only given for amounts suffered up to the rate of the UK corporation tax. Where a company is making losses, relief is claimed as an expense insofar as the foreign tax credit creates an allowable tax loss to carry forward into the future. Foreign tax suffered which is not available for offset as a credit in a company's corporation tax computation is not available for carrying forward against future corporation tax profits. It is important to consider the extent to which any overseas tax suffered can be used against a company's UK tax liability. There may be some element which is 'lost' and this will need to be considered in determining the overall commerciality of establishing an overseas presence.

As a result of having an overseas presence, it is normal to see costs being incurred in paying representatives in those foreign countries. Frequently, these are UK resident individuals which have been relocated overseas for a short period to carry out work. Following the recent Budget in March 1998, the Chancellor has tightened the rules for such individuals' exposure to UK income tax. Prior to the Budget, individuals going abroad under a full-time contract of employment were able to claim exemption from UK income tax on their earnings on the basis that the employment overseas would last at least 365 days. This enabled individuals to receive income without being liable to UK income tax. With effect from 17 March 1998, this relief, commonly known as the 'foreign earnings deduction' has been abolished. An individual must now become non-UK resident in order to escape liability to UK tax and must therefore be out of the UK for a complete tax year. In the worst case scenario, an individual leaving the UK on 7 April 1998 would need to remain out of the UK until 6 April 2000 in order to become non-UK resident for UK income tax purposes. 'Blame' for this change in legislation has been attributed by some to entertainers who have taken advantage of these rules and publicised the loophole to the UK Inland Revenue.

The reason for mentioning this point is that if individuals abroad become liable to overall higher tax on their earnings, they may seek to have their remuneration increased to reflect the potential additional tax burden to them. Furthermore, consideration would need to be given to the application of PAYE and National Insurance for such individuals.

To the extent that foreign subsidiaries are set up to run elements of a business overseas, consideration should be given to the effect of this on the company's effective rate of corporation tax. At present, a company's profits are subject to differing rates of corporation tax depending on the level of its taxable profit. Profits up to £300,000 are taxed at the small companies rate of tax. Profits from £300,000 to £1.5 million are taxed at the marginal rate and profits over and above £1.5 million are taxed at the full rate of corporation tax. To the extent that a company has subsidiaries the rates of £300,000 and £1.5 million are decreased. For example, if a UK company has two overseas subsidiaries the bands are reduced to £100,000 and £500,000 respectively. If the UK company were making profits of £500,000, if no overseas subsidiaries existed, the company would be liable to corporation tax at the small companies rate. However, in the event that two overseas subsidiaries existed, the UK company would be liable to tax at the full rate. This could have a significant impact on the tax burden to the group of companies and therefore is an area which should be considered prior to making the decision as to whether an overseas subsidiary or branch should be used.

To the extent that an overseas subsidiary is used, monies will generally be re-patriated to the UK. These will be treated as distributions and, where overseas tax has been suffered on these monies, relief should be afforded in the UK for this overseas tax. If the overseas company has borne tax, the relief will be given by the 'underlying tax' provisions. The extent to which tax is deducted from the distribution relief will be under the 'credit' or 'expense' relief provisions. As mentioned above, it is important to consider the extent to which any overseas tax suffered can be used against a company's UK tax liability as there may be some element which is 'lost'.

# 15.8   PAYE and P11D issues

As with any business entity, consideration needs to be given to PAYE and P11D issues. A couple of areas seem to crop up more often than not for travel businesses. These are discussed below.

Firstly, it is common for casual staff to be employed by a company due to the seasonal nature of the business of some travel companies. It is sometimes assumed that, as there is no written contract of employment as the period of the engagement is only for a short period, these casual workers can be paid gross. There are very few instances where a casual worker would be accepted as genuinely self-employed. Moreover care should be taken where students are employed who have signed form P38(S). They should not be employed in normal term time.

Another area which is commonly encountered is the benefit arising on the provision of cheap or free flights or holidays for employees. The benefit assessable on the employee is the additional or marginal cost of the provision of the flights and/or holidays to the employee, rather than a proportional part of the total cost incurred in their provision to both employees and public. Agreement should be sought from the company's tax office to ensure that the marginal cost of such holidays/flights are agreed.

It is also common to encounter living allowances being paid to couriers or other employees working abroad. Any round sum allowance, whether paid to employees in the UK or abroad, should be agreed in advance with the Inland Revenue to ensure that it can remain tax-free.

# 15.9   Other sundry matters

Another relief worthy of note for companies operating in the travel industry is the rollover relief afforded on the disposal of certain assets. Referred to as 'rollover relief', gains arising on disposals of freehold or long leasehold property (i.e., leases exceeding 60 years) and certain other specified assets can be rolled over into the acquisition costs of similar assets. To the extent that a company operating in the travel industry owns a freehold or long leasehold premises from which it carries out its trade with the public, any capital gain arising on the disposal of that property can be rolled over into the acquisition cost of another property.

As a direct result of the additional requirements of the various regulatory authorities, professional costs are incurred in meeting the reporting requirements. Furthermore professional costs may be incurred in negotiating with the authorities over a suitable level of required bonding. Such legal and professional costs will be allowed as trading expenses.

## 15.10   Summary

Although there are no specific tax provisions relating to the travel industry in isolation, as can be seen above there are various areas of the Taxes Acts that have a significant impact on companies operating in this industry. The importance of accounting treatment on a company's tax liability cannot be underestimated. The basis of income recognition has a significant bearing on the company's UK taxation liability. As with all tax matters, it is important to fully consider and plan a company's structure to ensure that, within the confines of commerciality, the structure is as tax efficient as commercially viable.

# Chapter 16 – VAT

## 16.1 Introduction

The application of VAT within the travel industry attracts various complications, not least in the definition on what constitutes a tour operator and the VAT implications for travel agents. These issues will be dealt with in this chapter.

The most significant issue in the VAT legislation concerns the provision of services by tour operators, which fall under the provisions of the infamous Tour Operators' Margin Scheme (TOMS).

This scheme is applicable to all businesses which buy in and resell certain designated travel services to travellers.

The legislation which is relevant in respect of TOMS is contained within the Sixth EC Directive, 77/388 Article 26, and the VAT Act 1994 s53 and the Value Added Tax (Tour Operators) Order 1987. The relevant parts of the legislation are reproduced in Appendices 4, 5, 6 and 7.

Unusually in VAT legislation certain elements of Public Notice 709/5 have the force of law, in that the Tour Operators Order 1987 provides for the Commissioners to specify the manner in which the scheme shall be implemented and this is contained in the Public Notice.

## 16.2 Scope

The definition of a tour operator within the provisions of the TOMS is:

- a travel agent acting as principal; or
- a person providing services of a kind enjoyed by travellers and commonly provided by tour operators or travel agents.

The difficulty arriving at a definition is exemplified by two VAT Tribunal cases, namely *Aer Lingus Plc* v *The Commissioners of HM Customs & Excise* and *Virgin Atlantic Airways* v *The Commissioners of HM Customs & Excise*. These cases were based on similar arguments that the TOMS did not apply where an airline company provided add on services of chauffeur driven cars or free nights' hotel accommodation.

The appellants were successful in one case but not the other, as a result of the Tribunal's decision that Virgin Atlantic Airways Limited was not a tour operator within the margin scheme, whereas in the Aer Lingus Plc case the Tribunal considered the company was a tour operator, and consequently subject to the TOMS regulations.

A current case at the time of writing has been referred before the European Court of Justice (ECJ), namely *Howden Court Hotel,* which was referred to the ECJ by the High Court to obtain opinions on, among other issues, the definition of a tour operator.

At the time of writing the Advocate General's opinion on this point in advance of the ECJ ruling was that this definition was in the hands of the UK legislator. (There are other issues within this case which are dealth with in **16.7.**)

The basic reasoning behind the TOMS is to provide uniformity of tax treatment in and between the Member States of the EU.

The basis of a supply of services is normally deemed to be where the supplier belongs.

Supplies of certain travel services are often made in more than one country, in addition to the supplier making its own supply and putting together a package.

Without the TOMS, suppliers of such services would be liable to register for VAT in every Member State where the services were enjoyed. The scheme enables the supplies to account for the correct amount of VAT without the need for multiple VAT registration.

The scheme provides for tour operators to account for VAT on the profit margin of such scheme supplies.

Designated travel services are defined in the *VAT Notice* as those which are:

- bought-in and resupplied without material alteration; and
- supplied by a tour operator based in the EU; and
- supplied for the benefit of the traveller.

The types of supplies which will always fall within the TOMS are:

- accommodation;
- passenger transport;
- hire of a means of transport for leisure purposes;

- use of lounges at airports;
- trips or excursions; and
- the services of a tour guide.

Other types of supplies which may fall within the definition of designated travel services are catering, theatre tickets and sports facilities if they are bought in and sold without material alteration for the benefit of the traveller, and provided as part of a package with one or more of the supplies detailed above.

The provisions of the TOMS must be applied by establishments in the UK which buy in designated travel services and resell them to a traveller, either singularly or in a package and as a principal or undisclosed agent and the supply is made in the UK.

Examples of businesses which fall under the provisions of the TOMS are:

- tour operators;
- travel agents acting as principals;
- seat-only operators selling to the public; and
- 'bucket' shops.

The following types of businesses *may* have to use the TOMS provisions:

- organisations running training courses;
- those selling admissions to certain events;
- clubs and societies which organise trips;
- hotels which provide transport and excursions for guests;
- language schools;
- schools;
- colleges; and
- universities.

The concept of bought-in supplies, or those which are deemed to be in-house, is fundamental in the application of the TOMS. As previously stated, margin scheme supplies being deemed to be bought in are supplied without material alteration, whereas in-house supplies are those which are made from a business's own resources and are deemed to be in-house as a result of purchases which have been materially altered, thus being sold on as being substantially different from that which was purchased.

If a package supply is made as one transaction which comprises both margin scheme supplies and in-house supplies, TOMS must be used to calculate the VAT due. The method specified by the Commissioners to apply the calculation is detailed in Appendices 7 and 8.

## 16.3   Application

### 16.3.1   Registration

The position with regard to VAT registration for tour operators which have to comply with the provisions of the TOMS regulations are as follows.

When calculating the value of taxable supplies which account towards VAT registration it is the total margin of the margin scheme supplies (not the total turnover) plus the full value of any other taxable supplies which are made in the UK, including those from in-house resources.

For VAT group registration purposes membership of a VAT group is barred if any other member of the group has an overseas establishment and makes supplies outside the UK, which would be taxable supplies if made in the UK and there are supplies of goods and services which will become, or are intended to become, margin scheme supplies.

### 16.3.2   Time of supply

There are special rules which apply to the time of supply (or tax point) for margin scheme supplies. The tax point rules also apply to a package of supplies for a single charge, which includes margin scheme and in-house supplies.

There are restrictions applied for changing from one method to another and any such change must be permitted specifically by HM Customs & Excise.

(a)   Tax point method one is based on the date of departure or the first date on which the traveller occupies any accommodation, whichever happens first.

(b)   Tax point method two is the same as method one, but with the alternative date of receipt of payment, depending on the value of the payment whichever happens first.

In other words, if a single payment is received for the supply the tax point is created on receipt of payment.

However, if a deposit is received prior to the main payment this will depend on the level of deposit. If a deposit is greater than 20 per cent of the selling price this creates a tax point in addition to the second tax point when the main payment is received, or alternatively if a deposit is less than 20 per cent the tax point for the whole supply is the date of main payment or the tax point under method one, whichever is the sooner.

### 16.3.3    Place of supply

The place of supply depends on where the business is established.

(a)    If the business is established in the UK solely, the place of supply of the margin scheme supplies is the UK.

(b)    If the business is established in more than one country, it is the place of establishment most directly connected with the supply which is crucial in establishing the place of supply. Thus the supply is deemed to be in the UK if the established business most connected with the margin scheme supplies is in the UK.

(c)    It thus follows that a business established outside the UK in another EU Member State which will be outside the scope of UK VAT but liable to be taxable in the other EU Member State.

(d)    It also follows that where the establishment is outside the EU the margin scheme does not apply and the provisions of the Place of Supply Order 1992 will be effective.

(e)    The place of supply for in-house supplies, whether or not part of a package, are determined using the normal VAT rules. See **16.6** below.

### 16.3.4    Accounting

The full details of how to calculate the VAT due under TOMS and the relevant formula are given in Appendices 8 and 9. The formula ensures that VAT is accounted for under the margin for margin scheme supplies and under the full selling price for other supplies.

VAT is not reclaimable as input tax on purchases designed to be resold as margin scheme supplies.

VAT may, however, be reclaimed in respect of that incurred on overheads, or the other purchases relating to in-house supplies, subject to the normal rules.

VAT incurred on purchases from other EU Member States may be reclaimed under the special refund procedure in respect of VAT incurred in other Member States.

## 16.4    Exceptions and concessions

The exception to the foregoing rules is that if a supply of designated travel services is to a business customer inside or outside the UK, and is for the use by that customer or an employee and is for the purpose of the customer's business, the normal VAT rules apply. This means that VAT must be calculated on the total sales value of the supplies, invoices must be issued and, conversely, VAT charged on the goods and services may be reclaimed, subject to the normal rules.

As a trade facilitation measure a tour operator can elect to treat such business supplies as margin scheme supplies under the TOMS, but permission must be sought from HM Customs & Excise.

These changes took effect from 1 January 1996 as a result of European Commission intervention that the UK was not implementing the TOMS legislation appropriately.

Specifically with effect from 1 January 1996 not only were wholesale supplies deemed to be outside the scope of the TOMS but from that date it was also deemed that all of the margin emanating from the calculation was liable to VAT at the standard rate.

Prior to this date the UK legislation provided for bought-in margin scheme supplies to be treated under the VAT liablity on which they were supplied.

In other words, the buying in of zero-rated transport and sold under the margin scheme was treated as a zero-rated element of the margin. Similarly, if exempt supplies were bought in and sold on in the same state as margin scheme supplies these were treated as an exempt element of the margin.

## 16.5   Calculations

The purpose of the calculation is to calculate the value of the supplies made under the TOMS and the VAT accordingly due. Thus the calculation provides details of the total margin achieved, how this is split between in-house and margin scheme supplies and how this should be split between alternative different rates of VAT.

The basic principle underlying the scheme is that the calculation is based on the costs incurred in making the supplies. This means that the total value of the margin scheme supplies, which includes the value of the packages incorporating bought-in margin scheme supplies, is calculated.

The costs incurred in the making of these supplies are then calculated under the different category headings, being standard-rated bought-in supplies, standard rated, zero rated, exempt and outside the scope, in-house supplies. This total cost figure is then deducted from the turnover figure resulting in the value of the margin. The margin is then subdivided into the same ratio as the various cost categories relate to the total costs as a whole.

Thus if 50 per cent of the costs relate to standard-rated bought-in margin scheme supplies, 50 per cent of the margin is liable to VAT at the standard rate. If the remaining 50 per cent relates to standard-rated in-house costs, then the 50 per cent remaining to the margin relates to the margin on standard-rated in-house activities and to this must be added the value of the standard-rated in-house costs in order to arive at a value for the supply of these in-house resourced items.

The formula for the calculation is included in Appendix 8. This is designed to take into account every eventuality and in all probability most businesses will only need to apply part of the calculation in order to calculate the VAT payable.

Because the TOMS calculation is based on annual figures extracted from the financial accounts, the scheme is by nature retrospective. In order for VAT to be calculated on a current basis a provisional application is made using the previous year's figures in order to calculate the VAT payable over-all. At a year end, the financial statements figures are used to perform an annual adjustment which is then applied to the provisional output tax cal-culated. The percentage calculated by this definitive method is then applied to the following year's VAT figures until such time as the annual adjustment is due again.

A simplified calculation is available where all of the supplies are made at the standard rate to avoid the necessity of calculating the standard-rated in-house costs, thus reducing the time spent on the administration of this and accounting for the scheme.

It is essential to maintain comprehensive records in order to apply the pro-visions of the TOMS, which incorporate the following.

(a)   The total value of the supplies made.

(b)   The costs relating to:

   (i)    margin scheme supplies.
   (ii)   standard-rated, zero-rated and exempt in-house supplies.
   (iii)  in-house supplies which are outside the scope of UK VAT.

   In addition to these records, if supplies are made outside the scope of the TOMS under the normal standard VAT accounting, records must be maintained to produce these figures accordingly.

(c)   The calculation of the selling price for TOMS purposes must include all margin scheme supplies, all in-house supplies where they have been supplied as a package together with margin scheme supplies.

   The turnover is net of any discounts given but must include sur-charges, must not be reduced by any commission paid to agents, and compulsory charges for insurance, including insurance premium tax.

(c)   The calculation of the costs for margin scheme supplies must be established net of any discounts received from suppliers and must not include costs of any supplies made from an agent and must not include costs of packages of supplies which do not include any TOMS supplies.

The calculation of in-house costs is crucial to the calculation in order to legitimately mitigate the amount of VAT payable. Whereas only direct costs may be included in the calculation, in the case of *RA, DL and GA Whittle* v *The Commissioners of HM Customs & Excise,* the Tribunal provided guidance on what could be included for the purposes of the TOMS calculations.

The appellants were bus and coach operators required to account for VAT under the TOMS. The appeal was in regard to the calculation of the in-house costs. While it was accepted that general overheads could not be included, other costs relating to the buildings in which the vehicles were parked could be included, specifically as depreciation costs of the building which would be regarded as an indirect cost of the tour operations and accepted as part of the scheme costs.

Examples of costs which HM Customs & Excise accept as in-house relevant costs are detailed as follows:
(i)   Passenger transport – costs include berthing fees, bridge and road tolls, depreciation on vehicles, drivers wages and employer's National Insurance contributions, etc., fuel for vehicles, garaging and parking of vehicles, insurance of vehicles, landing fees for aircraft, night subsistence and other allowances paid to drivers, rental or leasing of vehicles, road fund licences for vehicles, spares for and repairs and maintenance of the vehicles.
(ii)  Cost of in-house supplies and hotel accommodation, direct cost accepted by HM Customs & Excise include catering purchases, depreciation of buildings, fixtures and fittings, heating and lighting, rates and insurance of buildings, rental of equipment and furniture etc., repairs, maintenance and cleaning, staff costs including wages and employer's National Insurance contributions, etc.

These examples are not exhaustive and it is important to investigate all of the related costs, in particular where the in-house supplies are zero rated in order to reflect the cost of providing in-house resourced supplies, thus mitigating the VAT payable on the margin.

# 16.6   Non-TOMS issues

One of the main issues outside of the TOMS is whether a provider of travel services is acting as principal or agent. If a travel agent or tour operator is acting as principal the supply is deemed to be made entirely by the principal and consequently the value for the supply on which VAT is liable is the total income generated by the principal. However, if the business is acting on an agency basis VAT should be liable on the amount of commission due from the principal, or the fee that is charged.

It is possible for the tour operator acting as principal to make such responsibility for the invoicing of the agents supply or commission, which is known as self-billing, and this must be approved by H M Customs & Excise and satisfy various conditions.

As principal and supplying travel facilities, the place of supply depends on the nature of the service provided.

- *Transport* – is supplied where it takes place (there is, however, an EU-wide exemption for international air and sea transport).
- *Accommodation* – is supplied where it is situated.
- *Catering* – is usually supplied where it is made available to the consumer.
- *Entertainment* – is supplied where it is enjoyed.

The place of supply of travel agent services is an issue which must be closely addressed. The major services undertaken by travel agents are listed below, with the associated VAT treatment in respect of the place of supply.

(a)   For insurance and financial services, this falls under the scope of Sch 5, VAT Act 1994 and the place of supply is deemed to be where the services are received and thus in the country where the customer belongs if:
  (i)   the customer belongs outside the EU; or
  (ii)  the customer belongs in another Member State and receives the supply for the purposes of his business.
  If neither of these conditions applies, the place of supply of the service is in the UK.

(b)   For services supplied in the EU for a principal who is registered for VAT in any Member State, it is deemed to be supplied by the agent where the principal belongs.

(c)   Where services are arranged outside the EU or the agents act for a principal who is not registered for VAT in any Member State, the place of supply depends on the following.

(i)   In respect of a designated travel service as specified above and caught under the TOMS provisions, it is deemed to take place where the tour operator belongs.

(ii)  The place of supply for passenger transport, in respect of agents, supplies, is in the country or countries where it takes place.

(iii) In respect of accommodation, the agent's services are deemed to be supplied where the accommodation is situated.

(iv)  In respect of tuition and live entertainment, the place of supply for agents is where the services are performed.

(v)   For car hire, the place of agency supply is where the supplier belongs.

It is feasible that if the agent's place of supply is deemed to be outside the UK then there may be a liability to register for VAT in the Member State where the supply is deemed to take place; however, if the agent's principal is registered for VAT in a different Member State, the principal is responsible for accounting for VAT under the reverse charge procedure.

This means that the potential VAT liable is both accounted for by the principal and reclaimed as bona fide input tax (i.e., VAT to be reclaimed), providing the principal is fully taxable, thus in a position to reclaim all of the VAT.

The VAT liability of travel agent services in respect of commissions is detailed as follows. Where travel agents services are deemed to be supplied in the UK the VAT liability will depend on the nature of the supply.

The making of arrangements for certain passenger transport services is zero rated, while the arranging of some financial insurance services is exempt. In all other circumstances the agency supply is liable to VAT at the standard rate.

## 16.7   Summary

The biggest issue facing tour operators and travel agents buying-in and selling-on designated travel services is bound under the provisions of the TOMS.

As with other areas of VAT legislation the TOMS law is continually changing and a current case previously referred to above may well result in further significant changes to the UK implementation of the TOMS legislation.

The *Howden Court Hotel* case, before the ECJ as a result of a referral from the High Court, has recently been the subject of a preliminary opinion by the Advocate General.

In essence, this has a more significant effect on the matter of principle of the application of TOMS than the detail of the case itself. The Advocate General has as one of his opinions espoused that the implementation of the TOMS by the UK Government does not comply with European legislation.

This is because the TOMS is based on costs as opposed to sales values.

In practice, this would mean that while the TOMS supplies, i.e., the bought-in margin scheme services, should be accounted for on a margin basis, those of an in-house nature should be separated on an open market value of the sales and not as part of the cost-based method currently put forward by HM Customs & Excise.

The current implementation results in distortion due to the different profit margins made on the different categories of services within a package, and it is highly probable that the in-house activities reflect higher profit margins than those bought in and sold on. Thus the current method results in a tainting by the in-house values where these are of a different liability than the standard-rated bought-in margin scheme supplies. In practice this results in a higher amount of VAT being payable.

A change in the TOMS to the sales value being applied may lead to many tour operators applying the TOMS calculations to potentially account for less VAT, where the in-house VAT liability is not standard rated. For example, supplies of exempt tuition and zero-rated passenger transport from in-house resources.

It is important to note that where bought-in designated travel services are supplied in conjunction with other exempt or zero-rated in-house supplies, the TOMS legislation overrides the exempt or zero-rated legislation and thus institutions and suppliers of goods and services which do not incur VAT may be liable to VAT registration and accounting for VAT by dint of supplying bought-in margin scheme supplies.

For those supplies which are outside of the provisions of the TOMS the main issues concern the agency principal relationship and, following from this, where the supply is deemed to take place and the resulting VAT liability.

In an industry that involves highly significant turnover in the UK, the application of VAT is of paramount importance to ensure that VAT is accounted for correctly in order to mitigate the VAT payable and to avoid the risk of incurring interest charges and penalties on VAT which may be under-declared.

# Appendix 1 – CAA forms

## Auditor's Annual Report

| Licence Holder | ATOL Number |
|---|---|
|  |  |

| Twelve months from                          to |
|---|
|  |

This Report relates to the licensable turnover earned by the licence holder during the **four calendar quarters immediately prior to its latest financial year end.**

The turnover in this Report should relate to only **one** of the following categories of business. If the licence holder does more than one of these categories of business, please complete a separate form for each category. Please refer to the latest Guidance Notes for Auditors for an explanation of the different categories of licensable turnover.

Please indicate by ticking one box below which category of business this Report covers:

- *Fully bonded business:* scheduled or charter packages, and seat-only charters
- *Scheduled bonded business:* scheduled seat-only tickets covered by a bond
- *Agency business:* scheduled seat-only tickets covered by airline Deed(s) of Undertaking
- *ATOL to ATOL business:* licensable products sold to other ATOL holders for resale under the buyers' licences

## Report

In my/our opinion, based on tests I/we have carried out on the books and records of the licence holder and on the explanations given to me/us, the turnover which arose from licensable operation in the category and in the calendar quarters indicated is fairly stated as follows:

| Calendar Quarter | | Turnover |
| from | to | (£) |
| --- | --- | --- |
| | | |
| | | |
| | | |
| | | |
| | | |

**Tick one of the statements below: if the second applies, please indicate the number of other Reports submitted.**

- This Report covers all of the turnover which arose from licensable operations of the licence holder during the quarters indicated.

- I supply herewith ........ (number) other Reports relating to other categories of licensable business undertaken during the same periods.

**This report is your verification of the quarterly returns submitted by the licence holder. The CAA relies on the accuracy of this verification in granting the renewal of the licence. It must be a true and fair view of the category of licensable business undertaken during the quarters stated.**

| Signed | Date |
| --- | --- |

| Name of firm |
| --- |

| Address |
| --- |

(BLOCK LETTERS)

Dear

**AIR TRAVEL ORGANISERS' LICENSING – RELEASE OF BOND AND SUBORDINATED LOANS**

Thank you for your letter of        in which you have indicated that your firm will not be applying for the renewal of its Air Travel Organisers' Licence from 1 October 1998.

In order to release the bond of £    , we will require written confirmation from your auditors on the form enclosed with this letter. A template to guide them through completion is also enclosed. If they have any questions concerning the form, I shall be pleased to assist them.

In order to release the subordinated loan(s) totalling £     which we currently hold in favour of your firm, we shall require the following written confirmation from your auditors:

> **'All claims of other creditors in respect of liabilities incurred by the firm in the period during which it held an Air Travel Organisers' Licence, have been satisfied'.**

Yours sincerely

for the Civil Aviation Authority

# Confirmation from auditors for release of bond

1    We have acted as auditors for *[name of former ATOL holder]* ('our client') for *[number of]* years.

2    Our client has held Air Travel Organisers' Licence ('ATOL') number *[number]* issued by the Civil Aviation Authority ('the CAA').

3    As a condition of the grant of this licence, the CAA has required our client to procure a bond. As a consequence, our client provided a bond of *[£ amount]* from *[name of bond obligor]* to the CAA which expires on *[expiry date]*.

4    We acknowledge that:
  (1)   the purpose of the bond is, in the event of the failure of our client to meet its obligations to its customers who have paid for flights or holidays covered by the ATOL, to provide the CAA with a sum of money which it can then use *inter alia* to repatriate customers on holiday and refund those customers who have not yet commenced their holiday; and
  (2)   in the event that in a particular case the sum of money produced by a bond proves insufficient or no longer available for this purpose, as part of the ATOL system the CAA has recourse to a trust fund, the Air Travel Trust ('the ATT'), to meet liabilities to customers which would have been met by the bond if it had been sufficient and available.

5    Our client now has surrendered its ATOL and no longer carries on any business for which such a licence is required ('licensable business').

6    Our client wishes to cancel the bond prior to its specified expiry.

7    We acknowledge that:
  (1)   the CAA will agree to the early termination of the bond only if it is satisfied that neither it nor the ATT will suffer any loss as a consequence;
  (2)   this requires the CAA to be satisfied that all outstanding liabilities to customers in respect of licensable business have been met by our client; and,
  (3)   our client has therefore requested that we give to the CAA and to the ATT confirmation to that effect.

8    Accordingly, we have satisfied ourselves by inspecting our client's records that all outstanding liabilities to its customers in respect of licensable business have been met by our client, and hereby confirm that this is the case.

9     This statement is made for the benefit of the CAA and the ATT, to both of whom, in light of the foregoing, we acknowledge a duty of care in this regard.

10    We further acknowledge that:
    (1)    the CAA will rely upon this statement both for itself and on behalf of the ATT when deciding whether the bond should be cancelled before its specified expiry date; and,
    (2)    the ATT may suffer a loss in the event that there remain any outstanding liabilities to our client's customers after the cancellation of its bond.

Authorised signatory

Name [*actual name of the individual signing on behalf of the firm*]

On behalf of [*name of firm*]

Date

# Appendix 2 – ABTA travel agent forms

TO THE ASSOCIATION OF BRITISH TRAVEL AGENTS LIMITED

Member's Name . . . . . . . . . . . . . . . . . . . . . Head Office ABTA No. . . . . . . .

Auditor's Name . . . . . . . . . . . . . . . . . . . . . . . . . . . . . . . . . . . . . . . . . . . . . . .

We have audited the accounts of your above-named member for the period
from . . . . . . . . . . . . . . . . . . . . . . . . . . . to . . . . . . . . . . . . . . . . . . . . . . . . . . . . . .
In our opinion at the balance sheet date the net recoverable current asset
position was as follows:

|  | £ | £ |
|---|---|---|
| Net Current Assets/(Liabilities) as per balance sheet |  | . . . . . . . . |
| **Adjust for:** |  |  |
| Deposits or other current assets pledged as security for bonds |  | . . . . . . . . |
| Debtors amounts falling due for settlement after one year |  | . . . . . . . . |
| Brochure costs carried forward |  | . . . . . . . . |
| Other promotional costs carried forward |  | . . . . . . . . |
| Prepaid element of bond |  | . . . . . . . . |
| Amounts not demonstrably recoverable due from connected companies or persons |  | . . . . . . . . |
| Other (*please specify*): i) |  | . . . . . . . . |
| ii) |  | . . . . . . . . |
| iii) |  | . . . . . . . . |

**Net Recoverable Current Assets** ........

Value of freehold property in UK as per
  balance sheet ........

Less: Amount charged as security against this
  property ........

........

Value of long leasehold property in UK as per
  balance sheet ........

Less: Amount charged as security against this
  property ........

**Adjusted Net Recoverable Current Assets** ........

The information provided here is accurate to the best of our knowledge
and belief.

Signed .............. Qualification ............ Date ...........
(for the auditors)

Signed .............. Position ................ Date ...........
(for the member – for signature by a director, proprietor, partner or
responsible official)

**THIS FORM SHOULD ACCOMPANY THE MEMBER'S AUDITED
ACCOUNTS, TURNOVER CERTIFICATE AND ANALYSIS AND
AUDITOR'S STATEMENT WHEN SUBMITTED.**

Form Audit008 (Apr 96)

Association of British Travel Agents Ltd

## TOUR OPERATORS' QUARTERLY TURNOVER CERTIFICATE – BONDING YEAR ENDING 30 SEPT 199
### for all non-ATOL activities other than retail sales

I hereby certify that our non-ATOL turnover for the period . . . . . . . . . . . .
to . . . . . . . . . . . . . . . . . . . . . . .on a gross cash receipts basis was as follows:

| MONTH: | 1: | 2: | 3: | TOTAL |
|---|---|---|---|---|
| N/L TURNOVER* | £ | £ | £ | £ |
| BREAKAGE DEPOSITS** | £ | £ | £ | £ |
| UK TRANSPORTATION*** | £ | £ | £ | £ |
| **TOTAL** | £ | £ | £ | £ |

\* including UK inclusive arrangements

\* i.e., refundable deposits collected in the UK to cover possible breakages or losses, usually related to self-catering holidays or yacht hire

\*\*\* e.g., day tours

*N.B.* In accordance with Article 10(10) your auditor's confirmation of the returns for this bonding year will be required within six months following the final quarter.

Signed . . . . . . . . . . . . . . . . . . . . . . . . . . . . . Date . . . . . . . . . . . . . . . . . . . .
Director/Proprietor/Partner/Co. Secretary
(delete as applicable)

Company . . . . . . . . . . . . . . . . . . . . . . . . . . . . Head office ABTA No . . . . . .

Address . . . . . . . . . . . . . . . . . . . . . . . . . . . . . . . . . . . . . . . . . . . . . . . . . . . . . .

1st  Quarterly Certificate  (1 Oct–31 Dec)  to be submitted by
                                            31 January
2nd  Quarterly Certificate  (1 Jan–31 Mar)  to be submitted by 30 April
3rd  Quarterly Certificate  (1 Apr–30 Jun)  to be submitted by 31 July
4th  Quarterly Certificate  (1 July–30 Sep)  to be submitted by
                                            31 October

Would you please ensure that copies of any new brochures introduced during the quarter are sent to the Association's Legal Department with a completed Brochure Information form. Supplies of this form can be obtained from the Legal Department on 0171 307 1962.     Form FM003(m)

## <u>REGISTERED AUDITOR'S REPORT</u>

To the Association of British Travel Agents:

We have examined the information supplied above and confirm that in our opinion the information is in accordance with the member's books and records.

Signed .............................. Date ...................

Auditor's Name and Address (please use block capitals) ..............

...........................................................

...........................................................

Registered Auditor No ......................................

Form FM002(s) April 97
(New Members)

## TURNOVER CERTIFICATE AND ANALYSIS
(to be completed by a Director, Partner, Proprietor, Co. Secretary or Authorised Signatory of the member)

Member's Name _____H/O ABTA No. _____

Certificate for the period_____to_____

Number of offices including Head Office at the Balance Sheet date _____

TURNOVER ANALYSIS

|   |   | Section |   |
|---|---|---|---|
| (A) | Total Gross Turnover as a Travel Agent | 1 | |
| (B) | Total Licensable Turnover | 2 | |
| (C) | Total Non-Licensable Turnover | 3 | |
| (D) | Total Other Revenue | 4 | |
| (E) | Turnover per Financial Statements (total A, B, C & D) | Note 6 | |

**PLEASE ENSURE THAT SECTIONS 1, 2, 3 & 4 ARE COMPLETED**

**Section 1** – must be completed if you wish to claim a reduction in bond level

Details of Sales as a Travel Agent included in (A) above

|   |   | Note |   |
|---|---|---|---|
| (a) | Tour Operator Credit Turnover | 2(a) | |
| (b) | Car Hire Credit Turnover | 2(b) | |
| (c) | BSP Turnover – Travel Agent | 3 | |
| (d) | British Rail – Travel Agent | | |
| (e) | Scheduled Bus Ticket Turnover – Travel Agent | | |

**Section 2** – must be completed by members who hold an ATOL

ATOL Number _____

| Details of ATOL Turnover | 4(a) | |
|---|---|---|
| (a) Fully Bonded | | |
| (b) Lower Bonded | | |
| (c) Agency Bonded | | |
| Total Licensable Turnover | | |

FORM AUDIT 003 SEPT 96

1

**Section 3** – must be completed if you conduct Non-Licensable Activities

Details of Non-Licensable Turnover

| | | Note | |
|---|---|---|---|
| (a) | Overseas Non-Licensable Turnover | 4(b) | |
| (b) | Domestic Inclusive Holidays | 4(c) | |
| (c) | Breakage Deposits | 4(d) | |
| (d) | UK Transportation | 4(e) | |
| (e) | Foreign Transportation | 4(f) | |
| Total Non-Licensable Turnover | | | |

**Section 4** – must be completed if Other Revenue is declared

Details of other revenue

| | | | |
|---|---|---|---|
| (a) | Ground Handling Turnover | 5 | |
| (b) | Seat Sales to other ATOL holders | | |
| (c) | Inbound Tours | | |
| (d) | Travellers Cheques / Foreign Currency | | |
| (e) | Freight Traffic | | |
| (f) | Other (please give details below)* | | |
| Total of Other Revenue | | | |

I have read the notes on page 4 and confirm that the analysis of turnover shown on pages 1 and 2 are correct.

Signed_____
Director/Proprietor/Partner/Co. Secretary/or Authorised Signatory
(delete as applicable)

Name_____  Date_____
(Please Print in Block Capitals)

FORM AUDIT 003 SEPT 96

2

202

## AUDITOR'S STATEMENT
(to be completed by the member's Auditors)

Member's Name _____

Head Office ABTA Number_____

We act as auditors to the above named member of the Association of British Travel Agents Ltd. We confirm that we have audited the accounts for the period from _____ to _____ and that we have examined this Turnover Certificate and Analysis for the above period supplied to you by the directors/partners/proprietors/Co. Secretary/or Authorised Signatory* of the member. In our opinion the figures included on this certificate are in accordance with the books and records of the member and comply with Article 14 of the Association's Articles of Association.

Signed _____

Name_____

Qualification _____

Company_____

Date_____ Regd Auditors Status Held? Y/N*

*Delete as applicable        Regd Auditor No: _____

FORM AUDIT 003 SEPT 96

3

## AUDITORS REPORT TO THE ASSOCIATION OF BRITISH TRAVEL AGENTS

### IN RESPECT OF

. . . . . . . . . . . . . . . . . . . . . . . . . . . . . . . . . . . . .(Members name)

. . . . . . . . . . . . . . . . . . . . . . . . .(Head Office A.B.T.A. Number)

We confirm that we have audited the Financial Statements of the above named member for the period from        to       .

We confirm that, in our opinion, proper books of account have been kept by the member throughout this period and that satisfactory returns have been received and examined by us in respect of all branches not visited by us.

Having received all the information and explanations necessary for the purposes of this report, we confirm that, in our opinion, the Profit and Loss account for the above period shows a true and fair view of the member's profit/loss* for the period and that the Balance Sheet shows a true and fair view of the state of the members affairs as at that date. We confirm that the accounts are in accordance with Article 14 of the Articles of Association of the Association of British Travel Agents Limited.

. . . . . . . . . . . . . . . . . . . . . . . . . . Signed

. . . . . . . . . . . . . . . . . . . . . . . . . . Name (Block Capitals)

. . . . . . . . . . . . . . . . . . . . . . . . . . Qualification

. . . . . . . . . . . . . . . . . . . . . . . . . . Registered Auditor
Status Held (Y/N)

. . . . . . . . . . . . . . . . . . . . . . . . . . Company

. . . . . . . . . . . . . . . . . . . . . . . . . . Date

* Delete as appropriate

Form Audit 002 (Apr 96)

Association of British Travel Agents Ltd

## NON-LICENSED TOUR ACTIVITIES

### Auditor's Confirmation for the Bonding Period ending 30 September 199

Member . . . . . . . . . . . . . . . . . . . . . . . . . . . . . . . . . . . . . . . . . . . . . . . . .

Head Office Membership No. . . . . . . . . . . . . . . . . . . . . . . . . . . . . . . . . .

In my/our opinion based on the tests which I/we have carried out on the books and records of the above member, together with the explanations given to me/us, the turnover which arose from the operation of all non-licensed activities, other than retail sales, during the periods indicated is as stated below:

*N.B.* Where any of the figures shown below differ from those already submitted by the member, please provide an explanation.

| MONTH | TURNOVER | | |
| --- | --- | --- | --- |
| | NON-LICENSED TURNOVER | BREAKAGE DEPOSITS | UK TRANSPORTATION |
| OCTOBER | | | |
| NOVEMBER | | | |
| DECEMBER | | | |
| JANUARY | | | |
| FEBRUARY | | | |
| MARCH | | | |
| APRIL | | | |
| MAY | | | |
| JUNE | | | |
| JULY | | | |
| AUGUST | | | |
| SEPTEMBER | | | |
| TOTALS | | | |

*ABTA travel agent forms*

Signed .................................... Date ..............

Firm (Auditors) ....................................................

Qualification ......................................................

Address ...........................................................

Registered Auditor No. ............................................

Form Audit009(S) Apr 96

# Appendix 3 – ABTA tour operator forms

Association of British Travel Agents Limited

### QUARTERLY TURNOVER CERTIFICATE –
### TRAVEL AGENT MEMBERS

Member's Name . . . . . . . . . . . . . . . . . . . . . . . . . . . . . . . . . . . . . . . . . . . . . .

Head Office ABTA Number . . . . . . . . . . . . . . . . . . . . . . . . . . . . . . . . . . . . .

Quarterly Return for the three months ending . . . . . . . . . . . . . . . . . . . . . .

**SECTION A**                                                                          £

1.  Gross Turnover as a Travel agent – (Note 1)

2.  Gross Licensable Turnover – (Note 2)

3.  Gross Non-Licensable Turnover – (Note 3)

4.  Other Revenue – please specify

    TOTAL:

**SECTION B – ADDITIONAL INFORMATION
(OPTIONAL) (INCLUDED IN GROSS TURNOVER
AS A TRAVEL AGENT)**                                                                   £

Tour Operator Credit Turnover

Car Hire Credit Turnover

BSP Turnover (Note 4)

British Rail Turnover

Scheduled Bus Ticket Turnover

Signed . . . . . . . . . . . . . . . . . . . . . . . . . . . . . . . . . . . . . . . . . . . . . . . . . . . .
Director/Proprietor/Partner/Co. Secretary/Authorised Signatory
(delete as applicable)

Name . . . . . . . . . . . . . . . . . . . . . . . . . . . . . . . . . . . . . . . . . . . . . . . . . . . . .

Date . . . . . . . . . . . . . . . . . . . . . . . . . . . . . . . . . . . . . . . . . . . . . . . . . . . . . .

*Notes*

1. Travel Agent Turnover is defined as the gross amount (including commission and VAT) of passenger traffic revenue excluding travellers cheques and foreign currency in which you act as an agent.

2. Licensable Turnover is turnover bonded with the Civil Aviation Authority as either Fully, Lower or Agency Bonded Turnover.

3. Non-Licensable Turnover is turnover in which you act as a principal for which an ATOL is not required.

4. This should relate only to air tickets issued under the IATA BSP System by the member and not BSP tickets purchased from another supplier.

5. The turnover shown on this form should consist of Head Office Turnover and all Branch Turnover.

6. This form should be returned no later than one month after the end of the quarter to: The Financial Monitoring Department of ABTA.

Direct Fax number: 0171 580 9621.

Form/quarcer1wpd/dec96

# Appendix 4 – Accounting policies

## Travel agents

### Example (i)

*Total operating income comprises:*

**Turnover:** Turnover comprises commissions on travel arrangements, sales in respect of tour operations, traveller's cheque and foreign exchange commissions and margins on sale of currencies.

**Income arising from investment activities:** Income arising from investment activities comprises interest on deposits, bonds, debentures, bills and commercial paper and movements in the value of such investments listed on recognised stock exchanges, together with profits or losses on instruments used to hedge the value of the investment portfolio.

The profit and loss format has been adapted to include income arising from investment activities within total operating income. This is necessary to fairly reflect the operating income of the Group. Such income from investment activities principally arises from the investment of the funds, from the sale of traveller's cheques, needed to meet traveller's cheques awaiting redemption. The sale of traveller's cheques and the income arising therefrom are an integral part of the Group's trading operations which are considered to be one interrelated business.

**Inclusive tours:** Profit from inclusive tours and the cost of brochure publication relating thereto are taken to the profit and loss account in the financial year in which the tour is commenced or in the season to which they relate respectively.

**Costs of sales:** Cost of sales comprises the cost of travel arrangements, agents' commissions and management in respect of tour operations, the costs of operating retail shops, selling costs, and incentive commissions.

**Distribution costs:** Distribution costs include freight and insurance costs for the distribution of traveller's cheques and foreign currency notes.

**Traveller's cheques awaiting redemption:** A liability is recorded for all traveller's cheques issued but not encashed. This is then reduced to take account of the value of those cheques which it is anticipated will never be presented for payment. This amount is estimated by the Directors after consultation with a firm of independent actuaries. It is calculated at the beginning and end of each financial year with the difference being included in either other operating income or expenses as appropriate. This policy was first adopted in 1996 resulting in a prior year adjustment of £18,060,000.

**Foreign currencies:** Assets and liabilities in foreign currencies are translated into sterling at closing rates of exchange. The profit and loss account and cash flow statement are translated at average rates of exchange, except where income is matched with forward currency transactions. Where this occurs the differences arising between translation at the contract rate and the closing rate are shown as a reserve moment. Exchange differences resulting from the translation, at closing rates, of net investments in subsidiary and associated undertakings, together with differences between the profit and loss account translated at average rates and at closing rates, are dealt with in reserves. Forward contracts entered into as foreign exchange dealers and foreign currency assets and liabilities are valued at the rate of exchange ruling on the balance sheet date.

(Thomas Cook Group Ltd 31 December 1997)

## Example (ii)

**Foreign currencies:** The profits and losses on the overseas subsidiary undertakings and the group's net investments are translated at closing rates of exchange. Differences arising on translation are added to or deducted from reserves.

Transactions expressed in foreign currencies are translated into sterling and recorded at rates of exchange approximating to those ruling at the date of the transaction. Monetary assets and liabilities are translated at rates ruling at the balance sheet date.

**Travel transactions:** Transactions relating to customers travel bookings are recognised in the accounts at such time as payments are received from customers and deposited to the trust accounts (see note 11.) This treatment reflects the fact that customers retain the right to change or cancel their travel bookings at any time up to the date of payment.

Transactions relating to customer bookings are reflected in turnover when there is reasonable certainty that such transactions will be completed.

**Note 2: Turnover:** Turnover represents the gross sales value to customers of air tickets, travel insurance, hotel bookings and sundry related services. All operations giving rise to turnover and profits are continuing.

(Trailfinders Ltd 28 February 1998)

210

## Example (iii)

**Stocks:** Stocks represent tickets, publications and sundry items held for resale and are stated at the lower of cost and net realisable value.

**Foreign currency:** Transactions denominated in foreign currencies are recorded in sterling at the exchange rates as of the date of the transaction. Monetary assets and liabilities denominated in foreign currencies at the year end are reported at the rates of exchange prevailing at the year end. Any gain or loss arising from a change in exchange rates subsequent to the date of the transaction is included as an exchange gain or loss in the profit and loss account.

**Turnover:** Turnover represents the total value of sales and commissions receivable for goods sold and services rendered, excluding value added tax and trade discounts in the normal course of business.

(STA Travel Ltd 31 March 1997)

## Example (iv)

**Turnover:** Turnover is recognised when a travel ticket is issued.

**Stocks:** Stocks of tickets, travel card and guides are valued at the lower of cost and net realisable value.

**Foreign currencies:** Transactions denominated in foreign currencies are recorded at the rates of exchange ruling at the date of the transactions. All monetary liabilities and assets are translated at year end exchange rates and all resulting exchange differences are dealt with through the profit and loss account.

**Note 2: Turnover:** Turnover comprises revenue from ticket, travel card and guide sales and is exclusive of VAT. Turnover relating to each major geographic market is not disclosed.

(USIT Britain Ltd 31 October 1996)

## Example (v)

**Stocks:** Stocks are stated at the lower of cost and net realisable value. Prepaid stocks of brochures which will be distributed free are included at cost in prepayments.

**Turnover:** Turnover represents the sales value of air tickets, travel insurance, hotel bookings and related services, including non-refundable deposits, and excluding value added tax.

*Accounting policies*

**Foreign currencies:** Transactions in foreign currencies are recorded using the rate of exchange ruling at the date of the transaction. Monetary assets and liabilities denominated in foreign currencies are translated using the rate of exchange ruling at the balance sheet date and the gains or losses on translation are included in the profit and loss account.

(Travelbag Plc 31 March 1997)

## Example (vi)

**Turnover:** Turnover represents the net commissions earned, as travel agents, excluding VAT. These commissions are recognised for each element of the holiday as full payment is received and for Insurance sales, when the policy comes into force.

**Deferred revenue expenditure:** Expenditure incurred during the year, which relates to the following year's advertising campaign, has been carried forward. This is in order to match the income derived from the advertising campaign with expenditure incurred on it.

(Lunn Poly Ltd 31 December 1996)

## Example (vii)

**Turnover:** Turnover represents the amounts (excluding value added tax) derived from the sale of package holidays and scheduled airline tickets. All turnover arises in the United Kingdom.

In previous periods, turnover has been recognised upon the receipt of moneys from clients, however, with effect from 1 January 1996 turnover has been recognised at the point of booking confirmation. The revised policy provides a better matching of administrative expenditure with the sales generated by the activity and therefore gives a more fair representation of results. It is also in line with the group accounting policy.

The comparative figures have been restated where appropriate.

**Foreign currency:** Assets and liabilities denominated in foreign currencies are translated into sterling at closing rates. All revaluation differences are taken to the profit and loss account.

(Travelworld (Northern) Ltd 31 March 1997)

## Example (viii)

**Turnover:** Turnover, excluding value added tax, represents sales, net of rebates and discounts, earned during the year. Turnover now includes gross sales of Business Travel transactions. In previous years only commission and fees were reported. Comparatives have accordingly been restated.

**Foreign currencies:** Assets and liabilities expressed in foreign currencies are translated as follows:

on consolidation of an overseas subsidiary – Income and expenditure are translated into sterling at the average rate of exchange for the year. Adjustments are made for the effect of hedging instruments where applicable. Net assets of overseas subsidiaries are translated into sterling at the rate prevailing at the balance sheet date. Any resultant exchange differences are dealt with through the exchange reserve.

assets and liabilities denominated in a foreign currency – These are translated into sterling at the rate prevailing on the balance sheet date. Exchange differences arising on the translation of foreign currency borrowings are dealt with through the exchange reserve to the extent that there is a corresponding exchange difference on the translation of the related net investments. Exchange differences on sterling denominated Group loans to overseas subsidiaries which are of a permanent equity nature are dealt with through the exchange reserve. All other exchange differences are taken to the profit and loss account.

(Hogg Robinson Plc 31 March 1998)

# Tour Operators

## Example (i)

The following accounting policies have been consistently applied, with the exception of client money receivable in advance, in dealing with items considered material in relation to the Accounts. The balance sheet has been restated to reflect client money received in advance as deferred income. Previously, the Group's policy was to present moneys receivable as well as received as deferred income. The new policy reflects a fairer presentation of the Group's deferred income at the year end. As a result of this change there is no impact on the Group's net assets in either the current or the previous year.

**Foreign currencies:** Monetary assets and liabilities in foreign currencies are translated into sterling at the rates of exchange ruling at the balance sheet date except to the extent covered by forward exchange contracts. The benefit of foreign exchange contracts purchased to cover future seasons' requirements is accounted for in the season to which the contract relates. Exchange gains and losses arising on trading and translation of monetary assets and liabilities are dealt with through the profit and loss account.

213

The results of overseas subsidiaries are translated at weighted average exchange rates for the year and exchange differences arising on consolidation of the net investment in overseas subsidiaries are dealt with through reserves. The Canadian dollar exchange rates used are: opening rate – Can\$2.18, average rate – Can\$2.25 and year end rate Can\$2.36.

**Turnover:** Turnover represents the aggregate amount of revenue receivable in the ordinary course of business principally from the activity of tour operating in the UK, Ireland and Canada. Turnover excludes intra-group transactions and is stated net of commission and discounts. Revenue is recognised on the date of departure and related costs of holidays and flights are charged to the profit and loss account on the same basis. Turnover by destination is not materially different from such turnover by origin.

**Client money received in advance:** Client money received at the balance sheet date relating to holidays commencing and flights departing after the year end is included in creditors.

**Marketing costs:** Brochure and marketing costs are charged to the profit and loss account in the season to which they relate.

(First Choice Holidays Plc 31 October 1997)

## Example (ii)

**Turnover:** Turnover, which relates to continuing activities only, represents total invoiced sales in the United Kingdom, excluding VAT, in respect of tours and travel services for which the company acts as principal.

**Marketing costs:** All cost incurred in brochure production and distribution, advertising, promotions, exhibitions and market research which relate to the subsequent year's holidays are prepaid and charged in the year to which they relate.

**Foreign currencies:** Transactions in foreign currencies are translated at the rate ruling on the date of the transaction or the contracted rate if the transaction is covered by a forward exchange contract.

Monetary assets and liabilities denominated in a foreign currency are retranslated at the rate of exchange ruling at the balance sheet date or if appropriate at the forward contract rate.

**Note 2: Cost of sales:** Cost of sales comprises hotel costs, flight costs, transfer costs, travel agent's commission and VAT on margin. VAT on margin charged to cost of sales for the year ended 31 December 1997 amounted to £580, 937 (1996 – £432,411).

In previous periods commission received from airlines was recorded within other operating income. However, there has been a trend towards airlines quoting non-commissionable prices ('net fare contracts'). By showing the commission from other airlines (quoting commissionable prices) separately the disclosure is not as meaningful as used to be the case. Accordingly, the directors have decided to include commission in the cost of the sales figure. Prior year comparatives have been restated as appropriate.

(CIT Holidays 31 December 1997)

## Example (iii)

**Foreign currencies:** Assets, liabilities, revenues, and costs arising from transactions denominated in foreign currencies are translated into sterling either at the exchange rate in operation on the date on which the transactions occurred or at the contracted rate if the transactions are covered by a related or matching foreign exchange contract.

At the balance sheet date monetary assets and liabilities are translated at closing, or if appropriate, forward contract rates.

Exchange gains or losses on settled transactions and unsettled monetary items are dealt with in the profit and loss account as part of the results from ordinary activities.

**Turnover:** Turnover represents the amounts derived from the sales of services to customers within the United Kingdom during the period at invoiced amounts (excluding value added tax as calculated under the Tour Operators' Margin Scheme).

**Note 2: Turnover and operating loss:** The company's turnover and operating loss are derived from holiday operating activities originating in the United Kingdom.

(Shearings Holidays Ltd 31 December 1997)

## Example (iv)

**Turnover:** Turnover represents sales by the company to third parties (excluding value added tax) in the ordinary course of business for services provided as a principal.

**Foreign currency translation:** Foreign currency assets and liabilities have been translated into sterling at the rates of exchange ruling at the balance sheet date. Gains and losses due to currency fluctuations arising in the normal course of business are included in the profit on ordinary activities before taxation.

**Liquid resources:** Liquid resources comprise short-term deposits which have a maturity period of less than 12 months.

**Brochures and advertising:** Expenditure relating to brochures and advertising is written off in the financial period in which it is incurred.

(Page & Moy Ltd 31 October 97)

## Example (v)

**Income recognition:** Turnover represents the aggregate amount of revenue receivable from inclusive tours (net of agents' commissions), travel agency commissions received and other services supplied to customers in the ordinary course of business. Revenues and expenses relating to inclusive tours are taken to the profit and loss account on holiday departure. Certain expenses such as the cost of non-revenue earning flights, brochure and promotional costs are charged to the profit and loss account over the season to which they relate. Turnover and expenses exclude intra-group transactions.

**Foreign currencies:** Each year an estimate of the results of certain of the Company's overseas subsidiary undertakings are hedged and the actual results are translated using the hedged rates. Average exchange rates are used to translate the results of all other overseas subsidiary undertakings. The balance sheets of overseas subsidiary undertakings are translated at year end exchange rates and the resulting exchange differences are dealt with through reserves.

Transactions denominated in foreign currencies are translated at the exchange rate at the date of the transaction. Foreign currency assets and liabilities held at year end are translated at year end exchange rates, or the exchange rate of related hedging instruments where appropriate. The resulting exchange gain or loss is dealt with in the profit and loss account.

(Airtours Plc 30 September 1997)

## Example (vi)

**Turnover:** Turnover is the total amount receivable by the group for services provided, excluding value added tax.

216

**Foreign currencies:** Transactions during the year in foreign currencies are translated into sterling at the average exchange rate prevailing during the year. Monetary assets and liabilities in foreign currencies are translated into sterling at the rates of exchange ruling at the balance sheet date.

All exchange differences are taken into account in arriving at the operating profit.

**Brochure and promotional costs:** Brochure and promotional costs are charged to the profit and loss account in the season to which they relate. Prepaid costs are included in the prepayments and accrued income.

(Travelsphere Ltd 30 November 1997)

## Example (vii)

**Turnover:** Turnover represents income received in respect of passengers whose tours have been finalised at the balance sheet date. Cost of sales includes all costs in respect of this turnover.

**Foreign currencies:** Monetary assets and liabilities denominated in foreign currencies are translated into sterling at rates of exchange ruling at the accounting date. Transactions in foreign currencies are recorded at the rate ruling at the date of the transaction. All differences are taken to the profit and loss account.

**Brochure costs:** Brochure costs are written off in the year incurred as the directors consider this policy to be the most prudent.

(Destination Group 30 April 1997)

# Airline operators
## Example (i)

**Turnover:** Passenger ticket and cargo waybill sales, net of discounts, are recorded as current liabilities in the 'sales in advance of carriage' account until recognised as revenue when the transportation service is provided. Commission costs are recognised at the same time as the revenue to which they relate and are charged to cost of sales. Unused tickets are recognised as revenue on a systematic basis. Other revenue is recognised at the time the service is provided.

**Segmental reporting:**
*(a) Business segments:* The directors regard all Group activities as relating to the airline business.

*Accounting policies*

*(b) Geographical segments*

(i) *Turnover by destination:* The analysis of turnover by destination is based on the following criteria:

*Schedule and non-scheduled services:* Turnover from domestic services within the United Kingdom is attributed to the United Kingdom. Turnover from inbound and outbound services between the United Kingdom and overseas points is attributed to the geographical area in which the relevant overseas point lies.

*Other revenue:* Revenue from the sale of package holidays is attributed to the geographical area in which the holiday is taken, while revenue from aircraft maintenance and other miscellaneous services is attributed on the basis of where the customer resides.

(ii) *Turnover by origin:* The analysis of turnover by origin is derived by allocating revenue to the area in which the sale was made. Operating profit resulting from turnover generated in each geographical area according to origin of sale is not disclosed as it is neither practical nor meaningful to allocate the Group's operating expenditure on this basis.

(iii) *Geographical analysis of net assets:* The major revenue-earning assets of the Group are composed of aircraft fleets, the majority of which are registered in the United Kingdom. Since the Group's aircraft fleets are employed flexibly across its world-wide route network, there is no suitable basis of allocating such assets and related liabilities to geographical segments.

**Tangible fixed assets:**
Tangible fixed assets are stated at cost or valuation as stated below. Depreciation is calculated to write off the cost or valuation, less estimated residual value, on the straight line basis.

*(a) Capitalisation of interest on progress payments*
Interest attributed to progress payments made on account of aircraft and other assets under construction is capitalised and added to the cost of the asset concerned. Interest capitalised in respect of progress payments on those aircraft which subsequently become subject to extendible operating lease arrangements is carried forward and written off over the initial lease period.

*(b) Fleet*

(i) *Cost or valuation:* All aircraft are stated at cost, net of manufacturer's credits, with the exception of a small number that are stated at March 31, 1988 valuations, with subsequent expenditure stated at cost. The Concorde

218

fleet remains at nil book value. Aircraft not in current use are included at estimated net realisable value. Aircraft which are financed in foreign currency, either by loans, finance leases or hire purchase agreements, are regarded together with the related liabilities as a separate group of assets and liabilities and accounted for in foreign currency. The amounts in foreign currency are translated into sterling at rates ruling at the balance sheet date and the net differences arising from the translation of aircraft costs and related foreign currency loans are taken to reserves. The cost of all other aircraft is fixed in sterling at rates ruling at the date of purchase.

(ii) *Depreciation:* Fleet assets owned, or held on finance leases or hire purchase arrangements, are depreciated at rates calculated to write down the cost or valuation to the estimated residual value at the end of the planned operational lives. Cabin interiors, including those required for brand changes and re-launches, are depreciated over the lower of five years and the remaining life of the aircraft at the date of such modification. Residual values and operational lives are reviewed annually.

*(c) Property and equipment:*
Freehold properties and certain leasehold properties professionally valued at March 31, 1995 are included in these accounts on the basis of that valuation. Subsequent additions are included at cost. Provision is made for the depreciation of all property and equipment, apart from freehold land, based upon expected useful lives and, in the case of leasehold properties, over the duration of the leases if shorter.

*(d) Leased and hire purchased assets:*
Where assets are financed through finance leases or hire purchase arrangements, under which substantially all the risks and rewards of ownership are transferred to the Group, the assets are treated as if they had been purchased outright. The amount included in the cost of tangible fixed assets represents the aggregate of the capital elements payable during the lease or hire purchase term. The corresponding obligation, reduced by the appropriate proportion of lease or hire purchase payments made, is included in creditors. The amount included in the cost of tangible fixed assets is depreciated on the basis described in the preceding paragraphs and the interest element of lease or hire purchase payments made is included in interest payable in the profit and loss account. Payments under all other lease arrangements, known as operating leases, are charged to the profit and loss account in equal annual amounts over the period of the lease. In respect of aircraft, operating lease arrangements allow the Group to terminate the leases after a limited initial period, normally five to seven years, without further material financial obligations. In certain cases the Group is entitled to extend the initial lease period on pre-determined terms; such leases are described as 'extendible operating leases'.

**Aircraft and engine overhaul expenditure:**
Aircraft and engine spares acquired on the introduction or expansion of a fleet are carried as tangible fixed assets and generally depreciated in line with the fleet to which they relate. Replacement spares and all other costs relating to the maintenance and overhaul of aircraft and engines are charged to the profit and loss account on consumption and as incurred respectively.

**Frequent flyer programmes:**
The Group operates two principal frequent flyer programmes. The main airline schemes are run through the 'executive club' and 'frequent traveller' programmes where frequent travellers may accumulate mileage credits which entitle them to a choice of various awards, including free travel. The main United Kingdom scheme is run under the brand name of 'Airmiles' and principally involves the selling of miles of travel to United Kingdom companies to use for promotional incentives.

The incremental direct cost of providing free travel in exchange for redemption of miles earned by members of the Group's executive club, frequent traveller programmes and airmiles scheme is accrued as members of these schemes accumulate mileage. Costs accrued include incremental passenger service charges and security, fuel, catering, and lost baggage insurance; these costs are charged to cost of sales.

**Foreign currency translation:**
Foreign currency balances are translated into sterling at the rates of ruling at the balance sheet date, except for certain loan repayment instalments which are translated at the forward contract rates where instalments have been covered forward at the balance sheet date. Changes in the sterling value of outstanding foreign currency loans, finance leases and hire purchase arrangements which finance fixed assets are taken to reserves together with the differences arising on the translation of the related foreign currency denominated assets. Exchange differences arising on the translation of net assets of overseas subsidiary undertakings and associated undertakings are taken to reserves. Profit and losses of such undertakings are translated into Sterling at average rates of exchange during the year. All other profits or losses arising on translation are dealt with through the profit and loss account.

(British Airways Plc 31 March 1998)

## Example (ii)

**Fixed assets and depreciation:**
Depreciation is provided by the company to write off the cost or valuation less the estimated residual value of tangible fixed assets by equal instalments over their estimated useful economic lives as follows:

Short leasehold buildings: 10% of cost per annum
Plant and equipment: 10%–50% of cost per annum
Motor vehicles: 20%–25% of cost per annum
Computer hardware and software: 20% of cost per annum
Fixtures and fittings: 10% of cost per annum
Aircraft: 7–20% of cost per annum
Rotable aircraft parts: 10% of valuation per annum

**Foreign currencies:** Transactions in foreign currencies are recorded using the rate of exchange ruling at the date of the transaction. Monetary assets and liabilities denominated in foreign currencies are translated using the rate of exchange ruling at the balance sheet date and the gains or losses on translation are included in the profit and loss account.

**Aircraft rotables:** These comprise aircraft parts which have a renewable time/usage life which upon expiry are required by the Civil Aviation Authority to be serviced by approved engineers. Such parts are valued at a directors' valuation based on a proportion of manufacturer's list price.

**Aircraft consumables:** These comprise aircraft parts having a non-renewable life. These are valued at the lower of cost or net realisable value for each separately identified batch purchased.

**Aircraft maintenance costs:** Provision is made for costs of overhaul and major checks on the basis of hours flown and is designed to provide for the likely cost of bringing all lifed parts on the aircraft back to the condition existing when the aircraft was acquired or leased.

**Flying hour reserves:** Flying hour reserves are set up to provide for directors' estimates of future costs on maintenance contracts.

**Turnover – airline operations:** Represents the value of tickets flown in the year, together with the amounts (excluding value added tax) derived from the provision of services to customers during the year.

**Turnover – aircraft engineering services:** Represents the amounts (excluding value added tax) derived from the provision of goods and services to customers during the year.

**Turnover – aircraft leasing:** Represents the amounts (excluding value added tax) derived from the provision of services to customers during the year.

(Jersey European Airways (UK) Ltd 31 March 1997)

# Example (iii)

## (2) Fixed assets and depreciation – aircraft

Aircraft are depreciated on a straight line basis. The cost of each aircraft is depreciated over its remaining useful economic life after allowing for a 10 per cent residual value on original cost. The useful economic life of the aircraft is estimated to be 20 years.

**(4)** Monetary assets and liabilities denominated in foreign currencies have been translated into sterling at the rates of exchange ruling at the balance sheet date or, where forward cover has been taken, at the forward rate. Differences arising from changes in exchange rates are included in trading profits except for those which relate to advance payments for aircraft subsequently subject to operating leases. These exchange differences are amortised over the initial lease periods.

**(9)** Deferred revenue represents the unamortised element of:

(i)   aircraft disposal profits under leaseback arrangements which are included in earnings over the lease period;
(ii)  certain aircraft manufacturer credits relating to new aircraft which are included in earnings over five years from the date of delivery.

(Brittannia Airways Ltd 31 December 1996)

# Example (iv)

**Turnover:** Turnover is stated net of commission and comprises revenue from passenger ticket sales and freight arising from flights during the period. Revenue relating to flights after the accounting date, together with any commission thereon, is carried forward as deferred income.

**Administrative expenses:** Administrative expenses comprise overhead expenses together with marketing and promotional costs.

**Translation of foreign currencies:** Assets and liabilities denominated in foreign currencies are translated into sterling at the rates of exchange ruling at the end of the accounting period or where applicable at a hedged rate. Exchange differences arising through the translation of certain foreign currency borrowings and related fleet assets which are designated as foreign branches are taken to reserves.

**Depreciation:** Depreciation is provided at various rates in order to write off the cost or valuation of tangible fixed assets over their anticipated useful lives, or the periods of the underlying finance leases if shorter.

Aircraft and rotable spares are depreciated on a straight-line basis so as to reduce the cost or valuation to estimated residual value at the end of that period.

Expenditure incurred on modifications to aircraft under operating leases is depreciated on a straight-line basis to a non-residual value over a period not exceeding the lease period.

Other tangible fixed assets are depreciated at the following rates:

Fixtures and fittings: 25% on cost
Plant and equipment: 25%–33⅓% on cost
Computer equipment and software: 25% on cost
Motor vehicles: 25% on cost

**Aircraft maintenance costs:** Routine maintenance costs including annual airframe checks are written off to the profit and loss account as incurred. Heavy maintenance and engine overhaul costs are provided for in the profit and loss account on a flight-hour basis.

**Development expenditure:** Certain development expenditure, relating primarily to the setting up of new routes and introducing additional aircraft to the fleet, is deferred and written off over five years or the length of the underlying aircraft lease.

**Frequent flyer programme:** The estimated incremental cost of providing free travel and other rewards in exchange for redemption of miles earned by members of the Virgin Freeway frequent flyer scheme is accrued at the expected redemption rates as members of this scheme accumulate mileage.

(Virgin Atlantic Airways Ltd 30 April 97)

## Example (v)

**Turnover:** Turnover represents flown revenue from scheduled services, charter, freight and other activities net of value added tax.

**Development expenditure:** Any expenditure incurred on the start-up of new routes is charged to the profit and loss account as incurred.

**Foreign exchange:** Transactions denominated in foreign currency are translated into sterling at the exchange rate ruling at the dates of the transactions. Balances denominated in foreign currency are translated into sterling at the exchange rate ruling at the balance sheet date. Differences arising on translation are transferred to the profit and loss account.

**Depreciation of tangible fixed assets:** Depreciation is provided on the straight-line basis to write off tangible fixed assets to their estimated residual value over the following periods:

Leasehold improvements     – 10 years
Aircraft                               – 4–20 years
Motor vehicles, fixtures, fittings and equipment – 3–4 years

Depreciation on major additions is calculated from the month of acquisition.

Aircraft rotables are depreciated in accordance with the policy adopted for the respective aircraft.

**Hire purchase and lease agreements:** Assets acquired under finance leases and hire purchase agreements are treated as being owned and a liability equivalent to the cost is recognised. The finance costs are charged to the profit and loss account over the period of the lease in proportion to the balance outstanding.

Operating leases are charged to the profit and loss account on a straight-line basis.

**Maintenance provision and service costs:** Provision is made for the estimated cost of the future periodic overhaul of engines, propellers and parts of the airframe and is calculated with reference to the number of hours flown or other appropriate bases.

Other repair and service costs are charged to the profit and loss account as they accrue.

(Maersk Air Ltd 31 December 1996)

## Example (vi)

**Aircraft maintenance costs:** Future expenditure on each aircraft's next major airframe and engine overhaul is estimated and an accrual made on a flying hour or other appropriate basis so as to spread the cost of the maintenance over the period to the next major overhaul.

Routine maintenance is expensed in the year in which it is incurred.

**Foreign currency translations:** Monetary assets and liabilities denominated in foreign currencies are expressed at the rates prevailing at the balance sheet date or at the contracted rate where applicable.

Transactions during the year denominated in foreign currencies are translated using the rates prevailing at the date the transaction occurred, or at the contracted rate where applicable. Exchange adjustments due to fluctuations arising in the normal course of business are included in the profit or loss before tax except as explained in note 7.

**Depreciation:** Aircraft and technical spares are depreciated using a straight-line basis calculated to write down their cost to the current estimated residual values on the anticipated date of withdrawal from service or disposal. These estimates are reviewed regularly and adjusted as appropriate.

The current estimates of economic life are as follows:

| *Aircraft type* | *Economic life* |
|---|---|
| Boeing 737 – 500 | 19 years from date of construction |
| Rotables | 5 to 15 years |
| ATP Spares | Period to 31 July 2002 |
| BAe 146 aircraft and spares | Period to 30 June 2005 |
| Shorts 360 spares | Period to 31 March 1999 |
| Islanders | 13 years |
| Boeing 737 Simulator | 15 years |

All other plant and equipment is depreciated on a straight-line basis over five years except handling equipment, motor vehicles and certain computer equipment which are seven, four and three years respectively.

**Stocks:** Stocks consist of raw materials, consumable spares and sundry supplies and are valued at the lower of cost and net realisable value.

**Deferred expenditure:** Expenditure on new operations and aircraft introductory costs are charged over the following periods:

Introductory costs on aircraft fleet additions – within two years of commencement of passenger carrying services.

New routes – within one year of commencement of passenger carrying services.

Pilot training – within five years of commencement of flying.

(British Midland Plc 31 December 1997)

## Example (vii)

**Foreign currency:** Transactions in foreign currencies are recorded at the rate ruling at the date of the transaction.

Monetary assets and liabilities denominated in foreign currencies are retranslated at the rate of exchange ruling at the balance sheet date.

All differences are taken to the profit and loss account.

**Depreciation of tangible fixed assets:** Depreciation is provided to write off the cost of tangible fixed assets in equal annual instalments over their estimated useful lives as follows:

Motor vehicles: 4 years
Office furniture and equipment: 4–10 years
Handling equipment: 4–10 years
In-flight equipment: 4 years

No depreciation is provided for payments on account as the assets have not yet been brought into use.

**Operating leases:** Rentals paid under operating leases are charged to the profit and loss account as incurred.

**New route promotion and set-up costs:** Costs relating to the set-up and promotion of new routes are charged to the profit and loss account as incurred.

(GB Airways Ltd 31 March 1997)

# Appendix 5 – EC Directive 77/388, Article 26A

## Special scheme for travel agents

26(1)    Member States shall apply value added tax to the operations of travel agents in accordance with the provisions of this Article, where the travel agents deal with customers in their own name and use the supplies and services of other taxable persons in the provision of travel facilities. This Article shall not apply to travel agents who are acting only as intermediaries and accounting for tax in accordance with Article 11(a)(3)(c). In this Article travel agents include tour operators.

26(2)    All transactions performed by the travel agents in respect of a journey shall be treated as a single service supplied by the travel agent to the traveller. It shall be taxable in the Member State in which the travel agent has established the business or has a fixed establishment from which the travel agent has provided the services. The taxable amount and the price exclusive of tax, within the meaning of Article 22(3)(b), in respect of this service shall be the travel agent's margin, that is to say, the difference between the total amount to be paid by the traveller, exclusive of value added tax, and the actual cost to the travel agent of supplies and services provided by other taxable persons where these transactions are for the direct benefit of the traveller.

26(3)    If transactions entrusted by the travel agent to other taxable persons are performed by such persons outside the Community, the travel agent's service shall be treated as an exempted intermediary activity under Article 15(14). Where these transactions are performed both inside and outside the Community, only that part of the travel agent's service relating to transactions outside the Community may be exempted.

26(4)    Tax charged to the travel agent by other taxable persons on the transactions described in paragraph 2 which are for the direct benefit of the traveller, shall not be eligible for deduction or refund in any Member State.

# Appendix 6 – VAT Act 1994, section 53

53(1)    The Treasury may by order modify the application of this Act in relation to supplies of goods or services by tour operators or in relation to such of those supplies as may be determined by or under the order.

53(2)    Without prejudice to the generality of subsection (1) above, an order under this section may make provision:

(a)   for two or more supplies of goods or services by a tour operator to be treated as a single supply of services;
(b)   for the value of that supply to be ascertained, in such a manner as may be determined by or under the order, by reference to the difference between sums paid or payable to and sums paid or payable by the tour operator;
(c)   for account to be taken, in determining the VAT chargeable on that supply, of the difference rates of VAT that would have been applicable apart from this section;
(d)   excluding any body corporate from the application of section 43;
(e)   as to the time when a supply is to be treated as taking place.

53(3)    In this section 'tour operator' includes a travel agent acting as principal and any other person providing for the benefit of travellers' services of any kind commonly provided by tour operators or travel agents.

53(4)    Section 97(3) shall not apply to an order under this section, notwithstanding that it makes provision for excluding any VAT from credit under section 25.

228

# Appendix 7 – The Value Added Tax (Tour Operators) Order 1987 (as amended)

*Citation and commencement*

1 This Order may be cited as the Value Added Tax (Tour Operators) Order 1987 and shall come into force on 1 April 1988.

*Supplies to which this Order applies*

2 This Order shall apply to any supply of goods or services by a tour operator where the supply is for the benefit of travellers.

*Meaning of 'designated travel services'*

3 (1) Subject to paragraphs (2), (3) and (4) of this article, a 'designated travel service' is a supply of goods or services:
   (a) acquired for the purposes of his business; and
   (b) supplied for the benefit of a traveller without material alteration or further processing by a tour operator in a Member State of the European Community in which he has established his business or has a fixed establishment.

 (2) The supply of one or more designated travel services, as part of a single transaction, shall be treated as a single supply of services.

 (3) The Commissioners of HM Customs & Excise may on being given notice by a tour operator that he is a person who to the order of a taxable person:
   (a) acquires goods or services from another taxable person; and
   (b) supplies those goods and services, without material alteration or further processing, to a taxable person who ordered the supply for use in the United Kingdom by that person for the purpose of that person's business other than by way of resupply treat supplies within subparagraph (b) as not being designated travel services.

 (4) The supply of goods and services of such description as the Commissioners of HM Customs & Excise may specify shall be deemed not to be a designated travel service.

*Time of supply*

4  (1)  Sections 4 and 5 of the Value Added Tax Act 1983 shall not apply to any supply comprising in whole or in part a designated travel service.

   (2)  Subject to paragraphs (3) and (4) of this article, all supplies comprising in whole or in part a designated travel service shall, at the election of the tour operator making the supplies, be treated as taking place either:
   (a)  when the traveller commences a journey or occupies any accommodation supplied, whichever is the earlier; or
   (b)  when any payment is received by the tour operator in respect of that supply which, when aggregated with any earlier such payment, exceeds 20 per cent of the total consideration, to the extent covered by that and any earlier such payment, save in so far as any earlier such payment has already been treated as determining the time of part of that supply.

   (3)  Save as the Commissioners of HM Customs & Excise may otherwise allow, all supplies comprising in whole or in part a designated travel service made by the same tour operator shall, subject to paragraph (4) of this article, be treated as taking place at the time determined under one only of the methods specified in paragraph (2) of this article.

   (4)  Where:
   (a)  a tour operator uses the method specified in paragraph (2)(b) to determine the time of a supply; and
   (b)  payment is not received in respect of all or part of the supply; notwithstanding paragraph (3), the time of any part of that supply, which has not already been determined under paragraph (2)(b), shall be determined in accordance with paragraph (2)(a).

*Place of supply*

5  (1)  The application of sections 6 and 8 of the Value Added Tax Act 1983 shall be modified in accordance with paragraph (2) below.

   (2)  A designated travel service shall be treated as supplied in the Member State in which the tour operator has established his business or, if the supply was made from a fixed establishment, in the Member State in which the fixed establishment is situated.

230

6   [Revoked]

*Value of a designated travel service*

7   Subject to articles 8 and 9 of this Order, the value of a designated travel service shall be determined by reference to the difference between the sums paid or payable to and the sums paid or payable by the tour operator in respect of that service, calculated in such a manner as the Commissioners of HM Customs & Excise shall specify.

8   (1)   Where:

      (a)   a supply of goods or services is acquired for a consideration in money by a tour operator, for the purpose of supplying a designated travel service; and

      (b)   the value of the supply is (apart from this article) greater than its open market value; and

      (c)   the person making the supply and the tour operator to whom it is made are connected, the Commissioners of HM Customs & Excise may direct that the value of the supply shall be deemed to be its open market value for the purpose of calculating the value of the designated travel service.

   (2)   A direction under this article shall be given by notice in writing to the tour operator acquiring the supply, but no direction may be given more than three years after the time of the supply.

   (3)   A direction given to a tour operator under this paragraph, in respect of a supply acquired by him, may include a direction that the value of any supply:

      (a)   which is acquired by him after the giving of the notice, or after such later date as may be specified in the notice; and

      (b)   as to which the conditions in subparagraph (a) to (c) of paragraph (1) above are satisfied, shall be deemed to be its open market value for the purpose of calculating the value of the designated travel service.

   (4)   For the purpose of this article any question whether a person is connected with another shall be determined in accordance with section 533 of the Income and Corporation Taxes Act 1970.

9   (1)   Where:

      (a)   goods and services have been acquired prior to the commencement of this Order; and

      (b)   input tax credit has been claimed in respect of those goods and services; and

(c)   the goods and services are supplied as a designated travel service or as part of a designated travel service after the commence of this Order, article 7 of this Order shall not apply in determining the value of that part of a designated travel service referable to goods and services on which input tax has been claimed.

(2)   The value of that part of the designated travel service to which, by virtue of paragraph (1) of this article, article 7 of this Order does not apply shall be calculated in accordance with section 10 of the Value Added Tax Act 1983.

10   [Revoked]

11   [Revoked]

*Disallowance of input tax*

12   Input tax on goods or services acquired by a tour operator for resupply as a designated travel service shall be excluded from credit under sections 14 and 15 of the Value Added Tax Act 1983.

*Disqualification from membership of group of companies*

13   A tour operator shall not be eligible to be treated as a member of a group for the purposes of section 29 of the Value Added Tax Act 1983 if any other member of the proposed or existing group:
(a)   has an overseas establishment;
(b)   makes supplies outside the United Kingdom which would be taxable supplies if made within the United Kingdom; and
(c)   supplies goods or services which will become, or are intended to become, a designated travel service.

*Option not to treat supply as designated travel service*

14   (1)   Where a tour operator supplies a designated travel service he may treat that supply as not being a designated travel service if:
(a)   there are reasonable grounds for believing that the value of all such supplies in the period of one year then beginning will not exceed 1 per cent of all supplies made by him during that period; and
(b)   he makes no supplies of designated travel services consisting of accommodation or transport.

(2)   For the purposes of this article the value of any supplies shall be calculated in accordance with section 10 of the Value Added Tax Act 1983.

# Appendix 8 – TOMS: end of year calculation

## For all calculations you must use the actual figures from your financial records for the year ended

*Working out the total value of your supplies*

1    Add up the VAT inclusive selling prices of all of your supplies, or packages of supplies, that contain one or more margin scheme supplies (see Glossary of terms for margin scheme supplies). [Not reproduced here.]

Include all relevant supplies which fall within your financial year, according to the take point method you have chosen to use.

*Working out the costs of margin scheme supplies by liability of*
your *supply*

2    Add up the VAT inclusive cost to you of your **standard-rated** margin scheme supplies included in **1**.

Note: With effect from 1 January 1996 the only margin scheme supplies which may be treated as zero-rated are those which are enjoyed outside the EC.

*Working out the costs of your in-house supplies by liability of*
your *supply*

3    Add up the VAT exclusive cost to you of your **standard-rated** in-house supplies included in **1**.

Then add a percentage of that amount equivalent to the UK VAT rate (currently 17.5 per cent) to this total to give a notional **UK VAT** inclusive figure.

4    Add up the tax exclusive cost to you of your **zero-rated** in-house supplies included in **1**.

5    Add up the cost to you of your **exempt** in-house supplies included in **1**. Include any non-recoverable VAT you were charged on purchases relating to those supplies. Do not include any recoverable VAT.

*Working out the costs of your in-house supplies which are outside the scope of UK VAT*

6    Add up the cost to you of your in-house supplies which are outside the scope of UK VAT that are included in **1**. Do not include any VAT you were charged on purchases made to those supplies if it is recoverable in any country.

If you are liable to account for VAT in any other country on these supplies add to this total an uplift, using the relevant percentage VAT rate applicable in the country concerned.

## You must keep a record of how you have worked out your costs at steps 2 to 6 above

*Calculating your total margin:*

7    Totals at $2 + 3 + 4 + 5 + 6$   =   **total cost** of all relevant supplies.

8    Total at **1** − total at **7**   =   **total margin** for both margin scheme and in-house supplies.

*Apportioning the margin:*

9    $\dfrac{\text{Total at } \mathbf{2} \times \text{Total at } \mathbf{8}}{\text{Total at } \mathbf{7}}$   =   margin relating to **standard-rated** margin scheme supplies

10   $\dfrac{\text{Total at } \mathbf{3} \times \text{Total at } \mathbf{8}}{\text{Total at } \mathbf{7}}$   =   margin relating to **standard-rated in-house** supplies

11   $\dfrac{\text{Total at } \mathbf{4} \times \text{Total at } \mathbf{8}}{\text{Total at } \mathbf{7}}$   =   margin relating to **zero-rated in-house** supplies

12   $\dfrac{\text{Total at } \mathbf{5} \times \text{Total at } \mathbf{8}}{\text{Total at } \mathbf{7}}$   =   margin relating to **exempt in-house** supplies

13   $\dfrac{\text{Total at } \mathbf{6} \times \text{Total at } \mathbf{8}}{\text{Total at } \mathbf{7}}$   =   margin relating to supplies **outside the scope** of UK VAT.

*Calculating out output tax:*

14   Total at **9** × VAT fraction   =   **output tax due** on your standard-rated margin scheme supplies.

234

15   (Total at **3** + total at **10**)    =   **output tax due** on your standard-rated
    × VAT fraction               in-house supplies.

## Calculating sales values for VAT:

16   Total at **9** – Total at **14**    =   **Value for VAT** of your standard-rated
                                     margin scheme supplies.

17   Total at **3** + Total at **10**    =   **Value for VAT** of your standard-rated
    – Total at **15**               in-house supplies.

18   Total at **4** + Total at **11**    =   **Value for VAT** of your zero-rated in-
                                     house supplies.

19   Total at **5** + Total at **12**    =   **Value for VAT** of your exempt in-house
                                     supplies.

20   Total at **10** + Total at **13**    =   **Value of in-house supplies** which are
                                     outside the scope of UK VAT.

## Working out your annual adjustment:

21   Total at **14** + Total at **15**    =   **Total output tax due for the year.**

22   Add up the provisional output tax accounted for on your VAT returns
    during your financial year.

23   Total at **21** – Total at **22**    =   **VAT payable/deductible** to be included
                                     on your **VAT return** for the VAT period
                                     immediately following the end of your
                                     financial year.

## The steps of the calculation are as follows:

Step 1          =   total value of supplies.

Step 2          =   costs of margin scheme supplies.

Steps 3 to 6    =   costs of in-house supplies.

Steps 7 to 20   =   calculation of the margin and output tax due.

Steps 21 to 23  =   working out the annual adjustment.

You will need to use all 23 steps of the calculation for travel packages which include standard-rated, zero-rated and exempt margin scheme supplies and standard-rated, zero-rated, exempt, and outside the scope of in-house supplies. If you do not make all of these different types of supplies you will be able to omit some steps from the calculation.

*Example:*   If you do not make any standard-rated in-house supplies you need not carry out steps 3, 10, 15 or 17.

Though the steps of the calculation are numbered 1 to 23 provided you use the method shown it is not necessary to use the same step references or to carry them out in the same order.

# Appendix 9 – Provisional margins and output tax for the next year

First complete the procedure in Appendix 8.

*Working out your provisional percentages:*

1   Add the totals at **3, 9 and 10**        = VAT inclusive value of your
                                              **standard-rated** supplies.

2   $\dfrac{\text{Total at } \mathbf{1} \text{ above} \times 100}{\text{Total at Step } \mathbf{1} \text{ of Appendix 4}}$        =                          _____%

3   Add the totals at **18, 19 and 20**       = value of your **zero-rated,**
    of Appendix 4                              **exempt and outside the scope**
                                               supplies

4   $\dfrac{\text{Total of } \mathbf{3} \text{ above} \times 100}{\text{Total at Step } \mathbf{1} \text{ of Appendix 4}}$        =                          _____%

*Each VAT period you must apply these percentages to the total of any sales containing margin scheme supplies as follows:*

*Working out the VAT return figures:*

5   Add up the total selling prices of all your supplies in the period (i.e., sales with a tax point falling within that period) that contained one or more margin scheme supplies.

6   Total at **5** above × **% at 2 above**   = provisional **VAT inclusive** value of your **standard-rated** supplies.

7   Total at **6** above × VAT fraction       = provisional **output tax** to be
    (see Glossary)                             included on your **VAT return**.

*Provisional margins and output tax for the next year*

8     Total at **6** above – Total at **7** above    = provisional **VAT exclusive** value of your **standard-rated** supplies.

9     Total at **5** above × % **at 4 above**    = provisional value of your **zero-rated, exempt and outside the scope** supplies.

10   Add the totals at **8 and 9** above    = VAT exclusive value of supplies to be included in the outputs box of your VAT return.

*You must repeat the procedure in steps 5 to 10 at the end of each tax period.*

You must account for VAT in the normal way in each tax period, on any other standard-rated supplies that you make in the UK which are not included in Step 1 of Appendix 8.

# Appendix 10 – The Package Travel, Package Holidays and Package Tours Regulations 1992

| | |
|---|---|
| *Made* | *22nd December 1992* |
| *Coming into force* | *23rd December 1992* |

Whereas the Secretary of State is a Minister designated**(a)** for the purposes of section 2(2) of the European Communities Act 1972**(b)** in relation to measures relating to consumer protection as regards package travel, package holidays and package tours;

And whereas a draft of these Regulations has been approved by a resolution of each House of Parliament pursuant to section 2(2) of and paragraph 2(2) of Schedule 2 to that Act;

Now, therefore the Secretary of State in exercise of the powers conferred on him by section 2(2) of that Act hereby makes the following Regulations:

## Citation and commencement
1.   These Regulations may be cited as the Package Travel, Package Holidays and Package Tours Regulations 1992 and shall come into force on the day after the day on which they are made.

## Interpretation
2.—(1)  In these Regulations—

"brochure" means any brochure in which packages are offered for sale;

"contract" means the agreement linking the consumer to the organiser or to the retailer, or to both, as the case may be;

"the Directive" means Council Directive 90/314/EEC on package travel, package holidays and package tours;

"offer" includes an invitation to treat whether by means of advertising or otherwise, and cognate expressions shall be construed accordingly;

(a)   S.I. 1991/755.
(b)   1972 c.68.

239

"organiser" means the person who, otherwise than occasionally, organises packages and sells or offers them for sale, whether directly or through a retailer;

"the other party to the contract" means the party, other than the consumer, to the contract, that is, the organiser or the retailer, or both, as the case may be;

"package" means the pre-arranged combination of at least two of the following components when sold or offered for sale at an inclusive price and when the service covers a period of more than twenty-four hours or includes overnight accommodation:—

(a) transport;
(b) accommodation;
(c) other tourist services not ancillary to transport or accommodation and accounting for a significant proportion of the package,
   and
   (i) the submission of separate accounts for different components shall not cause the arrangements to be other than a package;
   (ii) the fact that a combination is arranged at the request of the consumer and in accordance with his specific instructions (whether modified or not) shall not of itself cause it to be treated as other than pre-arranged;

and

"retailer" means the person who sells or offers for sale the package put together by the organiser.

(2) In the definition of "contract" in paragraph (1) above, "consumer" means the person who takes or agrees to take the package ("the principal contractor") and elsewhere in these Regulations "consumer" means, as the context requires, the principal contractor, any person on whose behalf the principal contractor agrees to purchase the package ("the other beneficiaries") or any person to whom the principal contractor or any of the other beneficiaries transfers the package ("the transferee").

**Application of Regulations**

**3.**—(1) These Regulations apply to packages sold or offered for sale in the territory of the United Kingdom.

(2) Regulations 4 to 15 apply to packages so sold or offered for sale on or after 31st December 1992.

(3) Regulations 16 to 22 apply to contracts which, in whole or part, remain to be performed on 31st December 1992.

**Descriptive matter relating to packages must not be misleading**

**4.**—(1)  No organiser or retailer shall supply to a consumer any descriptive matter concerning a package, the price of a package or any other conditions applying to the contract which contains any misleading information.

(2)  If an organiser or retailer is in breach of paragraph (1) he shall be liable to compensate the consumer for any loss which the consumer suffers in consequence.

**Requirements as to brochures**

**5.**—(1)  Subject to paragraph (4) below, no organiser shall make available a brochure to a possible consumer unless it indicates in a legible, comprehensible and accurate manner the price and adequate information about the matter specified in Schedule 1 to these Regulations in respect of the packages offered for sale in the brochure to the extent that those matters are relevant to the packages so offered.

(2)  Subject to paragraph (4) below, no retailer shall make available to a possible consumer a brochure which he knows or has reasonable cause to believe does not comply with the requirements of paragraph (1).

(3)  An organiser who contravenes paragraph (1) of this regulation and a retailer who contravenes paragraph (2) thereof shall be guilty of an offence and liable:—

  (a)  on summary conviction, to a fine not exceeding level 5 on the standard scale; and

  (b)  on conviction on indictment, to a fine.

(4)  Where a brochure was first made available to consumers generally before 31st December 1992 no liability shall arise under this regulation in respect of an identical brochure being made available to a consumer at any time.

**Circumstances in which particulars in brochure are to be binding**

**6.**—(1)  Subject to paragraphs (2) and (3) of this regulation, the particulars in the brochure (whether or not they are required by regulation 5(1) above to be included in the brochure) shall constitute implied warranties (or, as regards Scotland, implied terms) for the purposes of any contract to which the particulars relate.

(2)  Paragraph (1) of this regulation does not apply—

  (a)  in relation to information required to be included by virtue of paragraph 9 of Schedule 1 to these Regulations; or

  (b)  where the brochure contains an express statement that changes may be made in the particulars contained in it before a contract is concluded and changes in the particulars so contained are clearly communicated to the consumer before a contract is concluded.

(3)  Paragraph (1) of this regulation does not apply when the consumer and the other party to the contract agree after the contract has been made

that the particulars in the brochure, or some of those particulars, should not form part of the contract.

**Information to be provided before contract is concluded**

**7.**—(1)  Before a contract is concluded, the other party to the contract shall provide the intending consumer with the information specified in paragraph (2) below in writing or in some other appropriate form.

(2)  The information referred to in paragraph (1) is:—

    (a)   general information about passport and visa requirements which apply to British Citizens who purchase the package in question, including information about the length of time it is likely to take to obtain the appropriate passports and visas;

    (b)   information about health formalities required for the journey and the stay; and

    (c)   the arrangements for security for the money paid over and (where applicable) for the repatriation of the consumer in the event of insolvency.

(3)  If the intending consumer is not provided with the information required by paragraph (1) in accordance with that paragraph the other party to the contract shall be guilty of an offence and liable:—

    (a)   on summary conviction, to a fine not exceeding level 5 on the standard scale; and

    (b)   on conviction on indictment, to a fine.

**Information to be provided in good time**

**8.**—(1)  The other party to the contract shall in good time before the start of the journey provide the consumer with the information specified in paragraph (2) below in writing or in some other appropriate form.

(2)  The information referred to in paragraph (1) is the following:—

    (a)   the times and places of intermediate stops and transport connections and particulars of the place to be occupied by the traveller (for example, cabin or berth on ship, sleeper compartment on train);

    (b)   the name, address and telephone number—

        (i)  of the representative of the other party to the contract in the locality where the consumer is to stay,

        or, if there is no such representative,

        (ii)  of an agency in that locality on whose assistance a consumer in difficulty would be able to call,

        or, if there is no such representative or agency, a telephone number or other information which will enable the consumer to contact the other party to the contract during the stay; and

    (c)   in the case of a journey or stay abroad by a child under the age of 16 on the day when the journey or stay is due to start, information enabling direct contact to be made with the child or the person responsible at the place where he is to stay; and

(d) except where the consumer is required as a term of the contract to take out an insurance policy in order to cover the cost of cancellation by the consumer or the cost of assistance, including repatriation, in the event of accident or illness, information about an insurance policy which the consumer may, if he wishes, take out in respect of the risk of those costs being incurred.

(3) If the consumer is not provided with the information required by paragraph (1) in accordance with that paragraph the other party to the contract shall be guilty of an offence and liable:—

(a) on summary conviction, to a fine not exceeding level 5 on the standard scale; and

(b) on conviction on indictment, to a fine.

**Contents and form of contract**

**9.**—(1) The other party to the contract shall ensure that—

(a) depending on the nature of the package being purchased, the contract contains at least the elements specified in Schedule 2 to these Regulations;

(b) subject to paragraph (2) below, all the terms of the contract are set out in writing or such other form as is comprehensible and accessible to the consumer and are communicated to the consumer before the contract is made; and

(c) a written copy of these terms is supplied to the consumer.

(2) Paragraph (1)(b) above does not apply when the interval between the time when the consumer approaches the other party to the contract with a view to entering into a contract and the time of departure under the proposed contract is so short that it is impracticable to comply with the sub-paragraph.

(3) It is an implied condition (or, as regards Scotland, an implied term) of the contract that the other party to the contract complies with the provisions of paragraph (1).

(4) In Scotland, any breach of the condition implied by paragraph (3) above shall be deemed to be a material breach justifying rescission of the contract.

**Transfer of bookings**

**10.**—(1) In every contract there is an implied term that where the consumer is prevented from proceeding with the package the consumer may transfer his booking to a person who satisfies all the conditions applicable to the package, provided that the consumer gives reasonable notice to the other party to the contract of his intention to transfer before the date when departure is due to take place.

(2) Where a transfer is made in accordance with the implied term set out in paragraph (1) above, the transferor and the transferee shall be jointly and severally liable to the other party to the contract for payment of the price of the package (or, if part of the price has been paid, for payment of the balance) and for any additional costs arising from such transfer.

**Price revision**

**11.**—(1) Any term in a contract to the effect that the prices laid down in the contract may be revised shall be void and of no effect unless the contract provides for the possibility of upward or downward revision and satisfies the conditions laid down in paragraph (2) below.

    (2) The conditions mentioned in paragraph (1) are that—

      (a)  the contract states precisely how the revised price is to be calculated;

      (b)  the contract provides that price revisions are to be made solely to allow for variations in:—

          (i)   transportation costs, including the cost of fuel,

          (ii)  dues, taxes or fees chargeable for services such as landing taxes or embarkation or disembarkation fees at ports and airports, or

          (iii) the exchange rates applied to the particular package; and

    (3) Notwithstanding any terms of a contract,

      (i)   no price increase may be made in a specified period which may not be less than 30 days before the departure date stipulated; and

      (ii)  as against an individual consumer liable under the contract, no price increase may be made in respect of variations which would produce an increase of less than 2%, or such greater percentage as the contract may specify, ("non-eligible variations") and that the non-eligible variations shall be left out of account in the calculation.

**Significant alterations to essential terms**

**12.**   In every contract there are implied terms to the effect that—

      (a)  where the organiser is constrained before the departure to alter significantly an essential term of the contract, such as the price (so far as regulation 11 permits them to do so), he will notify the consumer as quickly as possible in order to enable him to take appropriate decisions and in particular to withdraw from the contract without penalty or to accept a rider to the contract specifying the alterations made and their impact on the price; and

      (b)  the consumer will inform the organiser or the retailer of his decision as soon as possible.

**Withdrawal by consumer pursuant to regulation 12 and cancellation by organiser**

**13.**—(1)  The terms set out in paragraphs (2) and (3) below are implied in every contract and apply where the consumer withdraws from the contract pursuant to the term in it implied by virtue of regulation 12(a), or where the organiser, for any reason other than the fault of the consumer, cancels the package before the agreed date of departure.

(2)  The consumer is entitled—

(a)  to take a substitute package of equivalent or superior quality if the other party to the contract is able to offer him such a substitute; or

(b)  to take a substitute package of lower quality if the other party to the contract is able to offer him one and to recover from the organiser the difference in price between the price of the package purchased and that of the substitute package; or

(c)  to have repaid to him as soon as possible all the monies paid by him under the contract.

(3)  The consumer is entitled, if appropriate, to be compensated by the organiser for non-performance of the contract except where—

(a)  the package is cancelled because the number of persons who agree to take it is less than the minimum number required and the consumer is informed of the cancellation, in writing, within the period indicated in the description of the package; or

(b)  the package is cancelled by reason of unusual and unforeseeable circumstances beyond the control of the party by whom this exception is pleaded, the consequences of which could not have been avoided even if all due care had been exercised.

(4)  Overbooking shall not be regarded as a circumstance falling within the provisions of sub-paragraph (b) of paragraph (3) above.

**Significant proportion of services not provided**

**14.**—(1)  The terms set out in paragraphs (2) and (3) below are implied in every contract and apply where, after departure, a significant proportion of the services contracted for is not provided or the organiser becomes aware that he will be unable to procure a significant proportion of the services to be provided.

(2)  The organiser will make suitable alternative arrangements, at no extra cost to the consumer, for the continuation of the package and will, where appropriate, compensate the consumer for the difference between the services to be supplied under the contract and those supplied.

(3)  If it is impossible to make arrangements as described in paragraph (2), or these are not accepted by the consumer for good reasons, the organiser will, where appropriate, provide the consumer with equivalent transport back to the place of departure or to another place to which the

consumer has agreed and will, where appropriate, compensate the consumer.

### Liability of other party to the contract for proper performance of obligations under contract

**15.**—(1)  The other party to the contract is liable to the consumer for the proper performance of the obligations under the contract, irrespective of whether such obligations are to be performed by that other party or by other suppliers of services but this shall not affect any remedy or right of action which that other party may have against those other suppliers of services.

(2)  The other party to the contract is liable to the consumer for any damage caused to him by the failure to perform the contract or the improper performance of the contract unless the failure or the improper performance is due neither to any fault of that other party nor to that of another supplier of services, because—

    (a)   the failures which occur in the performance of the contract are attributable to the consumer;

    (b)   such failures are attributable to a third party unconnected with the provision of the services contracted for, and are unforeseeable or unavoidable; or

    (c)   such failures are due to—

        (i)   unusual and unforeseeable circumstances beyond the control of the party by whom this exception is pleaded, the consequences of which could not have been avoided even if all due care had been exercised; or

        (ii)  an event which the other party to the contract or the supplier of services, even with all due care, could not foresee or forestall.

(3)  In the case of damage arising from the non-performance or improper performance of the services involved in the package, the contract may provide for compensation to be limited in accordance with the international conventions which govern such services.

(4)  In the case of damage other than personal injury resulting from the non-performance or improper performance of the services involved in the package, the contract may include a term limiting the amount of compensation which will be paid to the consumer, provided that the limitation is not unreasonable.

(5)  Without prejudice to paragraph (3) and paragraph (4) above, liability under paragraphs (1) and (2) above cannot be excluded by any contractual term.

(6)  The terms set out in paragraphs (7) and (8) below are implied in every contract.

(7)  In the circumstances described in paragraph (2)(b) and (c) of this

regulation, the other party to the contract will give prompt assistance to a consumer in difficulty.

(8) If the consumer complains about a defect in the performance of the contract, the other party to the contract, or his local representative, if there is one, will make prompt efforts to find appropriate solutions.

(9) The contract must clearly and explicitly oblige the consumer to communicate at the earliest opportunity, in writing or any other appropriate form, to the supplier of the services concerned and to the other party to the contract any failure which he perceives at the place where the services concerned are supplied.

### Security in event of insolvency—requirements and offences

**16.**—(1) The other party to the contract shall at all times be able to provide sufficient evidence of security for the refund of money paid over and for the repatriation of the consumer in the event of insolvency.

(2) Without prejudice to paragraph (1) above, and subject to paragraph (4) below, save to the extent that—

    (a)    the package is covered by measures adopted or retained by the member State where he is established for the purpose of implementing Article 7 of the Directive; or

    (b)    the package is one in respect of which he is required to hold a licence under the Civil Aviation (Air Travel Organisers' Licensing) Regulations 1972**(a)** or the package is one that is covered by the arrangements he has entered into for the purposes of those Regulations,

the other party to the contract shall at least ensure that there are in force arrangements as described in regulations 17, 18, 19 or 20 or, if that party is acting otherwise than in the course of business, as described in any of those regulations or in regulation 21.

(3) Any person who contravenes paragraph (1) or (2) of this regulation shall be guilty of an offence and liable:—

    (a)    on summary conviction to a fine not exceeding level 5 on the standard scale; and

    (b)    on conviction on indictment, to a fine.

(4) A person shall not be guilty of an offence under paragraph (3) above by reason only of the fact that arrangements such as are mentioned in paragraph (2) above are not in force in respect of any period before 1 April 1993 unless money paid over is not refunded when it is due or the consumer is not repatriated in the event of insolvency.

(5) For the purposes of regulations 17 to 21 below a contract shall be treated as having been fully performed if the package or, as the case may

---

**(a)** S.I. 1972/223.

be, the part of the package has been completed irrespective of whether the obligations under the contract have been properly performed for the purposes of regulation 15.

### Bonding

**17.**—(1) The other party to the contract shall ensure that a bond is entered into by an authorised institution under which the institution binds itself to pay to an approved body of which that other party is a member a sum calculated in accordance with paragraph (3) below in the event of the insolvency of that other party.

(2) Any bond entered into pursuant to paragraph (1) above shall not be expressed to be in force for a period exceeding eighteen months.

(3) The sum referred to in paragraph (1) above shall be such sum as may reasonably be expected to enable all monies paid over by consumers under or in contemplation of contracts for relevant packages which have not been fully performed to be repaid and shall not in any event be a sum which is less than the minimum sum calculated in accordance with paragraph (4) below.

(4) The minimum sum for the purposes of paragraph (3) above shall be a sum which represents:—

   (a)   not less than 25% of all the payments which the other party to the contract estimates that he will receive under or in contemplation of contracts for relevant packages in the twelve month period from the date of entry into force of the bond referred to in paragraph (1) above; or

   (b)   the maximum amount of all the payments which the other party to the contract expects to hold at any one time, in respect of contracts which have not been fully performed,

whichever sum is the smaller.

(5) Before a bond is entered into pursuant to paragraph (1) above, the other party to the contract shall inform the approved body of which he is a member of the minimum sum which he proposes for the purposes of paragraphs (3) and (4) above and it shall be the duty of the approved body to consider whether such sum is sufficient for the purpose mentioned in paragraph (3) and, if it does not consider that this is the case, it shall be the duty of the approved body so to inform the other party to the contract and to inform him of the sum which, in the opinion of the approved body, is sufficient for that purpose.

(6) Where an approved body has informed the other party to the contract of a sum pursuant to paragraph (5) above, the minimum sum for the purposes of paragraphs (3) and (4) above shall be that sum.

(7) In this regulation—

"approved body" means a body which is for the time being approved by the Secretary of State for the purposes of this regulation;

"authorised institution" means a person authorised under the law of a member State to carry on the business of entering into bonds of the kind required by this regulation.

**Bonding where approved body has reserve fund or insurance**
**18.**—(1) The other party to the contract shall ensure that a bond is entered into by an authorised institution, under which the institution agrees to pay to an approved body of which that other party is a member a sum calculated in accordance with paragraph (3) below in the event of the insolvency of that other party.

(2) Any bond entered into pursuant to paragraph (1) above shall not be expressed to be in force for a period exceeding eighteen months.

(3) The sum referred to in paragraph (1) above shall be such sum as may be specified by the approved body as representing the lesser of—
    (a)  the maximum amount of all the payments which the other party to the contract expects to hold at any one time in respect of contracts which have not been fully performed; or
    (b)  the minimum sum calculated in accordance with paragraph (4) below.

(4) The minimum sum for the purposes of paragraph (3) above shall be a sum which represents not less than 10% of all the payments which the other party to the contract estimates that he will receive under or in contemplation of contracts for relevant packages in the twelve month period from the date of entry referred to in paragraph (1) above.

(5) In this regulation "approved body" means a body which is for the time being approved by the Secretary of State for the purposes of this regulation and no such approval shall be given unless the conditions mentioned in paragraph (6) below are satisfied in relation to it.

(6) A body may not be approved for the purposes of this regulation unless—
    (a)  it has a reserve fund or insurance cover with an insurer authorised in respect of such business in a member State of an amount in each case which is designed to enable all monies paid over to a member of the body of consumers under or in contemplation of contracts for relevant packages which have not been fully performed to be repaid to those consumers in the event of the insolvency of the member; and
    (b)  where it has a reserve fund, it agrees that the fund will be held by persons and in a manner approved by the Secretary of State.

(7) In this regulation, authorised institution has the meaning given to that expression by paragraph (7) of regulation 17.

**Insurance**
**19.**—(1) The other party to the contract shall have insurance under one or

249

more appropriate policies with an insurer authorised in respect of such business in a member State under which the insurer agrees to indemnify consumers, who shall be insured persons under the policy, against the loss of money paid over by them under or in contemplation of contracts for packages in the event of the insolvency of the contractor.

(2) The other party to the contract shall ensure that it is a term of every contract with a consumer that the consumer acquires the benefit of a policy of a kind mentioned in paragraph (1) above in the event of the insolvency of the other party to the contract.

(3) In this regulation:

"appropriate policy" means one which does not contain a condition which provides (in whatever terms) that no liability shall arise under the policy, or that any liability so arising shall cease:—

  (i)   in the event of some specified thing being done or omitted to be done after the happening of the event giving rise to a claim under the policy;
  (ii)  in the event of the policy holder not making payments under or in connection with other policies; or
  (iii) unless the policy holder keeps specified records or provides the insurer with or makes available to him information therefrom.

**Monies in trust**
**20.**—(1) The other party to the contract shall ensure that all monies paid over by a consumer under or in contemplation of a contract for a relevant package are held in the United Kingdom by a person as trustee for the consumer until the contract has been fully performed or any sum of money paid by the consumer in respect of the contract has been repaid to him or has been forfeited on cancellation by the consumer.

(2) The costs of administering the trust mentioned in paragraph (1) above shall be paid for by the other party to the contract.

(3) Any interest which is earned on the monies held by the trustee pursuant to paragraph (1) shall be held for the other party to the contract and shall be payable to him on demand.

(4) Where there is produced to the trustee a statement signed by the other party to the contract to the effect that—

  (a)  a contract for a package the price of which is specified in that statement has been fully performed;
  (b)  the other party to the contract has repaid to the consumer a sum of money specified in that statement which the consumer had paid in respect of a contract for a package; or
  (c)  the consumer has on cancellation forfeited a sum of money specified in that statement which he had paid in respect of a contract for a relevant package,

the trustee shall (subject to paragraph (5) below) release to the other party to the contract the sum specified in the statement.

(5) Where the trustee considers it appropriate to do so, he may require the other party to the contract to provide further information or evidence of the matters mentioned in sub-paragraph (a), (b) or (c) of paragraph (4) above before he releases any sum to that other party pursuant to that paragraph.

(6) Subject to paragraph (7) below, in the event of the insolvency of the other party to the contract the monies held in trust by the trustee pursuant to paragraph (1) of this regulation shall be applied to meet the claims of consumers who are creditors of that other party in respect of contracts for packages in respect of which the arrangements were established and which have not been fully performed and, if there is a surplus after those claims have been met, it shall form part of the estate of that insolvent other party for the purposes of insolvency law.

(7) If the monies held in trust by the trustee pursuant to paragraph (1) of this regulation are insufficient to meet the claims of consumers as described in paragraph (6), payments to those consumers shall be made by the trustee on a pari passu basis.

**Monies in trust where other party to contract is acting otherwise than in the course of business**

**21.**—(1) The other party to the contract shall ensure that all monies paid over by a consumer under or in contemplation of a contract for a relevant package are held in the United Kingdom by a person as trustee for the consumer for the purpose of paying for the consumer's package.

(2) The costs of administering the trust mentioned in paragraph (1) shall be paid for out of the monies held in trust and the interest earned on those monies.

(3) Where there is produced to the trustee a statement signed by the other party to the contract to the effect that—

    (a)    the consumer has previously paid over a sum of money specified in that statement in respect of a contract for a package and that sum is required for the purpose of paying for a component (or part of a component) of the package;

    (b)    the consumer has previously paid over a sum of money specified in that statement in respect of a contract for a package and the other party to the contract has paid that sum in respect of a component (or part of a component) of the package;

    (c)    the consumer requires the repayment to him of a sum of money specified in that statement which was previously paid over by the consumer in respect of a contract for a package; or

    (d)    the consumer has on cancellation forfeited a sum of money specified in that statement which he had paid in respect of a contract for a package, the trustee shall (subject to paragraph (4) below) release to the other party to the contract the sum specified in the statement.

(4) Where the trustee considers it appropriate to do so, he may require the other party to the contract to provide further information or evidence of the matters mentioned in sub-paragraph (a), (b), (c) or (d) of paragraph (3) above before he releases to that other party any sum from the monies held in trust for the consumer.

(5) Subject to paragraph (6) below, in the event of the insolvency of the other party to the contract and of contracts for packages not being fully performed (whether before or after the insolvency) the monies held in trust by the trustee pursuant to paragraph (1) of this regulation shall be applied to meet the claims of consumers who are creditors of that other party in respect of amounts paid over by them and remaining in the trust fund after deductions have been made in respect of amounts released to that other party pursuant to paragraph (3) and, if there is a surplus after those claims have been met, it shall be divided amongst those consumers pro rata.

(6) If the monies held in trust by the trustee pursuant to paragraph (1) of this regulation are insufficient to meet the claims of consumers as described in paragraph (5) above, payments to those consumers shall be made by the trustee on a pari passu basis.

(7) Any sums remaining after all the packages in respect of which the arrangements were established have been fully performed shall be dealt with as provided in the arrangements or, in default of such provision, may be paid to the other party to the contract.

**Offences arising from breach of regulations 20 and 21**
**22.**—(1) If the other party to the contract makes a false statement under paragraph (4) of regulation 20 or paragraph (3) of regulation 21 he shall be guilty of an offence.

(2) If the other party to the contract applies monies released to him on the basis of a statement made by him under regulation 21(3)(a) or (c) for a purpose other than that mentioned in the statement he shall be guilty of an offence.

(3) If the other party to the contract is guilty of an offence under paragraph (1) or (2) of this regulation shall be liable—
   (a) on summary conviction to a fine not exceeding level 5 on the standard scale; and
   (b) on conviction on indictment, to a fine.

**Enforcement**
**23.** Schedule 3 to these Regulations (which makes provision about the enforcement of regulations 5, 7, 8, 16 and 22 of these Regulations) shall have effect.

**Due diligence defence**

**24.**—(1) Subject to the following provisions of this regulation, in proceedings against any person for an offence under regulation 5, 7, 8, 16 or 22 of these Regulations, it shall be a defence for that person to show that he took all reasonable steps and exercised all due diligence to avoid committing the offence.

(2) Where in any proceedings against any person for such an offence the defence provided by paragraph (1) above involves an allegation that the commission of the offence was due—

    (a)   to the act or default of another; or,

    (b)   to reliance on information given by another,

that person shall not, without the leave of the court, be entitled to rely on the defence unless, not less than seven clear days before the hearing of the proceedings, or, in Scotland, the trial diet, he has served a notice under paragraph (3) below on the person bringing the proceedings.

(3) A notice under this paragraph shall give such information identifying or assisting in the identification of the person who committed the act or default or gave the information as is in the possession of the person serving the notice at the time he serves it.

(4) It is hereby declared that a person shall not be entitled to rely on the defence provided by paragraph (1) above by reason of his reliance on information supplied by another, unless he shows that it was reasonable in all the circumstances for him to have relied on the information, having regard in particular—

    (a)   to the steps which he took, and those which might reasonably have been taken, for the purpose of verifying the information; and

    (b)   to whether he had any reason to disbelieve the information.

**Liability of persons other than principal offender**

**25.**—(1) Where the commission by any person of an offence under regulation 5, 7, 8, 16 or 22 of these Regulations is due to an act or default committed by some other person in the course of any business of his, the other person shall be guilty of the offence and may be proceeded against and punished by virtue of this paragraph whether or not proceedings are taken against the first-mentioned person.

(2) Where a body corporate is guilty of an offence under any of the provisions mentioned in paragraph (1) above (including where it is so guilty by virtue of the said paragraph (1)) in respect of any act or default which is shown to have been committed with the consent or connivance of, or to be attributable to any neglect on the part of, any director, manager, secretary or other similar officer of the body corporate or any person who was purporting to act in any such capacity he, as well as the body corporate, shall be guilty of that offence and shall be liable to be proceeded against and punished accordingly.

(3) Where the affairs of a body corporate are managed by its members, paragraph (2) above shall apply in relation to the acts and defaults of a member in connection with his functions of management as if he were a director of the body corporate.

(4) Where an offence under any of the provisions mentioned in paragraph (1) above committed in Scotland by a Scottish partnership is proved to have been committed with the consent or connivance of, or to be attributable to neglect on the part of, a partner, he (as well as the partnership) is guilty of the offence and liable to be proceeded against and punished accordingly.

(5) On proceedings for an offence under regulation 5 by virtue of paragraph (1) above committed by the making available of a brochure it shall be a defence for the person charged to prove that he is a person whose business it is to publish or arrange for the publication of brochures and that he received the brochure for publication in the ordinary course of business and did not know and had no reason to suspect that its publication would amount to an offence under these Regulations.

## Prosecution time limit

**26.**—(1) No proceedings for an offence under regulations 5, 7, 8, 16 or 22 of these Regulations or under paragraph 5(3), 6 or 7 of Schedule 3 thereto shall be commenced after:

   (a)   the end of the period of three years beginning within the date of the commission of the offence; or

   (b)   the end of the period of one year beginning with the date of the discovery of the offence by the prosecutor,

whichever is the earlier.

(2) For the purposes of this regulation a certificate signed by or on behalf of the prosecutor and stating the date on which the offence was discovered by him shall be conclusive evidence of that fact; and a certificate stating that matter and purporting to be so signed shall be treated as so signed unless the contrary is proved.

(3) In relation to proceedings in Scotland, subsection (3) of section 331 of the Criminal Procedure (Scotland) Act 1975 (date of commencement of proceedings) **(a)** shall apply for the purposes of this regulation as it applies for the purposes of that section.

## Saving for civil consequences

**27.**   No contract shall be void or unenforceable, and no right of action in civil proceedings in respect of any loss shall arise, by reason only of the commission of an offence under regulations 5, 7, 8, 16 or 22 of these Regulations.

**(a)**     1975 c.21.

**Terms implied in contract**

**28.** Where it is provided in these Regulations that a term (whether so described or whether described as a condition or warranty) is implied in the contract it is so implied irrespective of the law which governs the contract.

*Denton of Wakefield*
Parliamentary Under-Secretary of State,
22 December 1992            Department of Trade and Industry

SCHEDULE 1            Regulation 5

**Information to be included (in addition to the price) in brochures where relevant to packages offered**

1. The destination and the means, characteristics and categories of transport used.

2. The type of accommodation, its location, category or degree of comfort and its main features and, where the accommodation is to be provided in a member State, its approval or tourist classification under the rules of that member State.

3. The meals which are included in the package.

4. The itinerary.

5. General information about passport and visa requirements which apply for British citizens and health formalities required for the journey and the stay.

6. Either the monetary amount or the percentage of the price which is to be paid on account and the timetable for payment of the balance.

7. Whether a minimum number of persons is required for the package to take place and, if so, the deadline for informing the consumer in the event of cancellation.

8. The arrangements (if any) which apply if consumers are delayed at the outward or homeward points of departure.

9. The arrangements for security for money paid over and for the repatriation of the consumer in the event of insolvency.

SCHEDULE 2            Regulation 9

**Elements to be included in the contract if relevant to the particular package**

1. The travel destination(s) and, where periods of stay are involved, the relevant periods, with dates.

2. The means, characteristics and categories of transport to be used and the dates, times and points of departure and return.

3. Where the package includes accommodation, its location, its tourist category or degree of comfort, its main features and, where the accommodation is to be provided in a member State, its compliance with the rules of that member State.

4. The meals which are included in the package.

5. Whether a minimum number of persons is required for the package to take place and, if so, the deadline for informing the consumer in the event of cancellation.

6. The itinerary.

7. Visits, excursions or other services which are included in the total price agreed for the package.

8. The name and address of the organiser, the retailer and, where appropriate, the insurer.

9. The price of the package, if the price may be revised in accordance with the term which may be included in the contract under regulation 11, an indication of the possibility of such price revisions, and an indication of any dues, taxes or fees chargeable for certain services (landing, embarkation or disembarkation fees at ports and airports and tourist taxes) where such costs are not included in the package.

10. The payment schedule and method of payment.

11. Special requirements which the consumer has communicated to the organiser or retailer when making the booking and which both have accepted.

12. The periods within which the consumer must make any complaint about the failure to perform or the inadequate performance of the contract.

SCHEDULE 3       Regulation 23

ENFORCEMENT

**Enforcement authority**

1.—(1) Every local weights and measures authority in Great Britain shall be an enforcement authority for the purposes of regulations 5, 7, 8, 16 and 22 of these Regulations ("the relevant regulations"), and it shall be the duty of each such authority to enforce those provisions within their area.

(2) The Department of Economic Development in Northern Ireland shall be an enforcement authority for the purposes of the relevant regulations, and it shall be the duty of the Department to enforce those provisions within Northern Ireland.

**Prosecutions**

2.—(1) Where an enforcement authority in England or Wales proposes to institute proceedings for an offence under any of the relevant regulations, it shall as between the enforcement authority and the Director General of Fair Trading be the duty of the enforcement authority to give to the Director General of Fair Trading notice of the intended proceedings, together with a summary of the facts on which the charges are to be founded, and to postpone institution of the proceedings until either—

(a) twenty-eight days have elapsed since the giving of that notice; or

(b) the Director General of Fair Trading has notified the enforcement authority that he has received the notice and the summary of the facts.

(2) Nothing in paragraph 1 above shall authorise a local weights and measures authority to bring proceedings in Scotland for an offence.

**Powers of officers of enforcement authority**

**3.**—(1) If a duly authorised officer of an enforcement authority has reasonable grounds for suspecting that an offence has been committed under any of the relevant regulations, he may—

(a) require a person whom he believes on reasonable grounds to be engaged in the organisation or retailing of packages to produce any book or document relating to the activity and take copies of it or any entry in it, or

(b) require such a person to produce in a visible and legible documentary form any information so relating which is contained in a computer, and take copies of it,

for the purpose of ascertaining whether such an offence has been committed.

(2) Such an officer may inspect any goods for the purpose of ascertaining whether such an offence has been committed.

(3) If such an officer has reasonable grounds for believing that any documents or goods may be required as evidence in proceedings for such an offence, he may seize and detain them.

(4) An officer seizing any documents or goods in the exercise of his power under sub-paragraph (3) above shall inform the person from whom they are seized.

(5) The powers of an officer under this paragraph may be exercised by him only at a reasonable hour and on production (if required) of his credentials.

(6) Nothing in this paragraph—

(a) requires a person to produce a document if he would be entitled to refuse to produce it in proceedings in a court on the ground that it is the subject of legal professional privilege or, in Scotland, that it contains a confidential communication made by or to an advocate or a solicitor in that capacity; or

(b) authorises the taking possession of a document which is in the possession of a person who would be so entitled.

**4.**—(1) A duly authorised officer of an enforcement authority may, at a reasonable hour and on production (if required) of his credentials, enter any premises for the purpose of ascertaining whether an offence under any of the relevant regulations has been committed.

(2) If a justice of the peace, or in Scotland a justice of the peace or a sheriff, is satisfied—

  (a)  that any relevant books, documents or goods are on, or that any relevant information contained in a computer is available from, any premises, and that production or inspection is likely to disclose the commission of an offence under the relevant regulations; or

  (b)  that any such an offence has been, is being or is about to be committed on any premises,

and that any of the conditions specified in sub-paragraph (3) below is met, he may by warrant under his hand authorise an officer of an enforcement authority to enter the premises, if need be by force.

(3) The conditions referred to in sub-paragraph (2) above are—

  (a)  that admission to the premises has been or is likely to be refused and that notice of intention to apply for a warrant under that sub-paragraph has been given to the occupier;

  (b)  that an application for admission, or the giving of such a notice, would defeat the object of the entry;

  (c)  that the premises are unoccupied; and

  (d)  that the occupier is temporarily absent and it might defeat the object of the entry to await his return.

(4) In sub-paragraph (2) above "relevant", in relation to books, documents, goods or information, means books, documents, goods or information which, under paragraph 3 above, a duly authorised officer may require to be produced or may inspect.

(5) A warrant under sub-paragraph (2) above may be issued only if—

  (a)  in England and Wales, the justice of the peace is satisfied as required by that sub-paragraph by written information on oath;

  (b)  in Scotland, the justice of the peace or sheriff is so satisfied by evidence on oath; or

  (c)  in Northern Ireland, the justice of the peace is so satisfied by complaint on oath.

(6) A warrant under sub-paragraph (2) above shall continue in force for a period of one month.

(7) An officer entering any premises by virtue of this paragraph may take with him such other persons as may appear to him necessary.

(8) On leaving premises which he has entered by virtue of a warrant under sub-paragraph (2) above, an officer shall, if the premises are unoccupied or the occupier is temporarily absent, leave the premises as effectively secured against trespassers as he found them.

(9) In this paragraph "premises" includes any place (including any vehicle, ship or aircraft) except premises used only as a dwelling.

**Obstruction of officers**

**5.**—(1) A person who—

    (a)  intentionally obstructs an officer of an enforcement authority acting in pursuance of this Schedule;

    (b)  without reasonable excuse fails to comply with a requirement made of him by such an officer under paragraph 3(1) above; or

    (c)  without reasonable excuse fails to give an officer of an enforcement authority acting in pursuance of this Schedule any other assistance or information which the officer may reasonably require of him for the purpose of the performance of the officer's functions under this Schedule,

shall be guilty of an offence.

(2) A person guilty of an offence under sub-paragraph (1) above shall be liable on summary conviction to a fine not exceeding level 5 on the standard scale.

(3) If a person, in giving any such information as is mentioned in sub-paragraph (1)(c) above,—

    (a)  makes a statement which he knows is false in a material particular; or

    (b)  recklessly makes a statement which is false in a material particular,

he shall be guilty of an offence.

(4) A person guilty of an offence under sub-paragraph (3) above shall be liable—

    (a)  on summary conviction, to a fine not exceeding level 5 on the standard scale; and

    (b)  on conviction on indictment, to a fine.

**Impersonation of officers**

**6.**—(1) If a person who is not a duly authorised officer of an enforcement authority purports to act as such under this Schedule he shall be guilty of an offence.

(2) A person guilty of an offence under sub-paragraph (1) above shall be liable—

    (a)  on summary conviction, to a fine not exceeding level 5 on the standard scale; and

    (b)  on conviction on indictment, to a fine.

**Disclosure of information**

**7.**—(1) If a person discloses to another any information obtained by him by virtue of this Schedule he shall be guilty of an offence unless the disclosure was made—

    (a)  in or for the purpose of the performance by him or any other person of any function under the relevant regulations; or

(b) for a purpose specified in section 38(2)(a), (b) or (c) of the Consumer Protection Act 1987**(a)**.

(2) A person guilty of an offence under sub-paragraph (1) above shall be liable—

(a) on summary conviction, to a fine not exceeding level 5 on the standard scale; and

(b) on conviction on indictment, to a fine.

**Privilege against self-incrimination**

**8.** Nothing in this Schedule requires a person to answer any question or give any information if to do so might incriminate him.

---

## EXPLANATORY NOTE

*(This note is not part of the Regulations)*

These Regulations implement Council Directive 90/314/EEC on package travel, package holidays, and package tours (OJ No. L158, 13 June 1990, p.59).

The Regulations control the sale and performance of packages sold or offered for sale in the UK. Packages are defined as the pre-arranged combination of at least two of the following when sold or offered for sale at an inclusive price and when the service covers a period of 24 hours or more or includes overnight accommodation:

— transport;

— accommodation;

— other tourist services not ancillary to transport or accommodation and accounting for a significant proportion of the package.

The Regulations set out what information must be given to the consumer before the contract is concluded (including information to be in brochures, where one is published) and information which must be given to the consumer before the package starts. They lay down terms which must be included in the contract and prescribe the circumstances in which price revisions may be made. They provide that the other party to the contract (ie the organiser and/or retailer, as the case may be) should be strictly liable to the consumer for the proper performance of the obligations under the contract, irrespective of whether such obligations are to be provided by that other party or by other suppliers of services. They also provide that the

**(a)** 1987 c.43.

other party to the contract shall provide sufficient evidence of security for the refund of money paid over and for the repatriation of the consumer in the event of insolvency.

The Regulations will be enforced by local weights and measures authorities in Great Britain and by the Department of Economic Development in Northern Ireland.

# Glossary

| | |
|---|---|
| **ABTA** | The Association of British Travel Agents Ltd. |
| **ABTOF** | The Association of British Tour Operators to France. |
| **AETA** | The Association of European Travel Agents. |
| **AITO** | The Association of Independent Tour Operators Limited. |
| **ART** | Applicable risk turnover. A term employed by ABTA in calculating bonding levels for travel agent members. |
| **ARTAC** | ARTAC World Choice (previously the Alliance of Retail Travel Agents Consortia). |
| **ATOL** | Air Travel Organisers' Licence. Under The Civil Aviation (Air Travel Organisers' Licensing) Regulations 1995 (SI 1995 No 1054) all 'organisers' (that is, tour operators and firms selling charter or discounted scheduled airline tickets on a flight-only basis) must obtain an ATOL. In order to obtain the licence a tour operator must, in practice, satisfy the requirements of the **CAA** which is the licensing authority under the Regulations. The regulator must also, in practice, provide a **bond**. |
| **BITOA** | British Incoming Tour Operators Association. |
| **Bond** | An agreement by a third-party bank or insurer to pay in specified circumstances (for example, on demand or in the event of insolvency of a tour operator) the specified sum of money to relevant bonding administrator. (*See also* **ATOL** and **Package Travel Regulations**.) |
| **BSP** | Billing and Settlement Plan; formerly Bank Settlement Plan. The credit settlement plan operated by **IATA** for the benefit of accredited agents. |
| **CAA** | The Civil Aviation Authority; empowered by statute to regulate the UK air travel industry. |
| **CDDA 1986** | The Company Directors Disqualification Act 1986. |
| **CRS** | Computer reservation system. |
| **De-racking** | The withdrawal by a travel agent of a particular tour operator's brochures from its display shelves. |
| **Direct selling** | The sale of holidays, often by telephone, where consumers book directly with the tour operator rather than through a travel agent. This method can be used to purchase products which are only sold direct (after distribution of a brochure to potential customers), those sold |

|  |  |
|---|---|
| | through advertisements in the press or on teletext and the Internet, and those which are advertised in a brochure previously obtained from a travel agent (*see also* **Telesales** ). |
| **DTI** | Department of Trade and Industry. |
| **Foreign package holiday** | A package holiday of which the components include transport between the UK and the place outside the UK, and accommodation outside the UK. |
| **Free assets** | A term employed by the CAA in assessing the financial rigour of applicants and existing ATOL holders. |
| **FTO** | Federation of Tour Operators. |
| **GDS** | Global distribution system. |
| **IA 1986** | The Insolvency Act 1986. |
| **IATA** | International Air Transport Association. An industry trade association formed by member airlines *inter alia* to regulate the operation of credit agents. |
| **Long haul** | A destination outside Europe and North Africa. |
| **MMC** | The Monopolies and Mergers Commission. |
| **MTAA** | Multiple Travel Agents Association. |
| **Multiples** | Retail travel agents with more than 200 outlets. (Those with more than 30 but less than 200 outlets are known as miniples.) |
| **NAITA** | The National Association of Independent Travel Agents. |
| **NATS** | National Air Traffic Services. |
| **Net asset deficiency surcharge** | A term employed by ABTA in calculating contribution rates of member firms. |
| **NRCA** | Net recoverable current assets. A term employed by ABTA in calculating contribution rates of member firms. |
| **Package Travel Regulations** | The Package Travel, Package Holidays and Package Tours Regulations 1992 (SI 1992 No 3288) which were introduced to give effect to a European Council Directive (90/314/EEC). One of the main requirements is that the holiday 'organiser' has to provide financial protection for the consumer. One of the ways in which this can be done is by **bond**ing with an approved body (for example, **ABTA**, **FTO** and **AITO**). |
| **Peak period bonding** | A concept applied by ABTA to recognise that certain tour operators have activity levels concentrated in short periods of the year. |
| **Racking** | A travel agent's display of tour operators' brochures on its shelves. |
| **Short haul** | A destination in Europe or North Africa. |

| | |
|---|---|
| **SSAP** | Statement of Standard Accounting Practice. |
| **Switch selling** | The practice by a travel agent of persuading consumers to buy a comparable product of one tour operator (e.g., a linked operator) when another operator's holiday is specifically requested. |
| **TABRS** | Travel Agents' Bond Replacement Scheme. A scheme introduced by ABTA in 1994 to calculate contribution rates of member firms. |
| **Telesales** | Telephone booking centres run by tour operators or travel agents which advertise in the press and on tele-text. |
| **TOMS** | Tour Operators' Margin Scheme. The Customs & Excise VAT margin scheme applicable to tour operators. |
| **TTA** | The Travel Trust Association Ltd. |
| **TTG** | Thomas Travel Group Ltd. |
| **Viewdata** | A computerised accessing system to tour operators' own computerised reservation systems. The latter also provide descriptions of tour operators' **foreign package holidays**. In **short haul** charter **foreign package holidays** most tour operators produce descriptions for viewdata, and bookings by travel agents are exclusively through viewdata. |
| **WTO** | World Tourism Organisation. |
| **WTTC** | World Travel & Tourism Council. |

# Index

*Please note that references are to paragraph and those to tables are in italics.*

**ABTA (Association of British Travel Agents)**
anti-competitive practices   6.5
CAA compared   3.2.2
forms
tour operators   Appendix 3
travel agents   Appendix 2
growth   3.2
internal structure   3.3
main aim   14.3
membership   1.3, 1.5.1, 3.3.1–3.7
new businesses   14.5
unincorporated members   8.2, 13.2
memorandum and articles   3.4, 3.5
regulations   1.3.1
reporting requirements   3.9.1–3.9.3,
3.11.2, 14.3, 14.4, 14.5
secured assets   12.6
subscriptions to   15.6.7
**ABTOF (Association of British Tour Operators to France)**   1.3
**Accommodation suppliers**   7.3.1
**Accounting policies**
airline operators   12.4.1–12.4.7,
Appendix 4
bonds   12.6
foreign exchange contracts   11.5.1,
12.5.1–12.5.3
overseas subsidiaries   12.5.2
stocks   12.3.2
tax implications   15.2
tour operators   3.11.2, 12.2.1,
13.7.1, Appendix 4
travel agents   12.3.1–12.3.2, 13.5
Appendix 4
VAT considerations   16.3.4
*see also* **Bonding; Euro accounting; Turnover**
**Accounting Standards**   9.1.2, 9.2,
12.4.3, 13.9, 15.2
**Accounts**
IATA review   4.6
management   3.11.2

**Accounts**—*contd*
projections   3.11.2
TTA members' trust   5.7.1
*see also* **Reporting requirements**
**Advance contracting**   7.4.4
**Advantage Travel Centres (formerly National Association of Independent Travel Agents)**   5.5
**Advertising**
taxation issues   15.6.6
tour operators   7.3.4
**Aer Lingus**   9.4.5, 16.2
**AETA (Association of European Travel Agents)**   1.3
**Africa,** tourism in   1.1.3
**Agency Accreditation Programme**
4.3–4.3.1
**Agency bonded licenses**   2.2.2
**Agency fees,** IATA   4.9
**Agency Programme Joint Council (APJC)**   4.3
**Agency sales agreements**   4.10
**Agents, travel**   1.5.1–1.5.4
**AIG Europe Limited**   5.7.2
**Air 2000 Ltd**   1.6.4
**Air Tour Organisers' Licensing System**
*see* **ATOL**
**Air Travel Trust Fund**   2.2.4
**Air (UK) airline**   1.6.2
**Aircraft**
asset valuation   12.4.3
audit considerations   9.2
capacity management   9.3.1–9.3.3
capital allowance claims   15.6.3
consumables   12.4.3
credit purchasing   9.1.2
leasing   9.1.3
maintenance issues   9.4.1–9.4.6
outright purchase of   9.1.1
rotables   12.4.3
**Airlines**
accounting policies   12.4.1–12.4.7,
Appendix 4

**Airlines**—*contd*
  alliances 9.6.1–9.6.5
  audit programmes 13.11.3
  charter 1.6.3–1.6.4, 9.3.1
  computer-assisted techniques 9.3.2
  income/cost recognition 13.10
  reservation systems 10.2
  scheduled 1.6.2, 9.3.2
**Airports** *1.18*, 7.2.7
**Airports Council International** 1.6
**Airtours group**
  charter airlines 1.6.4
  key player, as 1.4.3
  vertical integration *1.9*, 9.5.1
  *see also* **Going Places**
**Airworld** 8.1.1
**AITO (Association of Independent Tour Operators)** 1.3, 1.3.1, 5.6, 6.5
**All-inclusive tours** 1.4.1, *1.8*, Appendix 4
**Alliances of airlines** 9.6.1–9.6.5
**Amadeus reservation system** 9.6.3, 10.5
**Anite reservation system** 10.2
**Annual returns** 2.2.7, Appendix 1
**Anti-competitive practices** 6.5
**APJC (Agency Programme Joint Council)** 4.3
**Applicable risk turnover ('ART')** 3.12.3
**ARTAC (World Choice)** 1.3, 5.4, 6.5
**Articles of Association, ABTA** 3.4, 3.5
**Asia**, tourism in 1.1.3, 1.1.4
**Assets**
  fixed 12.4.3, 15.6.2, Appendix 4
  free 2.2.4, 14.4
**Association of British Tour Operators to France (ABTOF)** 1.3
**Association of British Travel Agents** *see* **ABTA**
**Association of European Travel Agents (AETA)** 1.3
**Association of Independent Tour Operators (AITO)** 1.3, 1.3.1, 5.6, 6.5
**AT Mays travel group** 1.4.3
**ATOL (Air Tour Organisers' Licensing system)**
  application process 2.2.3
  CAA returns 2.2.7
  financial monitoring 2.2.4
  forms of 2.2.2
  IATA 2.2.1, 2.2.2
  regulations 1.3.1

**ATOL (Air Tour Organisers' Licensing system)**—*contd*
  required by 2.2.1
  sales 2.2.3, 2.2.5
  turnover 2.2.4
**Audit programmes** 13.11.1–13.11.3
**Auditing**
  aircraft acquisitions 9.2
  alliance agreements 9.6.5
  annual accounts 3.9.1, 3.9.2
  charter flights 9.3.1
  euro accounting developments 11.6
  maintenance of aircraft 9.4.6
  reports, statutory 13.3, Appendix 1
  risk-based 13.4
  scheduled operations 9.3.2
  turnover certification 3.9.2
  understanding of client business 13.2
  vertical integration 9.5.1

**BA (British Airways)** 1.6.2
**Bank interest, tour operators** 7.2.3
**Bank Settlement Plan - later Billing and Settlement Plan (BSP)** 3.12.3, 4.7, 13.6
**Bankruptcy, ABTA membership** 3.5
**Billing and Settlement Plan (BSP)** 3.12.3, 4.7, 13.6
**BITOA (British Incoming Tour Operators Association)** 1.2.1, 5.2
**Bonding**
  accounting policies 12.6
  arrangements 2.2.4
  IATA 4.4
  lodging with regulators 15.6.1
  package holiday contracts Appendix 10
  peak period 3.10.5
  third-party 3.10.6
  tour operators 3.10.4–3.10.6, 7.3.6
  travel agents 3.12.4, 3.12.2
  variations in 2.2.4
**Bookings, transfer of** Appendix 10
**Bought-in travel services** 16.2, 16.7
**Breach of duty** 6.9.1
**Bridgeman, John (Director General)** 6.2
**Britannia Airways Ltd** 1.6.4
**British Airways (BA)** 1.6.2, 12.4.2, 12.4.3, 12.4.6
**British Incoming Tour Operators' Association (BITOA)** 1.2.1, 5.2

**British Midland airline**   1.6.2
**Brochures**
  costs   15.2, Appendix 4
  package regulations   Appendix 10
  racking of   6.5, 7.4.3
  stock control   8.2
  taxation issues   15.6.6
  tour operators   7.3.3, 12.2.1
  travel agents   12.3.1
**BSP (Billing and settlement plan -
    formerly Bank Settlement Plan)**
    3.12.3, 4.7, 13.6
**Businesses, new**   14.5

**CAA**
  *see* **Civil Aviation Authority**
**Caledonian Airways**   1.6.3
**Cancellation charges**   7.2.2
**Capacity management**   9.3.1–9.3.3, 9.4.4
**Capital allowances**   15.6.3
**Capital requirements**
  maintenance   9.4.1
  tour operators   3.10.1, 3.11.1, 7.4.1
  travel agents   3.12.1, 4.3.1
**Caribbean**,
  passenger travel growth   1.6
**Cash flow**,
  tour operators   7.2.3
**CDDA (Company Directors
    Disqualification Act) 1986**   6.12
**Channel Tunnel**   1.2.2
**Chartered airlines**   1.6.3–1.6.4, 7.4.5,
    9.3.1, 9.4.3
**Civil Aviation (Air Travel Organisers'
    Licensing) Regulations (1995)**
    2.1.1
**Civil Aviation Authority**
  financial monitoring   2.2.4
  forms   Appendix 1
  main aim   14.3
  net asset position monitoring   14.4
  policy implementation   2.1.1
  regulation structure and scope
    1.3.1, 2.1.2
  reporting requirements   13.2
  returns   2.2.7
  role   2.1
  subscriptions to   15.6.7
**Commission income, travel agents**
    8.2, 13.5.1, 16.6
**Companies**
  groups   15.3, 15.4
  names, restrictions on use
    6.10–6.10.3

**Companies Act (1989)**   13.1
**Company Directors Disqualification Act
    1986 (CDDA)**   6.12
**Compensation payments**   7.3.5
**Complex monopolies**   6.3, 6.4
**Computer reservation systems (CRSs)**
    10.2
**Computers, capital allowances**   15.6.3
**Conferences**   15.6.8
**Consortiums**   10.3
**Consumer demand**   1.4.2
**Consumer profile**
  tour operators   1.4.2
  travel agents   1.5.2
**Contracts**
  foreign exchange   12.5.1–12.5.3
  package regulations   Appendix 10
**Control procedures, financial**   13.8
**Corporation tax**   15.3, 15.4, 15.6.8,
    15.7
**Costs**   7.3.1–7.3.9, 7.4.3, 9.4.5, 15.2,
    Appendix 4
  *see also* **Expenditure; Income/cost
    timings**
**CRS (Computer reservation system)**
    10.2
**Currencies, foreign** *see* **Foreign
    exchange**
**Currency movements**   7.2.6

**Deeds of undertaking**   2.2.3
**Deferred expenditure**   12.4.5
**Department of Trade and Industry
    (DTI)**   3.2.1, 6.13
**Deposits**   7.2, 8.2, 12.3.1, 15.6.5, 16.3.2
**Depreciation of assets**   12.4.3,
    Appendix 4
  *see also* **Capital allowances**
**Deracking**   6.5
**Designated travel services**   Appendix
    7
**Destinations, popular**   *1.1*, 1.1.3
**Development expenditure**   12.4.5
**Digital television**   1.5.4, 7.3.3
**Direct selling**   6.3
**Directional selling**   6.5
**Director General of Fair Trading**   6.2
**Directors**
  disqualification   6.12–6.13
  insolvency   6.6, 6.14
  personal guarantees of   7.4.2
  shadow   6.8
**Distribution costs**   Appendix 4
**Domestic markets**   1.2.2

**Double booking**   7.3.1
**DTI (Department of Trade and Industry)**   3.2.1, 6.13
**Dual currency accounting** *see* **Euro accounting**
**Due diligence defence**   Appendix 10
**Duty, breach of**   6.9.1
**Duty of care**   14.7

**East Asia**, tourism   1.1.3
**EC Directive 77/388, Article 26A,**   1.3.1, 16.1, Appendix 5
**Ecotourism**   1.1.4
**Employees, cheap/free flights**   15.8
**Empty-leg provisions**   13.11.2
**Engine overhaul expenditure**   Appendix 4
**Entertaining**   15.6.8
**Equity ownership**   9.6.1
**EU (European Union)**
   regulation   2.1–2.1.2
   tourism   1.2.2
**Euro accounting**
   auditing implications   11.6
   competition   11.5.2
   invoicing implications   11.5.1
   timetable   11.2–11.4.0
**Europe,**
   tourism in   1.1.3, 1.1.4
**European Union (EU)**, visits to   1.2.2
*Ex-gratia* payments   7.3.5
**Expenditure**, aircraft   Appendix 4
**Expenditure** deferred   7.4.3, 12.4.5
**Expenditure** resorts   13.8
**Extras, holiday**   7.2.5

**Family Expenditure Survey (FES)**   1.4.2
**Federation of Tour Operators (FTO)**   1.3, 6.5
**FES (Family Expenditure Survey)**   1.4.2
**Finance leases**   9.1.2, 15.6.2, 15.6.4, Appendix 10
**Financial Reporting Standards**   15.2
**First Choice group**   1.4.3, *1.9*, 8.1.3
**Fixed assets, tangible**   12.4.3, Appendix 4
**Fleet sizes**   9.4.2
**Flying Colours**   1.4.3, 1.4.4
**Forecasts**   1.1.4
**Foreign exchange**
   contracts   12.5.1–12.5.3
   gains and losses   7.2.6, 9.1.2, 15.6.2

**Foreign exchange**—*contd*
   transactions, accounting for   13.9, Appendix 4
**Forms**
   ABTA tour operators   Appendix 3
   ABTA travel agents   Appendix 2
   CAA   Appendix 1
**Forward currency contracts**   12.5.1, 12.5.3
**Franchising**   8.2, 9.6.4
**Fraudulent trading**   6.9.2
**Free assets**   2.2.4, 14.4
**Freehold properties**   2.2.4
**Freesale arrangements**   9.3.1
**Frequent flyer schemes**   9.3.2, 12.4.6, Appendix 4
**FRS reservation system**   10.2
**FTO (Federation of Tour Operators)**   1.3, 6.5
**Fully bonded licenses**   2.2.2

**Galileo reservation system**   9.6.3, 10.3
**GDP (Gross Domestic Product)**   1.1.1, *1.2.1*
**GDS (Global distribution systems)**   10.2
**Global Travel Group (ITG)**   1.3
**Going Places**
   consumer profile   1.5.2
   formation   8.1.2
   key player, as   1.5.1, 1.5.3
   *see also* **Airtours group**
**Government regulation** *see* **Civil Aviation Authority**
**Gross Domestic Product (GDP)**   1.1.1, *1.2.1*
**Groups of companies**   15.3, 15.4
**Guarantees**
   directors   7.4.2
   travel agents   12.6

**Hayes & Jarvis**   1.4.3
**Hedging, currency costs**   7.2.6, 7.4.5
**Hire purchase agreements**   9.1.2, 12.4.3, 15.6.2, 15.6.4
**Holiday extras**   7.2.5
**Holiday insurance**   7.2.4
**Holiday representatives**   7.3.7, 13.8
**Holidays, income and cost recognition**   12.2.1
**Hoteliers**   7.3.1

**IA (Insolvency Act) 1986**   6.8, 6.9.1–6.9.3

**IAICL (Independent Advantage Insurance Company Limited)** 5.5
**IATA (International Air Transport Association)**
  Agency Accreditation Programme 4.3–4.3.1, 4.5, 4.6
  agency fees 4.9
  annual accounts 4.6
  ATOL requirements 2.2.1, 2.2.2
  bonding requirements 4.4
  changes, notification of 4.11
  defined 4.1
  duty of care 14.7
  passenger sales agency agreement 4.10
  quality reviews 4.12
  structure 4.2
  ticketing procedures 4.8
**IIP (Investors in People)** 1.5.3
**In-house supplies** 7.3.2, 16.5
**Inbound market** 1.2.2, *1.7*
**Incentive programmes** 12.4.6
**Income and Corporation Taxes Act (1988)**, s393(8) 15.6.1
**Income, deferred** 7.4.3
**Income/cost timings**
  airlines 12.4.1, 13.10
  auditing considerations 13.3
  tax implications 15.2
  tour operators 12.2.1, 13.7.1, Appendix 4
  travel agents 3.5, 12.3.1
  *see also* **Turnover**
**Independent Advantage Insurance Company Limited (IAICL)** 5.5
**India**, tourism in 1.4.1
**Information technology (IT)** 7.3.9, 7.4.4
**Inland Revenue** 15.2, 15.6.6
**Insolvency**
  company names 6.10–6.10.3
  defined 6.7
  directors' responsibilities 6.6, 6.14
  offences under 1986 Act 6.9.1–6.9.3
  package holiday contracts Appendix 10
  preferences 6.11
**Insolvency Act (1986)** 6.8, 6.9.1–6.10, 6.11
**Inspirations plc** 1.6.2, 1.6.3
**Insurance**, package holiday contracts 7.2.4, Appendix 10
**International Air Transport Association** *see* IATA

**Internet ('intranet') bookings** 1.5.3, 1.5.4, 7.3.3, 8.2, 10.7
**Investors In People (IIP)** 1.5.3
**IT** *see* **Information technology**
**ITG (Global Travel Group)** 1.3

**Joint purchasing** 9.6.2

**Latin America**,
  passenger traffic growth 1.6
**Lease agreements** 9.1.2, 9.1.3, 12.4.3, 15.6.2, 15.6.4, Appendix 4
**Licensable and non-licensable turnover** 14.3
**Liquidity**, IATA accreditation 4.3.1
**'Load factors'** 7.4.1
**Loans for aircraft** 9.1.2
**Long-haul destinations** 1.4.3, 1.4.1
**Lower bonded licenses** 2.2.2
**Loyalty schemes** 9.3.2
**Lunn Poly**
  consumer profiles 1.5.2
  formation 8.1.3
  key player, as 1.5.1, 1.5.3
  monopolies 6.3

**Maintenance of aircraft** 9.3.2, 9.4.1–9.4.6, 9.6.2, 12.4.4
**Management accounts**,
  tour operators 3.11.2
**Margin scheme supplies** 16.5
**Market forecasts** 1.1.4
**Market sectors** 1.2.2
**Market, UK travel and tourism** 1.2.1–1.2.2
**Marketing issues** *see* **Advertising**; **Brochures**
**'Matchmaker' concept** 1.5.3
**Mays, AT** 1.5.1
**Mexico**, tourism 1.4.1
**Middle East**
  passenger growth 1.6
  tourism in 1.1.3, 1.1.4
**Misfeasance** 6.9.1
**MMC (Monopolies and Mergers Commission)** 1.4.3, 6.2–6.4, 9.5
**Monarch Airlines** 1.6.4, 9.5
**Money Direct (foreign exchange delivery service)** 1.5.3
**Monies in trust** Appendix 10
**Monopolies** 6.3, 6.4
**Monopolies and Mergers Commission (MMC)** 1.4.3, 6.2–6.4, 9.5

**MTAA (Multiple Travel Agents
  Association)**  5.3
**Multiple chains**  1.5.1

**NAITA (National Association of
  Independent Travel Agents)**  1.3,
  5.5, 6.5
**Names, company, restriction on re-use**
  6.10–6.10.3
**National Air Traffic Services (NATS)**
  2.1
**National Association of Independent
  Travel Agents (NAITA)**  1.3, 5.5,
  6.5
**National Insurance**  15.7
**NATS (National Air Traffic Services)**
  2.1
**Net asset deficits**  3.10.3, 3.12.4
**Net asset position**  14.4
**New businesses**  14.5
**North America**  1.2.2, 1.6
**NRCA (Net recoverable current assets)**
  3.10.2, 14.4

**Off-peak business**  7.4.2
**Offences**
  breach of package holiday contracts
    Appendix 10
  Insolvency Act (1986)  6.9.1–6.9.3
**Office of Fair Trading**  6.2
**Operating leases**  9.1.3, 15.6.2, 15.6.4,
  Appendix 4
**Outbound markets**  1.2.2, *1.6*
**Output tax**,  Appendix 9
**Overcapacity**  7.4.5
**Overseas representation**  15.7

**P11D issues**  15.8
**Package holidays**
  MMC  6.2
  tour operators  1.4.1–1.4.4
**Package Travel, Package Holidays and
  Package Tours Regulations (1992)**
  defined,  Appendix 10
  introduction of  1.3.1, 3.2.1
  security for clients fees  2.1.1
  TTA  5.7
**Panic buying**  7.4.5
**Passenger sales agency agreements**
  4.10
**PAYE (Pay as you Earn)**  15.7, 15.8
**Peak period bonding**  3.10.5
**Policies, accounting** *see* Accounting
  policies

**Preferences**  6.11
**Prepayments**
  tour operators  13.7.1
  travel agencies  13.5
**Price considerations**
  airlines  9.3.2
  package holiday contracts
    Appendix 10
  tour operators  7.4.4
**Profitability,**
  IATA accreditation  4.3.1
**Programs, audit**  13.11.1–13.11.3
**Provisional margins,**  Appendix 9
**Prudence accounting concept**  13.5,
  13.7.1, 15.2, 15.6.6

**Quality reviews,**
  IATA  4.12
**Quarterly turnover certificates**
  3.11.2

**Racking**  7.4.3
**Rebates, airports charges**  7.2.7
**Receipt before ticketing**  7.4.4
**Record-keeping**, TOMS  16.5
**Regional trends**  1.1.3
**Regulations, travel industry**  1.3.1
  *see also* **ATOL; Civil Aviation Authority**
**Reporting requirements, travel industry**
  audited accounts  3.9.1–3.9.3, 13.2
  net asset statements  14.4
  new business documentation  14.5
  one-off statements  14.6
  turnover certification  14.3
**Representatives**
  holidays  7.3.7, 13.8
  overseas subsidiaries  15.7
**Reservation systems**  9.6.3, 10.2
**Resort expenditure**  13.8
**Restrictive practices**  6.4
**Retail turnover**  14.3
**Rewards, sales teams**  7.4.4
**Risk-based auditing**  13.4
**Rollover relief**  15.9

**Sabre reservation system**  9.6.3, 10.4
**Sales teams**  7.3.8, 7.4.4
**Sales techniques,**
  tour operators  7.4.5
**Scale monopolies**  6.3
**Schedule D**
  Case I  15.3, 15.6.2, 15.6.5, 15.7
  Case III  15.6.1, 15.6.5
  Case V  15.7

**Scheduled airlines**   1.6.2, 7.4.5, 9.3.2, 9.4.3
**Seat only sales**   2.2.5
**Sector forecasts**   1.1.4
**Sectors, market**   1.2.2
**Segmental reporting**   12.4.2, Appendix 4
**Selling**
  ATOL to ATOL   2.2.3, 2.2.6
  direct   6.3
  directional   6.5
  seat only   2.2.5
  switch   6.5
  telesales   6.3
  tour operators   7.2.1, 7.4.4
**Shadow directors**   6.8
**Short-haul market**   1.4.3
**Single currency**   11.6
**South Asia**, tourism   1.1.3
**Split plane charters**   9.3.1
**Sponsorship**   15.6.8
**Standard-rating**   16.5
**Standards, accounting**   9.2, 15.2
  SSAP 20 *Foreign Currency Translation* 13.9
  SSAP 21 *Leases and Hire Purchase Contracts*   9.1.2, 12.4.3, 15.6.4
**Stays, length of**   1.2.2
**Stocks**
  airline operators   12.4.7
  travel agents   12.3.2, Appendix 4
**Sub-leasing**   9.3.3
**Subscriptions**   15.6.7
**Subsidiary companies**   12.5.2
**Sunworld**   1.4.4, 8.1.1
**Supply structure**
  tour operators   1.4.3
  travel agents   1.5.1–1.5.2
**Switch-selling**   6.5

**TABRS (Travel Agents Bond Replacement Scheme)** 3.12.2–3.12.5
**Tangible fixed assets**   12.4.3, Appendix 4
**Taxation issues**
  accounting policies   15.2
  advertising   15.6.6
  bonding   15.6.1
  brochures   15.6.6
  capital allowances   15.6.3
  conferences   15.6.8
  deductions allowable   15.6.7, 15.6.8
  deposits   15.6.5

**Taxation issues**—*contd*
  foreign exchange gains and losses 15.6.2
  groups of companies   15.4
  hire purchase agreements   15.6.4
  lease agreements   15.6.4
  overseas represenation   15.7
  P11D   15.8
  PAYE (Pay as you Earn)   15.8
  rollover relief gains   15.9
  sponsorship   15.6.8
  subscriptions   15.6.7
  trading status   15.3
  year end, choice of   15.5
**Telesales**   6.3
**Teletext**   1.5.4, 7.3.3, 8.2
**Theme parks**   1.1.4
**Third-party bonding**   3.10.6
**Thomas Cook Group Limited**
  charter airlines   1.6.3, 1.6.4
  history   8.1, 8.1.1
  key player, as   1.4.3, 1.5.1
  vertical integration   *1.9*
**Thomson Travel Group**
  charter airlines   1.6.4
  floation of   8.1.3
  key player, as   1.4.3
  monopolies   6.3
  vertical integration   *1.9*, 9.5
**Ticketing procedures**   4.8
**Time Off**   8.1.1
**Timing, income and costs**
  tour operators   12.2.1
  travel agents   12.3.1
**TOMS (Tour Operators' Margin Scheme)**
  audit programmes   13.11.2
  calculations   16.5, Appendix 8
  European Community VAT standardisation   7.4.2
  legislation defined   16.1, 16.6, 16.7
  non applicable   16.6
  registration for VAT   16.3.1
  scope of provisions   16.2
  VAT exceptions and concessions 16.4
**Tour operators**
  ABTA membership rules   3.6
  new members   3.11–3.11.2
  accounting policies   3.11.2, 12.2.1, 13.7.1, Appendix 4
  anti-competitive practices   6.5
  audit programs   13.11.2
  bonding   3.10.4–3.10.6, 7.3.6

**Tour operators**—*contd*
capital requirements   3.10.1, 3.11.1,
    7.4.2
costs   7.3.1–7.3.9, 7.4.5, 12.2.1
financial regulations   3.10.1–3.10.6
income
    deferred   7.4.3
    sources   7.2.1–7.2.7
    timing with costs   12.2.1, 13.7.1
operating year   7.4.2
package holiday industry
    1.4.1–1.4.4
risks   7.4.2–7.4.5
selling considerations   7.4.4
**Tour Operators' Council**
ABTA membership rules   3.6
bonding requirements   3.10.4
**Tour Operators' Fund**   3.10.4
**Tour Operators' Margin Scheme** *see*
    **TOMS**
**Tour Operators Order 1997**   16.1
**Tourism**, economic impact and trends
    1.1.2, 1.1, 1.1.1
**Tours, all-inclusive**   1.4.1, *1.8*,
    Appendix 4
**Trading status**   15.3
**Transport**, tour operators   7.3.2
**Travel agents**
ABTA membership rules   3.7
    new members   3.13
accounting policies   12.3.1–12.3.2,
    13.5, Appendix 4
anti-competitive practices   6.5
audit programmes   13.11.1
benefits for users   8.2
bonding   3.12.2, 3.12.4
capital requirements   3.12.1, 4.3.1
commission income   8.2, 13.5.1,
    16.6
EC Directive 77/388, Article 26A
    Appendix 5
fees for services   8.2
financial regulations   3.12.1–
    3.12.5
functions   8.1
IATA accreditation   4.3.1
inclusive tours   1.4.1, *1.8*, Appendix
    4
income/cost recognition   3.5,
    12.3.1, 13.5
investment income   Appendix 4
key players   1.5.1–1.5.4
stocks   12.3.2
turnover   Appendix 4

**Travel Agents Bond Replacement
    Scheme (TABRS)**   3.12.2–3.12.5
**Travel Trust Association (TTA)**   1.3,
    5.7.1–5.7.2
**Travellers' cheques**   Appendix 4
**Trends, tourism**   1.1.2, 1.1.3
**TTA (Travel Trust Association)**   1.3,
    5.7.1–5.7.2
**TTG** *see* **Thomson Travel Group**
**Turnover**
ABTA reporting requirements
    3.9.1–3.9.3
airline operators   12.4.1, Appendix 4
ATOL holders   2.2.4
certification   3.11.2, 14.3
First Choice holidays   1.4.3
retail   14.3
tour operators   3.11.2, 12.2.1,
    Appendix 4
travel agents   12.3.1, Appendix 4
*see also* **Income/cost timings**

**Unijet**   1.4.3, 8.2
**Unincorporated businesses**   8.2, 13.2
**United States**, tourism in   1.1.3

**Value Added Tax (Tour Operators)
    Order 1987**,   Appendix 7
**Value Added Tax (Tour Operators)
    Order 1997**   16.1
**Value Added Tax (VAT)**
accounting considerations   16.3.4
calculation of supplies   16.5
concessions   16.4
designated travel services   Appendix
    7
exceptions   16.4
non-TOMS issues   16.6
place of supply   16.3.3, Appendix 7
registration procedures   16.3.1
time of supply   16.3.2, Appendix 7
TOMS provisions   16.1, 16.2, 16.4,
    16.5
**VAT Act 1994**
Schedule 5   16.6
Section 53,   16.1, Appendix 6
**Vertical integration**
anti-competitive practices   6.5
auditing matters   9.5–9.5.1
capacity management   9.6
charter airlines   1.6.3
customer relationships   10.1
key players   1.5.1
maintenance of aircraft   9.4

**Viewdata (traditional booking system)**
  1.5.4, 6.5, 10.2
**Virgin Atlantic Airways Limited**   16.2
**Vision (automated booking system)**
  1.5.3

**Westdeutsche Landesbank**   1.4.4, 8.1
**Whole plane charters**   9.3.1
**Working capital**   3.12.4, 3.12.5

**World Tourism Organisation (WTO)**
  1.1.4
**Worldspan reservation system**   9.6.3,
  10.6
**Wrongful trading**   6.9.3

**Year end, choice of**   7.4.1, 15.5

**Zero-rated items**   16.4, 16.6, 16.7